The Methuen Drama Anthology of
Playwrights: 1970–2

Wesley Brown is Professor Emeritus at Rutgers University and teaches literature and creative writing at Bard College at Simon's Rock, USA. He co-edited the multicultural anthologies *Imagining America* (fiction), *Visions of America* (non-fiction), edited the *Teachers & Writers Guide to Frederick Douglass* and wrote the narration for a segment of the PBS documentary, *W.E.B. DuBois: A Biography in Four Voices*. In addition, he is the author of four produced plays, *Boogie Woogie and Booker T, Life During Wartime, A Prophet Among Them,* and *Dark Meat on a Funny Mind*; three novels, *Tragic Magic, Darktown Strutters*, and *PushComes to SHOVE*; and a short story collection, *Dance of the Infidels*.

Aimée K. Michel is Associate Professor of Theater at Bard College at Simon's Rock, USA. She was the Artistic Director of the New Orleans Shakespeare Festival for over ten years where she produced and directed plays by Shakespeare and Louisiana writers as well as creating and launching *Shakespeare Alive*, an educational outreach program to New Orleans schools. Before this, she was Artistic Director of the Drama League's Directors Project in New York City where she created the New Directors/New Works program. As a freelance director, she has directed in theaters all over the country. She was a recipient of both the Drama League's Directors Project Fellowship and the Boris Segal Directing Fellowship at Williamstown Theater Festival.

The Methuen Drama Anthology of American Women Playwrights: 1970–2020

Gun

Spell #7

The Jacksonian

The Baltimore Waltz

In the Blood

Intimate Apparel

Edited and with introductions by

WESLEY BROWN *and* AIMÉE K. MICHEL

methuen | drama

LONDON · NEW YORK · OXFORD · NEW DELHI · SYDNEY

METHUEN DRAMA
Bloomsbury Publishing Plc
50 Bedford Square, London, WC1B 3DP, UK
1385 Broadway, New York, NY 10018, USA

BLOOMSBURY, METHUEN DRAMA and the Methuen Drama logo are trademarks of
Bloomsbury Publishing Plc

First published in Great Britain 2020

This anthology is dedicated to

Elizabeth Nell Dubus
a pioneering writer and constant inspiration

Ntozake Shange
who continues to inspire
1948–2018

our treasured colleague Karen Beaumont
1955–2019

Contents

Acknowledgments

We would like to thank first and foremost the playwrights whose work we honor in this volume: Susan Yankowitz, Ntozake Shange, Paula Vogel, Beth Henley, Suzan-Lori Parks, and Lynn Nottage. We are particularly grateful to Ntozake Shange, who agreed to be part of this anthology before she passed away in October 2018, and whose work continues to inspire us.

We would like to thank our editors at Methuen Drama: Camilla Erskine, who helped us launch the project, and Anna Brewer, who worked tirelessly and with great enthusiasm to bring this book to fruition. Thanks also to Meredith Benson for her support pulling it all together.

We would like to thank Terence Nemeth at Theatre Communications Group for supporting us in obtaining rights for those plays published by TCG.

We are indebted to our students at Bard College at Simon's Rock who provided us the impetus to create this anthology.

We are grateful to our colleague and dear friend Joan DelPlato for providing editorial feedback and for her enthusiastic support of our work.

Thank you always to John and Sebastian for their love and support.

Introduction

Wesley Brown and Aimée K. Michel

Susan Yankowitz's collaborative play *Terminal* premiered in 1969 with Joseph Chaikin's Open Theater, and she has continued writing politically charged experimental plays for fifty years, including her most recent drama *Gun*. Ntozake Shange's *for colored girls who have considered suicide/when the rainbow is enuf* burst onto the theatrical scene in 1975 giving powerful voice to black women and her linguistically innovative plays speak directly to the modern "poetry out loud" movement, yet they are not being produced, though Shange herself, at age seventy, was performing her own work in New York City until she passed away in October 2018. Her startling play *Spell #7* shocks us with even deeper truths about women's lives. While New York City recently celebrated the fiftieth anniversary of the 1969 Stonewall riots which shifted our consciousness about the rights of gay and lesbian people in our communities, Paula Vogel's play *The Baltimore Waltz* reminds us of the heartache that followed with the AIDS epidemic. Since the late 1970s Vogel has written with bold authenticity about women's lives and particularly the intimate lives of lesbian women, most recently in her 2017 Broadway production of *Indecent*. Beth Henley's first produced play *Crimes of the Heart* won her the 1981 Pulitzer Prize for Drama, and she has been writing the stories of American women with her razor-sharp comic wit for both film and theater for forty years. Her 2012 play *The Jacksonian* is wickedly funny at the same time that it lays bare the psychic pain and trauma that racism continues to bring to our country. Suzan-Lori Parks' 1989 play *Imperceptible Mutabilities of the Third Kingdom* revealed a uniquely original voice and was compared to Ntozake Shange and Adrienne Kennedy in style. She has become a major voice in American theater and her *Red Letter Plays: In the Blood and Fucking A* played in a double bill at the Pershing Square Signature Theater in fall 2017 where she was Playwright in Residence. More recently, she premiered *White Noise*, a provocative, controversial play about racism in America, at the Public Theater in the spring of 2019. Lynn Nottage's play *Crumbs from the Table of Joy* premiered in 1995, and her commitment to the American stage has won her two Pulitzer Prizes. Her play *Sweat* premiered on Broadway at Studio 54 in March 2017 and she was in residence at Signature Theater for the 2018/19 season where her plays *Fabulation or the Re-education of Undine* and *By the Way Meet Vera Stark* were presented.

These powerful women writers have brilliantly articulated the American psyche for the past fifty years, delving deeply into sociological and political issues while continuing to experiment with theatrical form. Yet they, and many other American women playwrights who have been writing for the theater for decades, have succeeded despite a continuing marginalization of women playwrights in this country. Since an American theater was established over a century ago the only legitimate voice that has been continually recognized has been that of the white male playwright. O'Neill, Williams, Miller, Albee, Shepard, Mamet, McNally, and other major male theatrical voices have been given the stages to develop their craft and voices in the not for profit and commercial theater with impunity while women were sidelined again and again. And in academia, women playwrights continue to be marginalized while the canon of dramatic literature on syllabi across the country is heavily weighted toward male playwrights.

In a March 2017 article in *The New York Times*, "Two Female Playwrights Arrive on Broadway. What Took So Long?" Michael Paulson celebrates the arrival of Lynn Nottage's play *Sweat* and Paula Vogel's *Indecent* on the Broadway stage. He asserts, "The fact that these two writers are just now making their Broadway debuts raises uncomfortable questions for the theater industry, which season after season sees plays by men vastly outnumber plays by women in the all-important commercial spaces where money can be made, reputations burnished and Tony Awards won."

The facts support his assertion. Though women have been writing, creating, and producing work for the American theater for over a hundred years, women's voices have overwhelmingly been outside of the mainstream dialogue. In the past fifty years alone, the Tony nomination committee for Best Play nominated Lorraine Hansberry and Lillian Hellman in 1960, Marjorie Barkentin in 1974, Ntozake Shange in 1977, Beth Henley in 1982, Marsha Norman in 1983, Joanna Glass in 1984, and Tina Howe in 1987, but in every case the award went to a man. Except for Frances Goodrich co-winning the award with her husband, Albert Hackett, in 1956, the first Tony Award for Best Play since the award was established in 1947 to be given solely to a female playwright went to Wendy Wasserstein in 1989 for *The Heidi Chronicles*. Since then, only one other woman has won a Tony for Best Play, Yasmina Reza, a French playwright, for *Art* in 1998 and again for *God of Carnage* in 2009. Thus, in seventy years of recognizing the best playwriting in the American commercial theater, where playwrights stand to get the most widespread recognition and financial compensation, only two American women have been found worthy of the award—and one shared it with her husband! It is difficult not to wonder what standards the committee is using to determine the outcome. Or perhaps one should look at the percentage of plays by women that even reach the Broadway stage.

Women have fared slightly better with the more literary Pulitzer Prize for Drama. Zona Gale was the first female playwright to win the Pulitzer Prize for Drama for her play *Miss Lulu Bett* in 1921. It took another ten years for another woman to be so honored—this time Susan Glaspell in 1931 for her full-length play *Alison's House*. Zoe Akins won the prize for *The Old Maid* in 1935. Another ten years later, Mary Coyle Chase won for her 1945 drama *Harvey*. The 1950s saw two winners: the husband and wife team Albert Hackett and Frances Goodrich for *The Diary of Anne Frank* in 1956 and Ketti Frings in 1958 for her dramatic adaptation of Thomas Wolfe's novel *Look Homeward, Angel*. It is striking that no woman was awarded the Pulitzer Prize for Drama again until 1981 when Beth Henley won for *Crimes of the Heart*. Though new plays by women like Adrienne Kennedy, Maria Irene Fornes, and Ntozake Shange were being produced during those two decades, none were given this recognition. In the 1980s Marsha Norman won for her 1983 play *'Night Mother* and Wendy Wasserstein won for her 1989 play *The Heidi Chronicles*. In the late 1990s Paula Vogel won for her 1998 play *How I Learned to Drive* and Margaret Edson, in 1999, for her play *Wit*. It was not until the twenty-first century that an African American woman, Suzan-Lori Parks, won the Pulitzer Prize for Drama for her 2002 play *TopDog/Underdog*. Parks' achievement was followed by playwright Lynn Nottage's recognition as the only female playwright to win the award twice, in 2009 for *Ruined* and again in 2017 for *Sweat*.

Though in the first decade of the twenty-first century only two women playwrights won Pulitzers, in the second decade half of the prizes went to female playwrights. In 2012 Quiara Alegria Hudes won for her play *Water by the Spoonful*. In 2014 Annie Baker won for *The Flick*. In 2017 Nottage won for *Sweat*. In 2018 Martyna Majok won for *Cost of Living*, and in 2019 Jackie Sibblies Drury won for *Fairview*. Progress indeed, though there is much to be made up for. Since the prize was launched, in 1917, over one hundred years ago, eighty-eight awards have been given to playwrights. Of these only eighteen have been given to female playwrights. And it is not that women weren't writing, nor that their plays weren't being produced.

In Paulson's article Nottage articulates what a Broadway production can mean for a playwright, "Suddenly I thought, 'Oh, this is what it feels like to be a playwright who is part of the cultural conversation.'" And Vogel adds, "You feel the ghosts in a really great way, and they're the kind of ghosts that are saying, 'Welcome home.'"

Welcome home indeed. Looking back through the history of women playwrights in the American theater, there was a time, early in the twentieth century, when plays written by women were appearing on Broadway and when women were a powerful force behind the budding community and regional theater movements. In the Introduction to her book *Plays By American Women 1900–1930*, Judith E. Barlow writes, "Women writing for the stage in this country today are the heirs of a neglected but not negligible tradition." In both this anthology and in the introduction to her *Plays by American Women 1930–1960*, Barlow traces the journeys of American women playwrights from the beginnings of our country through suffrage, World War I, the Depression, World War II and the Cold War era, ending, in her second volume, with "The dramatists and other women writers who came of age in the sixties and seventies owe a debt to those who preceded them."

And so, while the focus of this book is on the groundbreaking work of the playwrights in this anthology who have been writing and being produced for the past fifty years, we want to pay tribute to some of the many female playwrights who led the way and on whose shoulders we stand today.

American Women Playwrights before 1940

American women playwrights first emerge en masse during the first wave of feminism in the late nineteenth and early twentieth centuries when American women were finding their voices at last in every sphere of American life and demanding the right to vote. And because the suffrage movement was closely allied with the abolitionist movement, the trajectory of American women in the theater parallels the trajectory of the civil rights movement, which demanded full participation for all citizens of all races and genders. Also, because these women were speaking the unspeakable—women's rights and the abolition of slavery—their plays and methods of presenting them, from the beginning of the twentieth century right up to the present moment in the twenty-first century, were often innovative in form, both in writing (subject matter and stylistic innovation) and in presentation (agit prop, one-acts, one-woman shows).

In the middle of the nineteenth century, early American female writer Anna Cora Mowatt's play *Fashion* was a tremendous success on the New York stage. But it wasn't until the end of the nineteenth century that women's voices were heard more and more fiercely as they demanded their political and economic rights. The plays of suffragettes have been documented, though because they were written as political propaganda to spread the word to all women of the importance of working for the vote, they are seldom anthologized or considered alongside work that was presented on the legitimate stage. They seem to have varied in form from conventional one-act plays, which used comedy and humor to present the woman's perspective, to more radical agit-prop theater used to arouse the masses to protest. The importance of these early dramatic expressions of women's voices cannot be underestimated as they proved that women could speak boldly in the theater in a way that they were not yet allowed in public.

Perhaps surprisingly, women were also running and writing for the many small non-professional "community" theaters which sprang up all over the country in the early twentieth century. These women playwrights were writing one-acts, often domestic in theme, and having them produced in community theaters such as the Pasadena Community Playhouse in California. At the same time, African American women were writing anti-lynching plays, calling attention to the violent backlash to African American men getting the right to vote in 1870 that was killing black men and boys all over the US.

By the early twentieth century more women were writing for the stage as the suffrage movement grew stronger and the short plays written as propaganda were more widely produced. At the same time, women became instrumental in the professional American Little Theater movement, which was challenging the proliferation of commercial theater where profit, not art, was the overarching motivation. The professional Little Theater movement, which contrasted with the non-professional community theater movement, encouraged low-budget productions with a focus on experimentation. Influenced by non-realistic and expressionist theater trends in Europe, American theater artists of the Little Theater Movement wanted to explore new ideas in playwrighting and design in direct contrast to the formulaic melodramas which were so successful at the time. Many talented women were drawn to theaters such as the Chicago Little Theater, co-founded by Maurice Browne and Ellen Van Volkenburg, and one of the leading contributors to the Little Theater movement.

A major female playwright and theater practitioner of the early twentieth century, Alice Gerstenberg, was an early member of the Chicago Little Theater. Gerstenberg was producer and president of the Playwrights' Theater of Chicago for two decades beginning in the early 1920s, where she championed and produced the work of emerging Midwestern playwrights. She wrote plays throughout her life leaving a canon of over twenty full-length plays and numerous one-acts with her last play written in 1969 three years before her death at age eighty-six. Her 1913 play *Overtones* is often included in anthologies and is stylistically innovative, incorporating the playing of an "alter ego" for each of two characters.

Susan Glaspell, co-founder with her husband George Cram Cook of the Provincetown Players in 1915, another of the theaters launched during the Little Theater Movement, also strove to write and produce plays which embrace a new kind of theatricality. In two of her best-known plays, *Trifles* and *Alison's House*, the major female character in the story never appears. Glaspell was an iconoclast in her day. She was hired as a reporter for the *Des Moines Daily News*, covering murder cases. A particularly controversial case became the theme for her one-act *Trifles* which premiered at the Provincetown Playhouse with Glaspell playing a leading role and was an instant success. Her 1931 play *Alison's House*, based loosely on the poet Emily Dickinson, won the Pulitzer Prize for Drama that year. Glaspell was a celebrated and successful novelist and short story writer both in the US and in the UK, and her novels were bestsellers on both sides of the Atlantic. She continued to publish in all three forms until her death in 1948.

Rachel Crothers was a force on the Broadway stage. She moved from her home in Illinois to New York City where she began acting and ultimately writing plays, which she directed and starred in. From 1906, with the debut of *The Three of Us*, until the 1940s her plays were consistently well received on the Broadway stage. One of her best-known plays, the 1909 *A Man's World*, lays bare the double standard that existed in the early part of the twentieth century and continues to exist today. It is possible that the phrase "it's a man's world" is taken from a speech by Malcolm Gaskell as he admonishes the protagonist, Frank Ware (a female character), "You keep banging away about woman—woman and what she could do for herself if she would. Why—this is a man's world. Women'll never change anything." Another of her powerful plays, *He and She* (1911; revised and produced 1920), lays bare a revolutionary marriage between two sculptors in New York City. The protagonist Ann (played by Crothers in the premiere of the play) struggles between the maternal needs of her teenaged sixteen-year-old daughter and her own blossoming career as a sculptor. The play climaxes when Ann beats her own husband in a contest to win a major commission whose execution will keep her from giving her daughter the maternal focus that the girl needs. Despite an understanding husband, Ann makes a difficult and questionable decision as the play ends, exposing the complexity that women faced and still do concerning responsibility for the children in a marriage. Who, ultimately, bears it?

Zona Gale, born in Wisconsin and inspired to write about the people there, was the first woman to win the Pulitzer Prize for Drama in 1921 for *Miss Lulu Bett* (1920), a play which she adapted from her popular novel of the same name. Perhaps inspired by Ibsen's Nora, her heroine Lulu Bett lives a conventional life as a spinster in her sister's home until circumstances force her to re-examine her situation and choose a different, unconventional, life. The play ends with her mother asking: "Where you goin' now, for pity sakes?" And Lulu responds: "Away. I thought I wanted somebody of my own. Well, maybe it was just myself . . . Good-by. Good-by, all of you. I'm going I don't know where—to work at I don't know what. But I'm going from choice!" It is not surprising that after winning the Pulitzer Prize for this radical and shocking ending to the play Gale wrote a revised Act III which ended with Lulu marrying her brother-in-law's brother and settling down. Though Gale was a prolific writer, publishing many novels, plays, and short stories, like her heroine, she, too, was trapped in her own time.

Zoe Akins was another iconoclast. A highly successful writer for stage and screen, she maintained a long-term romantic relationship with actress Jobyna Howland until Howland's death in 1936. Her wildly popular play *Declassée* played the Broadway stage in 1919 starring Ethel Barrymore. She continued to write both for the stage and the screen and had another great success in 1930 with *The Greeks Had a Word for It*. This script formed the basis for her screenplay for the popular movie *How to Marry a*

Millionaire in 1953. In 1935, her adaptation of Edith Wharton's novel *The Old Maid* played on Broadway and won the Pulitzer Prize for Drama.

Sophie Treadwell was born in California to a mother of Scottish ancestry and a father of Mexican descent. Her father spent much of his early life in Mexico, and Treadwell's Mexican roots informed her dramatic writing. She was determinedly independent, marrying a fellow journalist and then maintaining separate residences from him throughout their marriage. She took her work directly to the Broadway theater with seven of her plays running on the Broadway stage between 1922 and 1941 usually to mixed reviews and for short runs. *Machinal* (1928), the best-known of these plays, is an expressionistic exploration of the dehumanization of the modern industrial world. More interesting perhaps are her many plays with multiracial casts set in Mexico and the Southwest. Beginning with *Gringo* (1922) set in a mine and camp in Mexico and featuring a cast of Mexican and American characters, she also wrote *The Island*, *The Last Border*, and *Lusita*, all set in Mexico, as well as *Highway*, set in West Texas. All of these plays feature multiracial casts, which include Mexican and Native American characters.

Though there were fewer venues for their work and therefore a more difficult struggle for them to get their stories out, African American women were also a forceful power in the American theater of the early twentieth century. Angelina Weld Grimke and Georgia Douglas Johnson, fellow poets and close friends, wrote anti-lynching plays to draw attention to the need for anti-lynching laws. After the 1918 armistice ended World War I, black and white troops returned home. During 1919, race riots erupted all over the US as whites struggled against the return of black men who had fought bravely as full US citizens. Lynching of blacks increased from fifty-eight in 1918 to seventy-seven in 1919. These anti-lynching plays brought home the human carnage and soul destruction that the rampant vigilante lynching had upon the black population and the nation as a whole. Other African American female playwrights wrote disturbing plays about their lives as wives and mothers in a segregated world where all opportunities were closed to them and their families.

Angelina Weld Grimke's heartbreaking play *Rachel* (1916) opened at the Neighborhood Playhouse in New York City in 1917 after receiving a production in Washington, DC, sponsored by the NAACP. *Rachel* tells the story of a young black woman whose father and brother were murdered by lynching. Her mother has protected her and her remaining brother and they have grown into loving adults. However, the institutionalized racism around them begins to break them as they discover that the murderers are thriving while they are being kept down by segregation laws, and as they witness young children around them spiritually and physically wounded and beaten by a system that condones violence toward black children. The play ends with Rachel rejecting a loving suitor and declaring that black women should not bring black children into the world to be so mistreated and that she will never marry or be a mother. Understandably, its production met with conflicted and controversial response.

Georgia Douglas Johnson, a contemporary and friend of Angelina Weld Grimke, was known as a poet, publishing four volumes of poetry and traveling often to give public readings. However, her marriage took her to Washington, DC, and there she began her Saturday Salons in her home on South Street. The S Street Salons, as they came to be called, provided a gathering place for black intellectuals and artists for some forty years. Fellow female African American writers May Miller, Marita Bonner, Mary Burrill, Alice Dunbar-Nelson, Zora Neale Hurston, and Angelina Weld Grimke joined in discussion and shared work with their male counterparts in what came to be called the Harlem Renaissance. Johnson wrote some twenty-eight plays directly addressing the experience of being black in America. One of the more commonly anthologized is *Plumes* (1927) which is inspired by the "folk plays" of the Irish playwright J. M. Synge, who wrote so feelingly about the hard lives of Irish peasants. In *Plumes*, an African American woman, alone with her very ill teenaged daughter, is visited by a neighbor. As they discuss the brutal options between using the little money the mother has to either pay a doctor for a surgery that might fail or to give her daughter a funeral which will honor her, the mother makes the heart-breaking decision to pay for death rather than life. The "choice" is grim—as is the world described by these black women in so many plays of this time which documented the cruelty that these American mothers had to endure toward themselves and their children.

Marita Bonner, a contemporary of Angelina Weld Grimke and Georgia Douglas Johnson, was born in Boston but moved to Washington, DC, for a teaching position and frequented the S Street Salon where she shared the ideals of Johnson and other black intellectuals. Bonner's work focused not only on her race but also her gender and her first essay, "On Being Young—A Woman—And Colored," written in 1925, asserted that one should not look only at race when seeing inequality, but also at gender. Her best-known one-act, *The Purple Flower*, written in 1928, is a poetic, mythic drama which portrays the white and black races in the moment right before revolution. The play ends with the "US's" representing the black race rising up against the "White Devils" with the rallying cry "You have taken blood; there can be no other way. You will have to give blood! Blood!" and Bonner's question "Is it time?"

American Women Playwrights, 1940s to 1960

Many of these pioneer American women playwrights were being produced up to and during World War II, which was a pivotal historic and cultural event in terms of women's rights and the power of women's voices. In the 1940s, emerging playwrights such as Shirley Graham, Lillian Hellman, Maxine Wood, Gertrude Stein, Fay Kanin, and Carson McCullers challenged the underlying assumptions of the American Dream, the sanctity of family, and, more specifically, how men and women defined themselves in their relationships to one another.

The outlines of the tensions within what constituted the accepted masculine and feminine roles were put in context by historian Susan Hartmann, who, in her book *The Home Front and Beyond: American Women in the 1940s*, argues that while in 1940 a little over 25 percent of American women worked outside the home, by 1945 this had risen to 36 percent. This was not received well by the male arbiters of culture. Theater critic Norris Houghton wrote in a 1947 article, appearing in an issue of *Theatre Arts Magazine*, that he hoped returning veterans would "hold the line against the Amazonian hoards ... [since American theater had] withdrawn too much from the world of men [becoming] content to reflect the trivialities of domesticity ... rather than face up to the sinewy and exacting life of our time." Two plays by women,

Rose Franklin's *Soldier's Wife* (1944) and Esther Hawley's *On the Way Home* (1945), echoed Houghton's sentiment, presenting female protagonists who defer to the needs of men to reclaim their dominant masculine role within the household. A slightly more assertive female protagonist is presented in Anita Loos' 1946 comedy *Happy Birthday*, written specifically for Helen Hayes, which centers around a timid librarian who eventually emerges from her inhibitions through the missing ingredient of love.

Adding to the giddiness accompanying the Japanese surrender on August 14, 1945, the prevailing feeling among Americans was that having won the "Good War" abroad, the next order of business was to sustain the peace at home and the belief in the boundless optimism for the future. As critic June Schlueter points out in her survey of plays and playwrights from 1945 to 1970, the post-war vision of the inevitability of prosperity and ultimate happiness through grit and perseverance, embodied in the 1940s Broadway musicals *Carousel*, *South Pacific*, *Brigadoon*, and *Kiss Me, Kate*, was countered in Eugene O'Neill's 1946 play *The Iceman Cometh* where the down-and-out regulars frequenting Harry Hope's saloon bear witness to the reality that, for better and usually for worse, their lives are insupportable without illusions.

For over a decade after World War II ended, American women struggled to keep the personal and political power they had gained during the war years when the men were away and they had to take up the men's work. Culturally, the US seemed to be living an illusion of peace, prosperity, and every race and gender in its proper place, though underneath boiled the growing rebellion of all women and people of color. The clash between the modern reality and a yearning for a return to an idyllic past found dramatic expression in plays of Tennessee Williams, Arthur Miller, and Eugene O'Neill whose characters yearn for a return to a world of innocence and a nostalgia that is more imagined than actual. These plays convey the theme that a poetic sensibility is unable to survive in a more abrasive post-war world where damaged men such as Stanley Kowalski or Willy Loman can reassert their masculinity within the domestic sphere, the most likely place where their authority will go unchallenged.

However, female playwrights like Lillian Hellman presented a different picture. Hellman, one of the most successful and powerful female voices on the American stage in the middle of the twentieth century, used the family to dramatize these seismographic disruptions in American life but from the woman's perspective. Working in a classically "well-made" form familiar to Broadway audiences and therefore "comfortable," Hellman launched theatrical bombs by exploring themes of lesbianism in *The Children's Hour* (1934), fascism in *Watch on the Rhine* (1941), and the warping of womanhood due to ongoing subjugation in *The Little Foxes* (1939). Plays such as *Another Part of the Forest* (1946) and *The Autumn Garden* (1951) examined, through her always dramatically endowed female characters, the underside of familial bonds as emblematic of societal failings.

In the middle of the twentieth century, within a decade of each other, in 1949 and 1959, two of the most influential plays of the American theater in what is called "the American Century" appeared on the Broadway stage: Arthur Miller's *Death of a Salesman* and Lorraine Hansberry's *A Raisin in the Sun*. Miller continued his dramatic excavation of the moral failings of ordinary and unremarkable men, achieving its fullest expression in his 1949 play *Death of a Salesman*. In the tragic figure of Willy Loman, we see how his outsized dreams of success are thwarted, but kept alive through deceit and delusions of grandeur that are passed on to his wife and two sons. But these delusions, which held sway in a more innocent time before the national trauma of war, can no longer preserve the sanctity of family and the matrimonial bond. Like Williams, in his memory play *The Glass Menagerie*, Miller makes effective use of expressionistic, interior monologues where Willy Loman reveals the self-justifying reconstructions of his own life that have sustained him, leading irrevocably to his inevitable suicide--which, tragically, seems the only alternative left to redeem himself and his family from his life misspent in the service of illusions.

The postwar 1950s concluded with the production of Lorraine Hansberry's 1959 paradigm-changing drama *A Raisin in the Sun*, which was the first play by a black American woman to be produced on Broadway. Hansberry's drama features the Youngers, a working-class black family on the Southside of Chicago, whose specific circumstances and hopes called into question the promises of the American Dream for black Americans in post-World War II America. As James Baldwin wrote at the time: "Never before in American theatre history has so much of the truth of black people's lives been seen on stage." In addition to the play dramatizing the efforts of the Younger family to buy a home in an all white neighborhood, there were issues raised about the significance to black Americans of the emergence of independent African nations from European colonialism, the struggle of Walter Lee Younger, Jr. to define his manhood in a manner different from his deceased father and apart from the dominant presence of his mother Lena Younger, and, most notably, the startling revelation of Walter Lee's younger sister Beneatha, a black woman whose intellectual aspirations were without precedent at that moment in American theater. *A Raisin in the Sun* became a play to be reckoned with in any subsequent attempts by American playwrights of any race or gender to dramatize the family as embodying the pressing issues confronting society as a whole.

Other female playwrights were challenging not only the prevailing dramatic content but also the form of the well-made play and traditional stagecraft during the 1940s and 1950s. African American playwright Shirley Graham (who would later marry W.E.B. Du Bois) was an actor and political activist, studied music composition at the Sorbonne, and wrote several plays, as well as *Tom Tom*, the first opera produced in the United States (1932) to examine racial issues. Graham's 1940 play *It's Morning* dramatizes the lengths to which a black slave mother goes to protect her child from growing up enslaved. Anticipating Toni Morrison's novel *Beloved*, the play used musical interludes, dance, verse, and a mixture of black vernacular and more formal verbal expression to capture the disparities of class existing under the system of slavery. The play opened on Broadway, but had only a brief run, a clear indication that an America about to enter into a war against fascism and Aryan supremacy abroad was unwilling to expose itself to the legacy of slavery and white supremacy at home seventy-five years after the end of the Civil War.

Like Shirley Graham, Gertrude Stein, in collaboration with composer Virgil Thompson, used American history in creating the 1947 opera *The Mother of Us All* reimagining the life of pioneering suffragette Susan B. Anthony, as well as imagined and actual figures such as Daniel Webster, Ulysses S. Grant, and Lillian Russell, who populate the historical past but speak directly to the contemporary moment of post-World War II America. The opera was invigorated by Thompson's original use of folk and Protestant church music and Stein's playfully serious libretto with her stylized prose that had the appearance of childlike simplicity but never lacked in surprising profundity.

Lesser-known dramatists such as Doris Frankel and Maxine Wood took on the controversial subject of racial bigotry at a time during and right after World War II when the country was reluctant to confront what sociologist Gunnar Myrdal would call, in his important 1944 study, "the American Dilemma." Frankel's play *Journey for an Unknown Soldier* (1943) took aim at the shameful internment of Japanese Americans held in concentration camps during the war, and Wood's *On Whitman Avenue* (1946) dramatized the court-sanctioned practice of denying blacks the opportunity to buy homes in all white suburban neighborhoods. The play was virtually ignored by mainstream theater critics except for the positive reviews it received from the black press and the subject was not taken up again until thirteen years later in Lorraine Hansberry's drama *A Raisin in the Sun.*

Fay Kanin's 1948 comedy *Goodbye, My Fancy* tapped into the broadening aspirations of women in post-World War II America beyond what was expected of them as wives and mothers. Carson McCullers' dramatic adaptation of her novel *The Member of the Wedding* (1950) and Jane Bowles' play *In the Summer House* (1953) depicted intimate portraits of unconventional young women grappling with societal expectations within and outside the family.

With America no longer pre occupied with a war abroad, it took refuge in the Cold War with its fixation on the threat of communism embodied in the Soviet Union as the greatest threat to democracy. There was a reluctance to look deeper into the home-grown psychic demons that were brought into sharp relief even as the country tried to slip into the willful ignorance of domestic tranquility. After generations of demeaning stereotypes of blacks in theater and film, many black women who were actors began to write their own plays with characters that revealed richly layered interior lives unknown to most of the theatergoing public. Actor and political activist Beah Richards wrote *A Black Woman Speaks* (1950), a single-figure performance piece in verse on the mutual oppression of black and white women that also indicted the latter for their complicity in the continuing denigration of women of color.

Alice Childress also responded to this absence of complicated black women characters in American theatre by writing the 1949 one-act play *Florence* that focused on an encounter between a Southern black woman and a white woman awaiting a train that will take them to New York City. The play dramatizes the extent to which the black woman, on her way to dissuade her daughter Florence from pursuing an acting career, discovers how much she has internalized the dominant white society's low expectations for blacks when the white woman offers to help her daughter get a job as a maid. In a later full-length play *Trouble in Mind* (1955) Childress presents a biting satire set in a theater where a group of black female and male actors commiserate about the caricatures of themselves that they are inevitably offered to play—which have not moved very far from the days of blackface minstrelsy.

American Women Playwrights, 1960s and Beyond

In the January 1960 issue of *Esquire* magazine, historian Arthur Schlesinger, Jr. wrote of the new decade that "At periodic moments in our history, our country has paused on the threshold of a new epoch in our national life . . . One feels that we are approaching such a moment now—that the mood which has dominated the nation for a decade . . . no longer interprets our desires and needs as a people; that new forces . . . energies (and) values are straining for expression and for release." Schlesinger's words couldn't have been more prescient. But it is unlikely that even he was prepared for the magnitude of what was about to be unleashed in the social, political, and cultural landscape of America.

Playwrights such as Hellman, Williams, and Miller had already torn away the illusion of cohesion and safety that marriage and family was supposed to provide for women and men. But their work was still bound, for the most part, to realistic depictions of a world that didn't depart very far from the features of experience easily recognizable to an audience. The 1956 American production of Samuel Beckett's *Waiting for Godot* not only challenged the perennial American embrace of optimism but also discarded any semblance of theatrical realism in its staging.

Edward Albee was one of the first American playwrights to take up the challenge presented in *Waiting for Godot*. One can see the emerging arc of Albee's work in two early 1960s plays, *The Zoo Story* and *The American Dream*. In the former, two men who are disaffected from society but completely opposite in their adherence to conventional values meet on a New York Central Park bench and play out the shocking absurdities of their efforts to make a human connection. In the latter, a caricatured American family is thwarted in its perverse desire to adopt a child that will fit into an idealized image of perfection. This need to create the illusion of a child that would fill the void in otherwise unfulfilled lives found its culmination in Albee's 1962 play *Who's Afraid of Virginia Woolf?*

Albee influenced his and subsequent generations of American playwrights. Two, in particular, whose first plays he helped to introduce to theater audiences, were LeRoi Jones' (a.k.a. Amiri Baraka) *Dutchman* and Adrienne Kennedy's *Funnyhouse of a Negro*. Both plays opened in 1964 and received Obie Awards. Kennedy's expressionistic play is a cross-fertilization of seemingly unreconciled images from the mind of Sarah, the daughter of a black father and a white mother. Historical figures such as Patrice Lumumba, Queen Victoria, the Dutchess of Hapsburg, and Jesus populate Sarah's psyche, culminating in her failure to find a way to bring any coherence to these disparate parts of her identity. The voices speaking through Kennedy's plays are figures who depart from the fixed identities of coherent and easily recognized individuals. As drama scholar Philip C. Kolin has written in his book *Understanding Adrienne Kennedy*, "her characters are fragmented, splintered, often dispersed into warring selves. They are dispossessed persons caught in the flux of rapidly shifting, alternating identities, all inside their own skin." Kennedy remains a major force in the American theater, premiering her newest work, *He Brought Her Heart Back in a Box*, in New York City in 2018 and influencing contemporary playwrights.

The year 1964 also witnessed a play by Lorraine Hansberry, *The Sign in Sidney Brustein's Window*. Hansberry's play focuses on a group of bohemians and lapsed radicals living in Greenwich Village in the late 1950s and early 1960s who must come to terms with the cumulative impact that too many small ethical compromises can have on lessening their grasp of matters of greater consequence. What took the critical establishment by surprise was that nearly all the characters were white. The unarticulated discomfort among many seemed to be that Hansberry refused to segregate her dramatic imagination as the American theater and society was continuing to do. Her audacity was a rarity in the theatre when the play opened in 1964, and it has been an example for subsequent generations of American women playwrights. Yet her powerful voice was silenced less than a year later when she died of cancer at the age of thirty-four.

The 1960s produced the work of other emerging women playwrights that included Megan Terry, Rochelle Owens, Barbara Garson, and Maria Irene Fornes. Cuban-born Fornes was arguably the most daring in her use of inventive staging and non-traditional dramatic techniques. Having been in Paris, studying to be a painter, she saw the French production of Beckett's *Waiting for Godot*, and returned to America determined to devote herself to writing plays. Fornes' first two plays were *Tango Palace* (1964) and *Promenade* (1965), which won an Obie Award. *Promenade* was notable for its mixture of music and literary borrowings from Beckett, *Candide*, and Lewis Carroll, as the play follows two escaped prisoners, identified only by the numbers 105 and 106, through the distorting images of a world resembling a funhouse mirror. Fornes continued to be recognized for her unconventional body of work with a total of nine Obie Awards and she is credited as an inspiration by playwrights such as Paula Vogel, Tony Kushner, and Sam Shepard. Fornes continued writing into the twenty-first century, passing away in 2018.

Not surprisingly, the civil rights and black empowerment movements of the late 1960s and early 1970s inspired an outpouring of dramatic works from writers who were loosely part of what came to be known as the Black Arts Movement. Although the numbers of plays produced were dominated by black male writers such as Amiri Baraka, Ed Bullins, Lonne Elder III, Charles Gordone, Bill Gunn, Paul Carter Harrison, Leslie Lee, Ron Milner, Joseph Walker, Jr., and Richard Wesley, plays by black women were making their presence felt: Alice Childress, who had been writing plays since the early 1950s, wrote *Wedding Band* (1966) and *Wine in the Wilderness* (1968); Sonia Sanchez, a central figure in the Black Arts Movement, wrote *Sister Sonji* (1969, produced at the Public Theater) and *The Bronx is Next* (1970); J.E. Franklin wrote *Black Girl* (1971 and made into a film directed by Ossie Davis); Aishah Rahman wrote *Unfinished Woman Cry in No Man's Land While a Bird Dies in a Gilded Cage* (1977) and *The Mojo and the Sayso* (1987).

Ntozake Shange, who saw herself primarily as a poet, was able to take full advantage of this creative explosion and added (to use a term coined by Alice Walker) a "womanist perspective" that was distinctly her own. Shange extended the interior journey that Adrienne Kennedy dramatized by writing herself into existence using a theatrical form she called a "choreopoem" in *for colored girls who have considered suicide/when the rainbow is enuf* (1975). Using dance and live music to animate black women's voices out of the silence imposed by racial and gender stereotypes, Shange also viewed language as a form of what she called "combat breathing" (a term she borrowed from Frantz Fanon) to "attack deform n maim the language that I waz taught to hate myself in." *for colored girls . . .* received both praise and condemnation, but not indifference, and should be considered one of the seminal theatrical events of the 1970s. Shange's daring work paved the way for playwrights such as Pearl Cleage, Wendy Wasserstein, Suzan-Lori Parks, and Lynn Nottage.

After the political tumult of the 1960s and 1970s when women again joined with people of color to demand rights that transcended the right to vote such as reproductive rights, the right to live where they chose, and the right to equal pay and equal opportunity to education and jobs, the 1980s felt like a time of licking wounds. Hard-won policies like affirmative action were being fought in court. A strong campaign was mounted against women's reproductive rights. Women who had fought on the front lines in the 1960s and 1970s were ready to hand the baton to the next generation, but that generation wasn't ready to take it on. Though lasting change had not yet happened, women had made gains in autonomy and economic freedom and younger women coming up didn't see the urgency to keep it moving forward.

Wendy Wasserstein's Pulitzer Prize and Tony Award-winning 1988 play *The Heidi Chronicles* seemed to speak directly to this crucial moment in women's empowerment. Heidi Holland, an art historian who has risen to the top in her academic field, has achieved her success at the cost of having a partner and family. The play poignantly documents the second wave of feminism as we watch Heidi grow from a sixteen-year-old high school student in 1965, navigating romance and career dreams, through college consciousness-raising Rap Groups, a feminist academic career in the 1970s and 1980s, holding the hand of her dearest friend through the AIDS crisis and finally choosing to adopt a child on her own in 1989. In the final scene, Heidi holds her daughter up to the heavens saying: "A heroine for the twenty-first!" in a rallying cry that resonates across the twentieth century and into the twenty-first.

Wasserstein's plays were being produced by André Bishop, first at Playwright's Horizons and later at Lincoln Center Theater, but except for Carole Rothman at Second Stage Theater and Julia Miles at The Women's Project, it was still very difficult for women to find commercial producers for their plays in New York City or anywhere in the US in the 1980s. Tina Howe and Theresa Rebeck found their home with Carole Rothman, and many women playwrights such as Maria Irene Fornes found tremendous support at The Women's Project where Miles was supporting both women playwrights and women directors. In the regional theater, playwrights Marsha Norman and Beth Henley were first produced at the Actors' Theater of Louisville Humana Festival of New American Plays. Founded by Jon Jory, Producing Director, in 1976, the Humana festival and Jory's support of women playwrights contributed greatly to the growth of plays by women being produced across the US in the latter part of the twentieth century. Not only was Jory committed to producing plays by American women, but many of the playwrights were produced year after year, allowing them to nurture and deepen their craft in front of audiences. Many women playwrights, when asked why plays by women weren't being produced in America, responded that it was probably because most artistic directors were men. Jory, André Bishop, and more recently Douglas Aibel at the Vineyard Theater, James Houghton at the Signature Theater, and George C. Wolfe at the Public Theater are the exception. Today female artistic directors Rothman at Second Stage, Emily Mann at the McCarter, Molly Smith at Arena Stage, and Lynn Meadows at Manhattan Theater Club, among others, continue to support the work of women playwrights.

While our anthology of plays from 1970 to 2020 could not include the many diverse voices of women writing for the American stage as the twentieth century ended and the twenty-first century began, we pay tribute to some who are not among these pages and encourage readers to seek out their work.

For over forty years Tina Howe (b. 1937) has pushed the boundaries of American drama with her highly stylized, female-centered plays. After launching her career with the fifty-five-character *Museum* (1976) and *The Art of Dining* (1979), she formed a creative partnership with Carole Rothman at Second Stage Theater in New York City and Rothman directed the premieres of her next three plays: *Painting Churches* (1983), *Coastal Disturbances* (1986) and *Approaching Zanzibar* (1989). Howe has been a finalist for the Pulitzer Prize for Drama for both *Painting Churches* and *Pride's Crossing* as well as a nominee for the Tony Award for Best Play for *Coastal Disturbances*. *Pride's Crossing* (1998) won the New York Drama Critics' Circle Award for Best American Play in 1998, and she has been honored with several awards for distinguished achievement in the American theater.

Marsha Norman (b. 1947), a native of Louisville, Kentucky presented her first play *Getting Out* (1979) at the Humana Festival of New American Plays at the Actors' Theater of Louisville where it was so well received that it went to Off-Broadway for a successful run there. She followed this with her best-known and Pulitzer Prize-winning play *'Night Mother* in 1983. Both plays put troubled women who are rarely seen onstage at the center of the story in a frank and confrontational way. Norman later turned to writing for the musical theater, winning the Tony Award for Best Book for a Musical for *Secret Garden* in 1991 and a nomination for the Tony Award for Best Book for a Musical for *The Color Purple* in 2005. She continues to work in theater, film, and television and to mentor emerging female playwrights through her teaching.

Throughout the 1990s and into the twenty-first century, several black female playwrights created works of theater where multiple characters were played by one or two actors and language made the vernacular poetic. The tradition of Ntozake Shange and Adrienne Kennedy, where drama is infused with poetry and lyricism, continues with Anna Deveare Smith and Dael Orlandersmith, both of whom perform the work they create.

Anna Deveare Smith (1950), born in Baltimore, has had a rich and rewarding career as both an actress and a playwright. Her documentary-style theater piece *Fires in the Mirror*, composed of interviews with twenty-six people about the riots in Crown Heights, Brooklyn in 1991, won her the nomination for the Pulitzer Prize for Drama and the Drama Desk Award for Outstanding One Person Show in 1993. Her next solo piece, *Twilight: Los Angeles, 1992*, also won her the Drama Desk Award for Outstanding One Person Show as well as two Tony Award nominations for Best Play and Best Actress. In both plays Smith explores the American character by speaking the words of Americans from all races, religions, and classes as they respond to two seismic events in recent American history. Her recent play *Notes from the Field: Doing Time in Education* confronts head on incarceration, the plague that continues to destroy young black men.

Dael Orlandersmith (1959) grew up in New York City's east Harlem neighborhood. Her play *Yellowman*, which explores colorism in the black community, premiered in 2002 at the McCarter Theater and was a Pulitzer Prize finalist for Drama winning Orlandersmith the Susan Smith Blackburn Prize for Drama. In it, Orlandersmith and another actor portray eight characters in the life of the main characters, Alma, a dark-skinned black woman, and Eugene, a fair-skinned black man. Orlandersmith herself played Alma in the premiere of the play at the Manhattan Theater Club. Orlandersmith's incredibly powerful body of work began in 1995 with *Beauty's Daughter* and continues through to her recent unsettling piece *Until the Flood* which documents the murder of Michael Brown in Ferguson, Missouri, in 2014 and premiered in New York City in January 2018.

In the first two decades of the twenty-first century, more and more female playwrights are being produced both in New York City and in theaters around the US. Lisa Loomer (1950), Amy Freed (1958), Theresa Rebeck (1958), Wendy MacLeod (1959), Regina Taylor (1960), Lisa Kron (1961), Tracey Scott Wilson (1966), Lucy Thurber (1970), Brooke Berman (1970), Sarah Jones (1973), Young Jean Lee (1974), Sarah Ruhl (1974), Julia Cho (1975), Quiara Alegria Hudes (1977), Dominique Morisseau (1978), Danai Gurira (1978), Amy Herzog (1979), Annie Baker (1981), Jackie Sibblies Drury (1982), and Martyna Majok (1985) are only some of the many diverse and powerful female voices that make up the current American theater.

In 2002 the results of a three-year study on women in the theater by the New York State Council on the Arts revealed that only 17 percent of all plays produced in theaters across America were written by women. It was no surprise that most of those produced were in not-for-profit or Off-Broadway houses. The industry took note and in the intervening years there has been a concerted effort to showcase not only female playwrights but also female directors, who have also been sorely underrepresented in the American theater. With more and more women at the helm of both New York and regional theaters as artistic directors, more opportunities are being given to women playwrights. Now, one hundred years after women like Alice Gerstenberg and Susan Glaspell founded their own theater companies in order to create and produce work that represented their lives and spoke their truths, and women like Angelina Weld Grimke and Georgia Douglas Johnson gathered in salons and found venues for their plays to be seen and heard, the American theater finally seems ready to embrace all voices, of all genders and all races in a profound way.

With such a wealth of voices to choose from in the period that we cover in this anthology, 1970 to 2020, our focus has been to bring together six playwrights whose form, in many ways, breaks with the dramatic tradition of their time in order to deliver their messages, which are equally revolutionary to their form—in use of language, in use of staging, in the very characters they portray, and in the confrontational subject matter that the plays present. These are voices for all time and, like the voices of every playwright we document in this anthology, they deserve to be not only heard again and again but also a significant part of the canon of American plays.

Introduction to Susan Yankowitz

Wesley Brown

Born in Newark, New Jersey, in 1941, Susan Yankowitz can be seen as a bridge, connecting the innovative work of Adrienne Kennedy and Maria Irene Fornes to that of Paula Vogel, Ntozake Shange, and Suzan-Lori Parks through their use of highly charged poetic language and departures from the linear structure of conventional dramatic form. She graduated from Sarah Lawrence College and the Yale School of Drama. Over the course of Yankowitz's theatrical career, her work has received support from the National Endowment for the Arts and the Guggenheim and Rockefeller Foundations.

One of Yankowitz's earliest works was the genre-breaking *Terminal, 1969* with Joseph Chaikin's Open Theater Group, which was produced again in a revised version in 1996. It was with this collaborative theatrical work that Yankowitz began her persistent engagement with our confrontation of the inevitability of death. In addressing this preoccupation, she has written that "As a writer, I am very drawn to the drama of people in extreme situations, people pushed by fate or accident or character to the edge of some abyss, personal or political." Adding to this theme is another emerging from her work, which is, in her words, "a nightmare of my own . . . which I know I share with many others: the terror of being locked in the self, unable to communicate." These thematic concerns play out in *Terminal, 1969* through fragments performed by a single actor or several, using stylized language to dramatize the seamless relationship between life and death and how the latter informs how we live.

The 1960s were notable for the emergence of the first works by several women playwrights that included Maria Irene Fornes (*Tango Palace*, 1964 and *Promenade*, 1965) and Adrienne Kennedy (*Funnyhouse of a Negro*, 1964 and *The Owl Answers*, 1965). What Yankowitz had in common with Fornes and Kennedy was the use of expressionistic language and interior monologues.

In 1991, Yankowitz was reunited with Joseph Chaikin in *Night Sky*, a play inspired by the director's own experience with aphasia after suffering a blood clot in his brain. In a series of time-bending, beautifully rendered short scenes that are, alternatingly, unsettling and hilarious, Anna, a woman astronomer is diagnosed with aphasia after an automobile accident. In Yankowitz's words aphasia "is an injury to the language center in the brain, which causes the words to get lost somehow in the mind. The intelligence is there—the person knows what he wants to say but just can't find the right words." The extremity of Anna's situation in *Night Sky* is reminiscent of Yankowitz's 1976 novel *Silent Witness*, in which a blind woman accused of murdering her lover must come to terms, not only with being held captive by grief and the absence of sight, but by the captivity of prison. In an interview about the play *Night Sky*, she addressed her obsessive preoccupation with our failure as human beings to communicate: "I guess I have always had the sense that I am not able to really articulate what is inside of me, and why words only approximate either my thought or my feeling. The second thing is a sense that I am not understood—that what I have to say doesn't really communicate in the way I would like it to to other people, so they don't really understand who I am, [or] what I'm trying to express."

Yankowitz's *Phaedra in Delirium* (1998) is an updating of the Greek myth of Phaedra embodied in a contemporary woman's mid-life crisis, who marries her sister's philandering husband, falls in love with her stepson, but is ultimately abandoned by the former and rejected by the latter. With the juggling of events and time, Yankowitz employs heightened poetic language to expose the passions driving human behavior that are fated to confound our efforts to communicate in ways that are not destructive. A year later in 1999, Suzan-Lori Parks' play *In the Blood* also took up the challenge of reimagining an iconic literary figure. Produced at the Public Theater in New York City, the play was a late twentieth-century variation on Hawthorne's *The Scarlet Letter*, where the protagonist, Hester Prynne, is portrayed as a black American woman who is besieged by poverty and demonized by a society, embodied in the helping institutions charged with assisting a woman barely eking out a living for herself and five children. Yankowitz continued this examination of how we lockdown our own humanity and that of others in the 2012 play *A–Z Boxes*, an ensemble piece with several actors playing many roles and occupying boxes of various types that are either chosen by or imposed upon them.

Gun, a recent play, is an intimate dissection of a family whose young adult son is responsible for a mass shooting. The play is all of a piece with the themes that have consistently dominated Yankowitz's work, such as people unable to communicate and finding themselves in desperate circumstances that take on larger social and political implications beyond the fates of specific individuals. The main characters are Donald Holt, in his late teens or early twenties, and his parents, both in their forties. Following a practice in her previous plays, the playwright has other characters take on three or four roles. In her notes on the play Yankowitz indicates that the staging should approximate the unsettling and chaotic nature of what unfolds, dramatically, within the play where "[p]hysical and vocal stylization is required to achieve a sense of heightened reality . . . [and] . . . [s]tyles overlap . . . as time and place do. While we are sure of where we are at a given moment, we cannot predict where we will be going. It is a world in which anything can happen."

Gun opens with intense violin playing over a dream sequence where Mrs. Holt rises from a bed and witnesses several surreal and nightmarishly violent scenes involving a young boy, causing her to scream. This initial scene is the first of many flashes back and forward, as the Holts become surrogates for the audience, in an effort to discover what was hiding in plain sight in the life of their son Donald making him capable of shooting seven people, three fatally, and among them a charismatic governor running for president whom he greatly admired. As Mr. and Mrs. Holt seek explanations for Donald's heinous acts in predictable theatrical spaces such as a bedroom, a psychiatrist's office, a courtroom, or an interview room Yankowitz upends these typically pedestrian scenes used in naturalistic drama by accelerating them through rapid bursts of dialogue, making the horrifying events depicted in the play all the more compelling when they are quickened into dramatic time.

Susan Yankowitz's play *Gun* is the culmination of a body of work that began with *Terminal, 1969*, and dramatizes the dangers of living isolated within ourselves in the mistaken belief that we are separate from what is common to us all: mortality. Similarly, in *Gun*, the forces imposed upon the characters and those that are self-generating are always in an intimate conversation with one another. As Yankowitz mentions in the stage directions at the end of the play, "Mrs. Holt flings opens the door. It leads to OUTSIDE. And gunshots are heard. [There] is now a fusillade of GUNSHOTS. The DOOR collapses. The OUTSIDE and the INSIDE are now one and the same."

Gun

Susan Yankowitz

Note: Please do not be intimidated by the size of this characters list. Many characters only appear once. Seven actors will suffice to play all roles.

Characters

Mrs. Holt, *late forties*
Mr. Holt, *late forties*
Donald Holt, *their son, at ages sixteen to twenty-four*
Doctor Loeb, *a psychiatrist, fifty*
Milly, *a friend of Mrs. Holt, forty*
Kay, *also a friend*
Butcher
Jordan, *the lawyer, thirty-five to forty-five*
Salesman
Newscaster/Reporter
Eyewitness
Linda Ritter, *twenty*
Annie Soltan, *twenty-two*
Mrs. Diamond, *a matriarch, seventy*

Suggested Doubling
(allowing **Mr., Mrs.,** and **Donald Holt** their individual roles)
Dr. Loeb/Salesman/Eyewitness
Mrs. Diamond/Kay/Office Worker
Linda/Annie/Milly
Jordan/Butcher/Newscaster/Reporter

Notes on Sets and Staging

Essentially, the actors are working on a bare stage in which specific environments are evoked by basic objects. A bed, for instance, defines the Holts' bedroom. A panel of bars creates a prison cell. A straight-backed chair (possibly placed on a wooden box) becomes the witness stand and, by extension, the courtroom. Free-standing mirrors and doors evoke the almost surreal atmosphere of the play.

In this play, visual images are as important as dialogue. Physical and vocal stylization is required to achieve a sense of heightened reality. Styles overlap here, as time and place do. While we are sure of where we are at a given moment, we cannot predict where we will be going. It is a world in which anything can happen.

This is a work of fragments, of parts that suggest a whole. The simplest moment should stand for the most complex. Like the set, the staging should never attempt to gussy up the bones.

Sound

Whatever type of score is chosen, the sound design should incorporate the staccato of gunshots. After all, the other main character—the GUN—is both inside the play and hovering over it, jolting any complacency.

Prologue

Violin music—Beethoven—gentle at first, growing more agitated.

Downstage center, a series of doors, one behind the other. Only the first is fully visible. On it, a baby plaque, decorated with animals and angels, reads "Donald's room."

At one side of the stage, two people are sleeping in a double bed.

Mrs. Holt, *wearing a shapeless nightgown, bolts upright, gasping. She climbs out of bed—but her movements are infinitely slow, as if she were traversing dreams.*

She flings open the first door. Behind it stands a crib: an infant's blue head is wedged between the slats. Her mouth opens in a scream but no sound comes from it.

She walks to the second door. On it is a sheet of paper announcing in a childish scrawl: "Donald's room." She opens the door. For an instant we see a small child's back; then there is the sound of a match striking and the room erupts in flames. **Mrs. Holt** *tries to enter the room but freezes, repeatedly, as if trapped in molasses.*

She runs to the next door and opens. The floor is littered with the bodies of dead animals. Her breathing changes—short bursts, on the verge of hyperventilation, as she slams the door.

Her terrified breathing accompanies her to the next door. On it hangs a computer-designed sign: "DONALD'S ROOM. KNOCK BEFORE ENTERING—THAT MEANS YOU!" She knocks, soundlessly, then enters. The body of a young boy swings from a noose. She backs away in horror.

Behind this is yet another door with no sign at all. The violin music is louder now, as though she were nearing its source, and there is a frenzy in it.

She flings the door open. There, his back to her, is the teenaged **Donald** *playing the violin. For the first time, her body relaxes. She listens for a moment. Then* **Donald** *turns around: he has no face.*

This time her scream is audible. It merges with the piercing notes of the violin.

At the sound, **Mr. Holt** *is startled awake.*

Mr. Holt   Omigod. The baby!

Runs toward his wife.

What is it? What happened?

Mrs. Holt (*still disoriented*)   I don't know . . .

Mr. Holt   You're shaking. Why did you scream?

Mrs. Holt   It must have been a nightmare. That's all. A nightmare.

Mr. Holt   I got so frightened. I thought he'd stopped breathing or fallen out of the crib—

Mrs. Holt   No, no. I just looked in on him. He's fine.

Together they climb back into bed as the violin music, subdued now, continues into the next scene.

Act One

Lights up in an upstairs room. A sixteen-year-old boy, **Donald Holt**, *is playing the violin. His playing is heart-felt and precise, but ungifted.*

The walls of his room are postered with photographs and newspaper blowups of famous men: political leaders, actors, rock stars, athletes, musicians.

Donald *is dressed meticulously. Everything about him, like the house itself, is immaculate and orderly.*

He hits a false note. His face registers disgust. Immediately he stops playing and carefully puts away the violin.

He lies on his bed and stares at the ceiling.

Mrs. Holt *has begun mounting the stairs to this room. She appears fifteen years older than in the prologue. Now she is at the door, knocking.*

Donald   Who is it?

Mrs. Holt   Mother.

Donald   You can't come in. I'm undressed.

Mrs. Holt   Aren't you practicing anymore?

Donald   I wasn't practicing; I was *playing* the violin.

Mrs. Holt   I know. I heard. It sounded very good.

Donald   To you.

He lies back in bed as:

In another area of the stage, lights encircle the psychiatrist, **Doctor Loeb**, *from his office. He addresses* **Mrs. Holt** *on the landing outside* **Donald**'s *room.*

Doctor Loeb   You say Donald was a good boy, Mrs. Holt.

Mrs. Holt   Yes.

Doctor Loeb   Exactly what do you mean by that?

Mrs. Holt   What any mother means. Well-behaved, respectful. A good student. He liked to read, play the violin.

Doctor Loeb   So while he was growing up, you had no concerns at all about him?

Mrs. Holt   Well. Naturally. Sometimes.

Doctor Loeb   Can you tell me why?

Mrs. Holt   Why? Because he didn't have a transitional object. Because he didn't hit back. Because he picked his nose. For God's sake, what mother doesn't worry about everything?!

Doctor Loeb   Maybe you worried that he was *too* good.

Mrs. Holt   Too good? How do you measure that, Doctor?

*Lights fade there as **Donald***'s words overlap hers.*

Donald   If I were really any good, I wouldn't be here.

Mrs. Holt   Where would you be then?

Donald   Giving a recital. Touring the country. Playing in a symphony orchestra. In Europe. That's where.

Mrs. Holt   But if you don't practice . . .

Donald   What's the point? I'll never be good enough, Mom. Anyway, I don't really care.

Mrs. Holt   Please, Donald. Let me in.

Donald   I told you: I'm naked.

Mrs. Holt   Isn't Annie coming over?

Donald   Yeah.

Mrs. Holt   Then you'd better get dressed fast.

Donald   I'm going to take a nap.

Mrs. Holt   That's not right, Donald. You made a date with her.

Donald   She'll find something else to do. Annie's got lots of friends.

*Spotlight on **Doctor Loeb**, overlapping, as before.*

Doctor Loeb   Did Donald have friends, Mrs. Holt?

Mrs. Holt   A few.

Doctor Loeb   Girls?

Mrs. Holt   Girlfriends, you mean? . . . Who knows? Teenagers are famous for keeping secrets, aren't they?

Doctor Loeb   How did he spend his time? When he wasn't in school?

Mrs. Holt   Reading. Listening to music. Doing homework. Doing something on the web.

Doctor Loeb   Those activities are all solitary.

Mrs. Holt   He didn't hang out, if that's what you mean, but he was hardly a "loner" in the sense that you are implying.

Doctor Loeb   Do you think he felt fearful somehow? Alienated?

Mrs. Holt   Don't we all?

Doctor Loeb   Yes, to some degree, but—

Mrs. Holt   Wasn't Kafka alienated? Fearful?

Doctor Loeb   He was, Mrs. Holt. But Kafka picked up a pen, not a gun.

Mrs. Holt   But were his *feelings* different, Doctor? Or just what he did with them?

Doctor Loeb   That's a very good question . . .

Mrs. Holt   Obviously one that you can't answer.

Wheels away and tries the knob to **Donald's** *room. It's locked.*

Mrs. Holt   Open up, Donald, open.

Donald   Give me a little privacy, will you?

Mrs. Holt   What am I going to say to Annie when she gets here?

Donald   Tell her I've flown the coop.

Mrs. Holt   You've had this date for a week.

Donald   So? Tell her I'm under the weather. That's easy. Tell her I have a cold. No. Tell her I'm burning up. I have a fever.

Mrs. Holt   I'm not going to lie for you.

Donald   Be creative, Mom. Tell her I'm out to lunch, okay? Tell her I'm far out. Tell her I turned into a mole and went underground. Yeah. Tell her I went under.

Blackout in **Donald's** *room.*

Mrs. Holt *goes downstairs, puts on her black coat, and ages. Then she walks from her house toward another area: the local* **Butcher** *shop.*

Lights. Two women are inside; the **Butcher** *is grinding meat.*

Butcher   There. Two pounds of chopped chuck. Anything else?

Kay   No, thanks. That's all.

Butcher   That'll be $15.90.

Mrs. Holt *enters. The atmosphere grows tense.*

Butcher   'Morning, Mrs. Holt.

Kay   Carol. What are you doing here?

Mrs. Holt   I still have to eat, don't I, Kay? Good morning, Milly.

Milly (*awkwardly; as* **Kay** *pays*)   How are you, Carol? I wanted to call, really I did, but . . . I just couldn't bring myself to—

Mrs. Holt   Everyone hates paying condolence calls.

Milly   Yes, yes, that's true, I mean, no. It's not exactly the same thing. I mean, Donald's not dead . . .

Mrs. Holt   Not exactly.

Butcher   What can I do for you, Mrs. Holt?

Mrs. Holt   A standing rib roast. Four or five pounds, please.

Kay   Come on, Milly. We have to go. Have a good day, Carol.

Mrs. Holt   Thanks. You too.

Milly   How are you bearing up? You and Lloyd?

Mrs. Holt   Well, we've decided against suicide.

Kay   Milly, please. I have to get home.

Milly   Just a minute, Kay!

*The **Butcher** is cutting the roast from a side of beef. He is nervous; his knife seems to saw against bone.*

Butcher   I think this cow has a few extra ribs. In the wrong places.

Mrs. Holt   Be gentle. God might decide to make women out of them.

Milly   It was such a shock, Carol. A real tragedy, everyone says so.

Kay   That's right. We all feel so sorry. Come on, Milly.

Mrs. Holt *is watching the rather bloody operation with grim fascination. When the* **Butcher** *finally severs the section of beef, he tosses it up on a scale to weigh it. He misses. The meat starts to fall to the floor.*

Instinctively, **Mrs. Holt** *reaches out to catch it, holds it in her hands for a second, and then flings it away from her with a scream. She is terribly shaken.*

Milly   Oh Carol, Carol . . .

Runs to embrace her. When she does, **Mrs. Holt** *breaks down in tears.*

Mrs. Holt   Forgive me. I didn't mean to—

Milly   No, no, don't apologize, I'm the one who should apologize, it must be devastating for you. I'm so sorry. I can't imagine anything more terrible—

Kay (*trying to tug* **Milly** *away*)   Don't, Milly. This isn't the time. Let's go. Please.

Mrs. Holt   Why are you in such a hurry? Do you think I'm contagious? Do you think you'll catch it from me?

Milly   No, no, of course she doesn't, Carol.

Mrs. Holt   It could have happened to you. It could have been your boy.

Kay   My James? Never. Never! These things are not accidents, Carol. There are causes, reasons. There had to be something . . . something sick in him, in you, in your home . . . Are you coming, Milly?

Milly   No. No, I'm not.

Kay *leaves. Lights dim on* **Milly** *comforting* **Mrs. Holt** *and come up in* **Donald**'s *bedroom.*

He is standing in front of a full-length mirror, in his underwear, holding a policeman's uniform. Nearby stands a rack of clothing. At one end hang suits; at the other are uniforms of various sorts: a sailor's, a surgeon's, a deep sea diver, etc. as desired.

Donald   I'm a cop. Everyone in town knows me. I stand at an intersection and tell the traffic which way to go. Stop, I say. No, I don't even have to say it; I just hold up my hand. And the cars stop. Then what? Then I help the kids cross the street. Kids and old people. Then what? Then . . . then . . . someone starts running across the street against my command, he's got a scared look on his face. I bet he's a crook. I whip out my gun. Stop, I yell. He keeps running. He's a sneaky little guy with long legs. But I chase after him. Why? Why? Because it's my job. Stop, I shout, in the name of the law! That doesn't work. So what do I do? I let my gun shout for me. Bang bang bang. He sprawls out flat on the pavement. Then what happens? Then what? Then I grab the wallet from his hand, a wallet belonging to Mrs. Cassell, with her social security check already endorsed. Okay. I . . . I bring the wallet back to Mrs. Cassell. Then what? Maybe she gives me ten bucks, which I'm not supposed to accept. Maybe she calls my mother, to tell her what a great guy I am, how I do my uniform proud. Then what?

Falters as the story becomes anticlimactic, not bringing him to the peak of excitement and heroism he craves.

I guess I go back to directing traffic . . . No. No, that's not it. I go into . . . into . . . into . . .

Flings down policeman's uniform and picks up soldier's motley camouflage.

. . . into the jungles, the forests, on my hands and knees. I'm searching for the enemy with my rifle and bayonet.

Mrs. Holt *has been walking up the stairs to his room. Now she knocks. There is no answer. She knocks again, waits.*

Donald   . . . I stab the bayonet spear into dead leaves; I'm getting in practice. Then I hear a noise behind me. I spin around—rat-a-tat-tat!—but after the sound clears, I don't see anyone, just trees that maybe aren't trees; everybody looks like a tree in war; even I do; that's my protection. Over my head planes are dropping big bundles—bombs or enemy people, I don't know which, they both make a scream when they fall—and I cover my head. I crouch down. It's so quiet I can forget where I am. The stars are like little candles.

Crouched down, he lies very still for a few moments. **Mrs. Holt** *knocks again.* **Donald** *makes no response, as if he's sleeping.*

Mrs. Holt   Donald, I know you're in there. We want to order the film tickets for this weekend . . .

Donald   . . . But I can't sleep. A soldier can't sleep . . . So what do I do? What?

Becomes inspired.

There's a fire, that's it, an enormous fire . . .

He throws down the soldier's uniform and wraps a firefighter's coat around his shoulders, puts the helmet on his head. **Mrs. Holt** *knocks.*

Mrs. Holt   Donald? Open up . . . Are you all right?

Still no response. Worried, she peeks through the keyhole.

Donald   . . . I hear the alarm. It's shrilling in my head. The engines come shrieking out of the firehouse and there I am, on the running board with the rest of them, and we ride, we ride till we get there, it's a house, no, it's an apartment house, all forty stories ablaze, and we unwind the hoses from the spools, we lug them close, and on comes the water, so powerful it's like we've got the ocean roaring through that hose. But that's not enough. Water doesn't do it. A man's needed to do it.

Mrs. Holt (*beginning down the stairs*)   Well, think about what you want to see and we'll decide at dinner.

Donald (*oblivious to* **Mrs. Holt***'s words, her presence or absence*)   There are people screaming from the top windows. I run through the flames and up the stairways. The smoke is in my lungs. I burst through a door into the corridor. There are bodies everywhere. I drag two kids under my arms like they were footballs and I run with them, I run back down the stairs and into the icy air. Here they are, here they are, I did it, I yell. These kids are saved, the only ones, and I did it! Then what? My picture's in the paper. I saved two kids. Then what? What?

Frantically drops the fireman's outfit, puts on the surgeon's gown.

I save more. And more. I take hearts from dead people and make them pump again for dying ones. I cut out cancers, sew on severed limbs. I keep on operating. There's an emergency a minute. Someone almost dies every minute. But I save them. Then what? Then what? Then what?!

Stares at his reflection in the mirror.

Mrs. Holt *goes to her husband, who is reading a newspaper in the living room.*

Mrs. Holt   He won't let me in, Lloyd. He tunes me out.

Mr. Holt   You know what the pros say about that. You have to give teenagers their space.

Mrs. Holt   I peeked through the keyhole. He's dressing up again.

Mr. Holt   Dressing up—like putting on costumes, like pretending. Didn't you do stuff like that?

Mrs. Holt   Yes . . . but I was a girl.

Mr. Holt   So? What's your point? He's not putting on women's clothes, is he?

Jordan, *the lawyer, rolls the rack of clothing out of* **Donald***'s room into another area, where a straight-backed chair is spotlit.*

Donald   Hey! Where are you taking my stuff?!

Donald *follows him.* **Mr.** *and* **Mrs. Holt** *follow with their eyes.*

A gavel pounds thrice, evoking the courtroom.

Jordan   You have been sworn in and your obligation to the truth remains.

Donald *sits in the spotlit chair.*

Jordan   You recognize these clothes, I see.

Donald   Oh, yes, they're mine.

Jordan (*selects the cop's uniform from the rack*)   This is yours?

Donald   Yes, sir.

Jordan (*holding up a priest's vestments*)   And this?

Donald   Yes, sir. All of them.

Jordan (*showing the court a judge's robe*)   Even this?

Donald   I told you: they're all mine!

Jordan   What did you do with these uniforms, Donald?

Donald   I dressed in them.

Jordan   Why?

Donald   I like to get out of myself.

Jordan   Could you be more specific?

Donald   Look at it this way: you're wearing a certain kind of suit, you're carrying a certain kind of briefcase. You'd wear something different to a ballgame. You're wearing what you're wearing so you can feel like a lawyer.

Jordan   But you're not a policeman, Donald. You're not a priest or a judge.

Donald   But I could be. Maybe one day I will be. I just wanted to see what it felt like. What's wrong with that?

Jordan   I didn't say anything was wrong with it. But you have to admit that your mode of dressing is not usual.

Donald   Well, sir, it is not my goal in life to be usual.

Jordan   Why didn't you actually try to become a policeman? Or a surgeon, a lawyer?

Donald   I don't like taking tests.

Jordan   Is that why you graduated from high school with only a C average? Why you did so poorly on your college boards?

Donald   I didn't try. I didn't even study, I really didn't give a sh- . You know.

Jordan   But your parents did. They wanted you to go to college. They thought you'd get into a top school.

Donald   Well, sure they did. I'm their son. They think I'm great.

Jordan   What did they think about these uniforms you wore?

Donald   They didn't know about them. I only wore them in my room.

Jordan   Not outside?

Donald *shakes his head.*

Jordan   Never?

Ditto.

Why not?

Donald   It would have seemed like lying.

Jordan   And it was important to you to be honest.

Donald   Yes, sir.

Jordan   Is that why you wore no disguise on the day of the murder?

Donald   *Excuse me*?!

Jordan   Is that why you wore an ordinary suit and tie?

Donald   My suit and tie were not ordinary! They were the best.

Jordan (*taking from the rack a bloodstained suit*)   Is this the suit you wore?

Donald (*descending from the stand to look at it*)   Yes. That's it.

Strokes the sleeve and begins to slip into the jacket.

Look at those lines. Feel that fabric. It makes your fingers melt. I bet you've never in your whole life worn such a fine suit . . .

Walks toward a full-length mirror in another area, still putting on the suit. Lights go up there and out on the courtroom.

Salesman (*overlapping*)   An elegant suit—Italian, you know.

Donald   Excellent. I'll be wearing it to a very special event.

Salesman   Are you getting married?

Positions **Donald** *for measuring, takes out his tape and begins chalking in the necessary alterations.*

Donald   Oh no. Television.

Salesman   Really? What show?

Donald   News channel.

Salesman   Oh. Yes. You do look familiar . . .

Donald   No, I don't.

Salesman   Wait. Aren't you the guy who won the lottery last week?

Donald   Sorry. I'm under orders to stay mum or—

Gestures: off with his head.

And you can imagine what *that* will do to your suit!

Salesman   Okay. But listen. You'll be wearing my suit, I mean the suit I'm selling you. Just give me a little hint about how soon this is happening and I'll watch out for you.

Donald   As soon as you can turn up the cuffs.

Salesman (*making chalk marks at the cuff line*)   You can pick up the suit tomorrow.

Donald *stands there smiling at himself in the mirror as the* **Salesman** *exits.*

Donald (*to his reflection*)   Well, Donald Holt. You do look great.

He turns around slowly, observing himself from all angles, and doesn't notice **Mrs. Holt** *entering and standing still, watching him.*

Mrs. Holt   Is that a new suit, sweetheart?

She comes up close to touch the fabric. **Donald** *jerks away.*

Donald   Don't, Mom! You'll wrinkle it.

Her hand is still stretched toward him and reflected in the mirror, almost touching his bloodstained sleeve.

Mrs. Holt (*anguished*)   Donald! Tell me it isn't true! Donald!

Calling into the darkness.

How could this happen? He was a wanted child, a loved child . . .

Doctor Loeb *now becomes visible, taking notes.*

Mrs. Holt   We'd been trying for three years before I conceived.

Doctor Loeb   And your pregnancy was normal?

She nods.

No bleeding? Migraines?

Shakes her head.

You weren't sick at all? No flus, fevers . . .?

Again no.

Drugs? Alcohol?

Mrs. Holt Aspirin? Sugar, artificial sweeteners, caffeine, red meat, sushi—no no no. I took excellent care of myself—and him. To my surprise, I loved being pregnant.

Doctor Loeb Yes? Why?

Mrs. Holt Why?

As if confidentially.

Because I was really really fat, Doctor, and I felt justified being fat, and for the only time in my life I felt beautiful being fat.

In a different mood.

I did everything I was supposed to do—and I loved him, I loved him . . .

Doctor Loeb It must be very painful for you, Mrs. Holt.

Mrs. Holt You have a talent for understatement, Doctor.

Doctor Loeb I'm sorry.

Noting her expression, offers a tissue.

Really, you can cry.

Mrs. Holt I've discovered that on my own, thank you.

But she accepts the tissue.

A phone rings. In his living room, **Mr. Holt** *answers.*

Mr. Holt Yes? . . . No, we are not planning to sell our house!

Hangs up.

Doctor Loeb Donald was your first—

Mrs. Holt —my only—

Doctor Loeb So is it fair to say that you lavished all your affection on him?

Mrs. Holt I wouldn't say "lavished." As you may have observed, I'm not a very demonstrative person.

Doctor Loeb And why is that?

Mrs. Holt If you want an answer to that question, I suggest you interview *my* mother!

The phone rings again.

Mr. Holt (*answering it*) Hello? . . . No, Mother, thanks anyway. This wouldn't be a good time for you to visit. I know you'd help out . . . Yes, I know he's your only grandson . . . But not now. Later, when everything settles down . . . Well, I'm sorry, Mother. I didn't mean to hurt your feelings.

Puts down the phone.

Doctor Loeb   Did Donald ever show signs of violence?

Mrs. Holt   Not really. No.

Doctor Loeb   Please. Tell me anything that comes to mind; it may be useful.

Mrs. Holt   Well . . . When the army rejected him, he smashed his violin.

Doctor Loeb   He wanted to serve?

Mrs. Holt   At one time.

Doctor Loeb   He obviously was very disappointed.

Mrs. Holt   Obviously.

Doctor Loeb   You don't have much respect for psychiatrists, do you, Mrs. Holt?

Mrs. Holt   The lawyer asked me to talk to you. I'm talking.

Doctor Loeb   No, you're fighting. Why? Why don't you want to help me?

Mrs. Holt   You're trying to cut me open, to dissect me. You call that help? Do you think dissection helps the frog?

Doctor Loeb   It can help your son. We're looking for a psychiatric defense.

Mrs. Holt   Looking into *me*! Into my mind, my heart, my life! Why don't you look into the air? Boys breathe it—and kill.

Doctor Loeb   . . . Not most boys.

Mrs. Holt   Hundreds! Thousands! Don't you know what's going on? It's an epidemic. Boys carry their teddy bears in one hand and guns in the other! They walk into a school and instead of opening their books, they open fire. Why? Who can explain it? There are endless influences on a child. God knows what happened to mine, God knows!

Doctor Loeb   But God can't speak in his defense. You and I have to do that. We need to look at everything about him, about your family, if we want to understand what happened.

Mrs. Holt   I'll be looking for the rest of my life.

Again the phone rings.

Mr. Holt   This is he. . . . A support group for the parents of murderers? Such a thing exists? What a statement! What a terrible statement!

Hangs up.

Mrs. Holt   I made mistakes, I know I did. But I wasn't cruel or negligent; I was a good mother . . .

Doctor Loeb   I don't doubt it. But you do. You blame yourself.

Mrs. Holt   How can I help it? Everyone else does. Have you seen the so-called news? The blogs? Don't you know what I did to that boy? I tried to abort him, not once but three times, which caused brain damage that caused—etc., etc. I whipped him to practice the violin, I roasted him over an open fire, committed incest with him—

Doctor Loeb   No one believes those things.

Mrs. Holt   Yes, they do. If it's allowed into public discourse, there are people who lap it up. Anyone can publish anything these days—and of course the most shocking stories are always the ones that stick. My husband calls it the price of a free press. I call it a free-for-all.

Doctor Loeb.   I'm sure he shares your—

Mrs. Holt   My what? My outrage? My pain? He's not the one being vilified. Is he suffering, too? Ask him. I don't know what he's feeling. We hardly talk anymore.

Doctor Loeb   I have an appointment with him tomorrow.

Mrs. Holt   How progressive of you! But really, why pretend? It's always the mother who's at fault. Oh, maybe the father had some small part in it, but all the attention is on her, what she did, what she didn't do. Whether she breastfed or didn't, made him breakfast in the morning or not . . . toilet trained him too early or too late . . . dressed him in the right clothes . . . overprotected him or underprotected him, you name it. Whatever the mother did, it was wrong. And don't we have your profession to thank for that?

Doctor Loeb   I frankly don't know what to say to you, Mrs. Holt.

Mrs. Holt   Then, frankly, Doctor, don't say anything!

She turns on her heel and leaves. At the same time, the phone rings.

Mr. Holt   Do I have a quote for the newspaper? Well, I don't know . . . When I heard? My first reaction? . . . Okay. It's like Truman said when Mrs. Roosevelt told him he'd succeed to office. "I felt like the moon, the stars, and all the planets had fallen on me." Well, that's exactly how it hit me. . . . Well, yes, of course I realize that's not the same as . . . what happened here . . . but they're cut from the same cloth, aren't they? Big unexpected events that change lives . . .

From his office, **Doctor Loeb** *addresses* **Mr. Holt**.

Doctor Loeb   But how did *you* feel, Mr. Holt? In your own words.

Mr. Holt   See, Doctor, I sort of sound stupid when I talk about important things. So I find some better words. I follow Emerson in that. He said: "Next to the originator of a good sentence is the first quoter of it."

Doctor Loeb   You're the boy's father, though. You know him better than almost anyone. What do you think was going through his mind? Why do you think he did what he did?

Mr. Holt   My opinion? He was used, he was misled. There must have been a conspiracy to assassinate the governor. Diamond had his enemies, we all know that. And these people seized upon my son, sir; they flattered him, they whispered their poison into his ears—and what did he hear? Not political intrigue, not murder—he heard triumphal music. My boy loves music, Doctor, he's a dreamer, a romantic, but I guess . . . well, maybe, he was sort of susceptible, you know?

Doctor Loeb   You mean weak?

Mr. Holt   Not exactly weak, no, but he'd sort of jump onto a horse before he looked it in the mouth, counted its teeth, you know?

Doctor Loeb   Impulsive.

Mr. Holt   Yeah, that's the word, but it never led him into anything you'd take seriously, you know? I just don't understand how he went along with them. I did everything I could to give him my values—everything!—but sadly, as Thomas Paine said, "virtue is not hereditary."

Doctor Loeb   You really know your American history, don't you?

Mr. Holt   Oh yeah. Been teaching it for twenty-six years, in the same high school. Fascinating subject: the story of our country, and the folks who made it great.

Doctor Loeb   And was Donald interested, too?

Mr. Holt   Well, you know kids these days. They spend all their time on the computer or with headphones in their ears. I bought him a bunch of games about the presidents, the Civil War, that sort of thing, but I don't think he installed any of them.

Lights up in **Donald**'s *room. Sixteen-year-old* **Donald** *is lighting up a joint.*

Doctor Loeb   Did you spend much time with him?

Mr. Holt   When he was little, oh yeah. I used to take him to the zoo and to the amusement park, go on every ride with him. Then we'd go to the arcades and stand in front of those funhouse mirrors. The ones that make you look squashed down or like your legs are stilts. He loved that. And we did Sunday swimming at the "Y." Later, though, it was sort of hard to . . . connect, you know? But I tried. I did. I don't think any man could have tried harder . . .

Mr. Holt *walks upstairs to* **Donald**'s *room and enters.*

Donald (*startled*)   Hey, Dad. Shame on you! You didn't even knock.

Mr. Holt   I thought you'd stopped that.

Donald   I did. Mostly. It's no big deal, Dad. Come on. Lighten up. Have a toke.

Mr. Holt   It's illegal, son.

Donald   So is cheating on your income tax.

Mr. Holt   I don't cheat. You know that.

Donald   Never?

His father shakes his head.

Not even on a test?

Mr. Holt *shakes his head again.*

Donald   Not even once?

Mr. Holt   Wellllll, maybe once. I wasn't very good in French.

Donald   Well, this joint is pure American. Grown in the state of California. Come on, Dad. Give it a try.

Mr. Holt   I can't.

Donald   Aren't you even curious?

Mr. Holt   Maybe. Maybe a little. But a man can be curious about lots of things. That doesn't mean he has to try them all. Thomas Jefferson said it: "Ignorance is preferable to error."

Donald   Yeah, Dad, but Jefferson's dead. He's been dead for ages.

Mr. Holt   So? So is your fabulous Beethoven. That doesn't stop him.

Donald   It stopped him, Dad. He's not here. His music is here, that lives on, but the man is stopped, he's gone gone gone for good.

Mr. Holt   I used to like music, too, you know. I played the piano for a while.

Donald   I never saw you—heard you. Why did you quit?

Mr. Holt   No talent.

Donald   Guess I'm a chip off the old block.

He's been smoking all this time and is rather loopy.

The old cock!

Laughs.

Mr. Holt   Hey! That's no way to talk to your father. Listen. It's still light outside. How about we go out for an hour or two? Throw the ball around a little.

Donald   Throw the *bull* around.

Laughs.

That doesn't sound funny to you? That's because you're not stoned. Come on, Dad. Live it up. Before Mom gets home. You want to go through life not knowing what generations of kids experience every day? Let's share, okay?

Mr. Holt   This will be just between us?

Donald   Just the two of us. Like father and son.

Mr. Holt   What do you mean, like? We *are* father and son.

He accepts the joint.

Donald   Take a drag. Right. Now breathe it in. Way into your lungs.

Mr. Holt (*coughs*)   I don't really . . . know how to . . . inhale . . .

Donald   I've heard that one before!

Both laugh.

Try again, Dad. Suck it in. That's the way! Now keep it trapped there. Terrific.

He turns on the CD player: the Kreutzer Sonata.

Now lie down on the floor. Right here, next to me. Yeah, like that. On your back. Oh. You can exhale now. Good. Now listen. Open your ears. Don't think about anything. Let the sound come flooding in.

They listen.

Mr. Holt   Hey. I see why you like this stuff, Donald. It . . . puts a little air in your head, doesn't it?

Donald   . . . And the music, the music . . . Can you hear how beautiful it is?

Mr. Holt   Yes, yes . . . I think I do, son.

Donald   Better than your Francis Scott Key?

Mr. Holt   Now don't poke fun at me! They have a lot in common, Donald, really they do. They're both grand, you know, sweeping, sweeping . . .

Donald   Sweeps you away, huh? Sweeps you off your feet . . . Hey! That's an idea. Off your feet, onto your head. You can do that, right?

Mr. Holt   Stand on my head? . . . I don't know. I haven't tried for ages.

Donald   You used to be a super athlete. You always said you were.

Mr. Holt   I was. You could be, too, if you ever got out of this room of yours and—

Donald   Come on, Dad. You can do something silly; you're stoned! . . . Roll onto your head . . .

Downstairs, **Mrs. Holt** *enters the house with her parcels from the* **Butcher**'s. *She takes off her coat, puts the meat away.*

Mr. Holt (*laughing, but trying*)   I don't think I can . . .

Donald   What do you mean? In America, a man can do anything! Sweep those legs up!

Sings, as he helps his father.

  Oh, say can you see
  By the dawn's early light
  What so proudly we hailed
  At the twilight's last gleaming . . .

Mr. Holt *is standing on his head, wobbling but triumphant.*

Mr. Holt   I did it, I did it!

Donald   Congratulations, Dad! You're upside down!

As he leaves the room.

> O'er the land of the free,
> And the home of the brave.

Mr. Holt *holds himself upside down for as long as he can, then collapses to the floor with a loud thud.*

At the sound, **Mrs. Holt** *gives way.*

Mrs. Holt   Donalllld! What happened to you?

Mr. Holt *picks himself up and runs downstairs as she runs up.*

I thought I knew him . . .

Mr. Holt   So did I.

Mrs. Holt   Were we blind?

Mr. Holt   I don't know. We were . . . parents. That's all. Parents.

They fall into each other's arms and cling together.

Mrs. Holt   This is the first time you've touched me since it happened.

Mr. Holt   I wanted to, Carol, I did. But I was afraid . . . afraid . . . you'd break.

They embrace more lovingly.

Or I would.

But just as they attempt to regain their closeness, they are barraged by the voices of the public besieging them, one after the other, relentlessly. These may be the letterwriters themselves physically coming between them, or a rain of letters accompanied by voices, or any other stage action that visually expresses the violation of their intimacy and grief.

A Christian   "Dear Mr and Mrs. Holt: What did you do to that boy? How did you destroy his reverence for human life, you who gave him life? How did you manage to kill every decent, normal feeling in him? You must bear the guilt for this sinful act through eternity. I cannot believe that God will forgive you though I am, and remain, yours truly, A Christian."

A Young Woman   "Dear Mrs. Holt: I consider birth control to be one of science's greatest contributions to mankind. Through it, I have been spared anguish like yours."

Mr. Holt   The lawyer wants to enter an insanity plea. He says prison's hell, much worse than a mental hospital. And then, if the worst happens, there's the possibility of—

Mrs. Holt   No, don't say it.

A Caterer   "We are writing to offer you our catering services in your time of need. We can prepare meals for groups as large as—"

A Mother   "Dear Mrs. Holt: The store of maternal suffering is endless. You too now share in that vast sorrow that unites women throughout the ages. I am the fortunate mother of five children. Every one of them is a blessing. My heart goes out to you."

A Politico   "Please pass this on to your son, Donald Holt. Dear Donald Holt: Thank you thank you thank you for getting rid of that traitor Diamond, he was going to make this country a commie junkyard and we should all be glad he's not going to get the chance to run for president like he planned. Thank God we still have a few real men left."

An Insurance Agent   "We regret to inform you that we have to raise the cost of your automobile insurance. Persons under severe stress are involved in 36 percent more accidents than—"

Mr. Holt   What? That is bogus statistic fraud! "We boil at different degrees." Emerson knew that more than a hundred years ago.

An Avenger   "Why don't you kill yourself, Mrs. Holt? Why don't you take that gun and shoot yourself in the heart and—"

Mrs. Holt   I wish I *could*! Then I wouldn't feel, I wouldn't hurt. Oh, when will it stop? When?

Annie   "Dear Mr. and Mrs. Holt: Do you remember me? Annie Soltan. Donald's friend when we were sixteen, seventeen? I used to come to the house sometimes . . ."

Annie *runs into the house and throws her arms around* **Mrs. Holt**.

Annie   I had to come. I can't believe it. I mean, I do believe it, but I can't take it in. That someone I know—Donald—did that. I can't even imagine how you must feel.

Mrs. Holt   Really, Annie. It's very nice of you to drop by. You're looking wonderful.

Annie   Oh . . . well . . . I don't know . . . older.

Mr. Holt   Same age as Donald, right? Sure. You graduated in the same class. We thought he'd take you to the prom.

Annie   He said he wasn't much of a dancer. Even though you tried to teach him, Mrs. Holt. He told me you were so patient. Anyway, he just didn't like parties.

Mr. Holt   Well, that's no crime. . . . Hey, you and Carol want to have a talk? Catch up?

Mrs. Holt   That would be good.

Annie   Whatever. I don't want to disturb you, Mr. Holt.

Mr. Holt   No problem. I have a thousand things to do. "If you are idle, be not solitary. If you are solitary, be not idle." . . . Richard Burton's last words. Not the actor Richard Burton. The explorer fella.

Pause; pecks his wife on the cheek before leaving.

Well. Right.

Annie   Please, Mrs. Holt, sit down.

Mrs. Holt   Can I get you a drink? A glass of—

Annie   Oh, no. No. Please. I don't want anything. I just thought maybe I could say something . . . I don't know . . . I spent so much time with Donald.

Mrs. Holt   He liked you: I remember. And you seemed to like him.

Annie   Oh, I did, I did. He wasn't like the other boys, and I thought that was great, you know, sort of exciting, like being in a foreign country. I mean, I got so bored with those other guys, all they wanted to do was get wasted, you know, hang out at clubs and—

Mrs. Holt   And Donald? What did he want to do?

Annie   Oh, listen to music or watch a movie, you know . . . He always had something way interesting to say. Not that he was a big talker—sometimes he wouldn't say anything for a half hour, and I'd tease him a little, I'd say: "Where are you now, Donald? Can I come sit on your cloud? Move over, Donald, make some room for me." But he didn't move. He was deep, Mrs. Holt.

Mrs. Holt   All those afternoons—you just listened to music?

Annie   Uh-huh. And did homework.

Mrs. Holt   That's all? . . . Nothing else? . . . He never . . . kissed you?

Annie   No, Mrs. Holt. He never did.

Mrs. Holt   Never? Not even once?

Annie *shakes her head.*

Mrs. Holt   Were there other girls? Boys? Annie, tell me, please.

Annie   Well . . . Well . . . he was . . . different, you know? He didn't kiss me. He never even tried. The thing that he liked to do was . . . play strip poker. Oh. Now I've said it. That's what we did upstairs.

*Lights up in **Donald**'s room. He is half-dressed. **Annie** walks upstairs to his room. She drops her shoes atop a pile of **Donald**'s forfeited clothes and sits down to continue playing.*

Annie (*as she drops the shoes*)   My first forfeit. I never realized I was such a good player.

*They play their own version of poker. **Donald** loses a hand: he takes off his undershirt. He loses again, takes off his socks. She starts to play with his toes.*

This little piggy went to market, this little piggy stayed—

He jerks his toes away.

Well, sorry! I wasn't going to eat them, you know!

They play another hand; now she loses, almost triumphantly.

Donald   How could you be so stupid? You just threw that hand away.

Annie   Yeah. Stupid me.

She unbuttons her blouse coyly and takes it off.

Donald   Well, put it on the pile. What are you playing around for? Come on. The game's not over.

She tosses the blouse onto the pile. **Donald** *doesn't even glance at her. He is already dealing the next hand. They play.* **Donald** *loses.*

He takes off his shorts and stands up, completely nude. **Annie** *turns away, embarrassed. He pulls her around to face him.*

Donald   You have to look. It's part of the game.

Annie   I looked, I looked.

Donald   No, you have to really look.

She looks.

Well?

Annie   Well—what?

Donald   What do you see?

Annie   I see—I don't know what you want me to say. I just see . . . you.

Donald   What do I look like?

Annie   Like . . . yourself. Without clothes on. God! What else would you look like?

Donald   I don't know. That's what I'm asking.

Annie   Well, I don't know either. I mean, how many naked guys do you think I've seen?

Donald   I don't care about that. I just want to know what you see, okay? Come on, Annie. Just look.

He turns around slowly, deliberately, almost like a model, so that she can see all of him. As he is turning, she puts on her shirt and shoes, and runs downstairs.

Mrs. Holt   He didn't want to see you undressed?

Annie   I guess not. I never got to strip all the way. Not once. Donald always lost.

Mrs. Holt   But why did he want to do that?

Annie   I don't know, I never asked, I guess I was sort of relieved, you know? That I didn't have to get naked.

Rising to leave.

I'm sorry, Mrs. Holt. I have to get home.

Mrs. Holt   I thought he'd go into music. Or law. He had so many talents.

Annie   He did. He could have done a thousand things.

Reaches out her hand.

It was great to see you—

Mrs. Holt   Annie! Is that an engagement ring?

Annie (*embarrassed*)   Mmmmhmmmmmmm.

Mrs. Holt   Oh. Well. Well! Congratulations, dear. Who's the lucky man?

Annie   A guy I met at college. A real sweetheart—you'll meet him, I hope, maybe come to the wedding? He's getting a Master's in Social Work so it's going to be a struggle, both of us being students . . .

Mrs. Holt (*fighting back tears*)   A struggle, well, that's all right, you'll be struggling together. Together, that's the important thing, isn't it?

Annie   I'm so sorry, Mrs. Holt. Honestly I am. I really liked Donald.

Leaves. **Mrs. Holt** *sits where she is.*

Lights have remained on **Donald***, who has begun dressing in his elegant suit.*

He talks to an imaginary **Reporter***.*

Donald   I had to educate myself about everything. It was really interesting. And easy—like the information was waiting to fall into my brain. Every Sunday, for weeks, for months, it told my feet to take me to an arcade or a fair. I felt like a magnet was pulling me and I just went with the flow, you know. Each time, I'd find myself at the same booth. I'd pick up a little fake rifle and aim at a little fake duck. It took a while to get the hang of it but once I did, every time, I'd shoot a duck off the track— pop!—yeah! It flipped off the track backward and bye-bye!—a little fake dead duck. No, I didn't hide. Why would I? Lots of guys were there, doing the same thing. Nobody noticed me, nobody knew what was in my mind—hey, even *I* didn't know what was in my mind. Not at first.

He pulls a gun and fires.

Offstage, the **Eyewitness** *screams.*

Eyewitness   He's got a gun!

He keeps firing. And firing. And firing.

Lights go up on a **Newscaster** *addressing the nation.*

Newscaster   There were seven victims in today's rampage. Three people are dead, including a baby who was asleep in her father's lap. Four others have been hospitalized.

In her living room, **Mrs. Holt** *casually turns on the television.*

Newscaster   We will not be releasing the names of the dead or injured until the families are notified.

Mrs. Holt   Lloyd! Come here. Something terrible has happened.

Newscaster   One survivor, a thirty-five-year-old office worker, is in critical but stable condition. She was willing to talk to us from her hospital bed.

Office Worker   The bullet ripped through my back. I was just in the way, that's all: I was in the way, you know? He didn't want me, so he kept on shooting. For the first time in my life, I feel blessed that I was unwanted.

Mr. Holt *joins his wife in front of the television. Both watch intently.*

Newscaster   The target of this shocking attack was Governor Philip Diamond, who was expected to announce his candidacy for president next week. No governor in the history of the state had so captivated the imagination of the electorate. He had just finished his address and was taking questions from the audience when—I'll leave it to an eyewitness to describe what happened.

Eyewitness (*spotlighted*)   The governor was standing at the podium, he'd already answered three or four questions, and this guy right in front of me stands up and waves his hand to be recognized and the governor recognizes him, and and and the hand is holding a gun, and the guy starts shooting, pop pop! it was crazy, he was spraying the room—pop pop! Pop pop!—

Donald *walks into another spotlight, soundlessly shooting his gun.*

Eyewitness   —and everybody starts screaming and running, the place goes from civilized to chaos in the blink of a second, thank God I was behind him not in front because people in front, I don't know how many, got shot before security tackled the guy, but it was too late. Our governor was dead.

Newscaster   The perpetrator of this shocking act has been identified as—

Donald   My name is Donald Holt. I am twenty-three years old and an employee at Starway Supermarket in Crescent Park. You may have seen me there. I work Monday to Saturday, four to midnight. I bought my suit at Ultimos on Cedar Street.

Mr. *and* **Mrs. Holt** *stare at each other in disbelief. For a long frozen moment, they cannot move. Then they run toward* **Donald**.

Donald   I am not resisting arrest, I am not running away, I will be cooperating with the investigation.

Just as they reach him, a panel of bars bangs down: **Donald** *is in jail.*

Mr. *and* **Mrs. Holt** *speak through them.*

Donald   Hey, Mom. Dad.

Mr. Holt   We came as fast as we could, son.

Mrs. Holt   Are you all right? Did they hurt—

Donald   I'm fine, Mom.

Mr. Holt   We couldn't believe our eyes, son.

Mrs. Holt   There were so many people in the crowd and somehow, somebody got the impression it was *you* who—

Donald   It was me, Mom.

Mrs. Holt   No. You couldn't have done such a thing.

Donald   Why not? History's filled with men who did.

Mr. Holt   Who led you into this, son? Whose idea was it?

Donald   It was my idea.

Mr. Holt   Don't try to protect anyone, Donald. Somebody must have influenced you. Somebody must have forced you to—

Donald   Why do you think that? Don't you think I have ideas of my own? Don't you think I can act for myself?

Mrs. Holt   Shhh, shhhh, sweetheart. Don't say anything else.

Mr. Holt   You need a lawyer. He'll advise you.

Donald   I don't want a lawyer. No briefcase can speak for me.

Mrs. Holt   Please, Donald, please! You'll incriminate yourself.

Donald   I already have. People caught it on their cell phones, I saw them, I'm probably viral by now, on YouTube, with the gun in my hand.

Mr. Holt   A lawyer can find a defense—

Donald   Like what?

Mrs. Holt   You didn't know what you were doing—

Donald   I did, too. "I cannot tell a lie." George Washington, regarding the cherry tree. That's a saying you always liked.

Mr. Holt   "Thou shalt not kill." I liked that better.

Donald   Why are you staring at me like that? . . . Are you going to cry?

He studies his father.

You *are* going to cry! I can't believe it. I've never seen you cry.

Mr. Holt   Oh, Donald.

Donald (*unsettled*)   Don't look at me like that! Go away! Both of you!

Mrs. Holt   It's all a mistake. It has to be. A tragic mistake.

Donald   Whose mistake? Whose tragedy do you mean?

In the distance, "Taps" is played softly.

Lights hold on **Donald** *and the* **Holts** *in tableau as, encompassed in the same light,*

Mrs. Diamond, *dressed in mourning, lowers the American flag to half-mast.*

Mr. *and* **Mrs. Holt** *bow their heads.*

Blackout on the three of them and:

Spotlight on **Linda Ritter**, *sitting on a porch, writing on a pad.*

Linda

Dear Donald: My name is Linda Ritter. I read about you on the internet and saw you on TV. You are one good-looking and brave guy. I think what you did was wonderful, I wish I could have done it. But I live in Omaha and, besides, my dad doesn't let me out of the house much. I know you play the violin and I think that's beautiful. I play the piano. We could play duets together. Do you like the Kreutzer Sonata by Beethoven? It's my favorite, especially the second movement. But there's no one around here who plays the violin, so I don't get to play it much. I hope it's not too terrible, being in jail. A person with your bursting soul shouldn't be confined like that. I wish we could talk on email because then we could communicate back-and-forth but I guess you can't have a computer in there, so please write back to me right away.
    Your friend, Linda Ritter

P.S. Don't put your real name or prison address on the envelope or my folks won't give me the letter.

She folds the letter, slips it in an envelope, and kisses it.

Lights out on her and up on **Mr.** *and* **Mrs. Holt** *in bed.*

Mrs. Holt   What happened? What went wrong? We wanted that child so much . . .

Mr. Holt   And there are so many people who don't want their kids.

Mrs. Holt   If we'd waited one more month . . . if we'd gone to bed an hour later, had another glass of wine . . . or stopped to blow out the candles . . . If you'd kissed me one more kiss . . . If I hadn't raised my legs so high . . . it would have been a different sperm, a different egg. A different child.

Mr. Holt   Shhh . . . Shhhhh . . . It's out of our hands now.

Mrs. Holt   Out of our bodies. Out of us. You and me. Out of us . . . Twenty-two years ago . . .

They embrace, returning to that night.

Mr. Holt   Tonight's the night. You said so.

Mrs. Holt   The thermometer said so. . . . Will he have your eyes?

Mr. Holt   I sure hope so.

Mrs. Holt   Lloyd!

Mr. Holt   But your hair. A child should have your gorgeous hair.

Mrs. Holt   Do you want a boy?

Mr. Holt   I don't care. As long as it's healthy.

Mrs. Holt   I love you.

Mr. Holt   Which way is the best?

Mrs. Holt   The deepest.

They start to make love.

In his cell, **Donald** *is writing a letter, possibly onstage, possibly offstage.*

Donald   . . . It felt like joy. You want the truth, right? That's how it felt—like joy, the way the bow feels in my hand, like it's part of the skin, part of the bone, the part that sings. You understand, don't you, Linda? I think you do . . .

Music from the Kreutzer Sonata *becomes a background to the scene. But for a moment more, the sounds of orgasm dominate, and then a bit of* tristesse.

Mrs. Holt   And with all that love, all that hope and planning, look what we created.

Mr. Holt   Something went wrong in him, in *him*, Carol, not us. Something snapped or got twisted. How could we, how could anyone, see inside him?

Mrs. Holt   Well, you couldn't, that's for sure. You didn't even try. You hid yourself away in the newspapers, TV, in your history books.

Mr. Holt   I wasn't hiding! Those are my interests. You know that.

Mrs. Holt   Did you ever *ever* have a real conversation with him?!

Mr. Holt   I tried. Ten times, a hundred times. What more could I do? I was afraid of putting too much pressure on him, afraid—

Mrs. Holt   Afraid afraid afraid—your theme song! Afraid of anger, afraid of tears, afraid to be too close or too far away, afraid of sunstroke, darkness, Mexican food, tunnels, airplanes, and the ocean and the mountains, too! Afraid even to speak your own words!

Mr. Holt   I'm speaking now.

Mrs. Holt   You left everything to me: choosing his schools, helping with the homework, teaching him about girls—

Mr. Holt   —pushing him, yes, goading him to be a great student, a great violinist, a great . . . something someone somebody—anything, as long as he was the best!

Mrs. Holt   And I suppose you wanted him to be the worst! Well, congratulations! Your wish has come true!

Mr. Holt   I wanted him to be a man. That's all. A man.

Mrs. Holt   Yes? And whose definition did you use? Your Jefferson's? Your Lincoln's? Whose?

Mr. Holt   At least I had models! But you—you wanted him to be yourself. The self you never found. And why? Why? I've never understood it. The museum begged you to come back to work—in a few years you would have been running the damn place!

Mrs. Holt   I didn't want to run a museum! I wanted to educate myself—to read the books I never read, and I did—listen to music, and I did—to be at home as much as I could so I could give my child everything I had!

Mr. Holt   Well, I guess what you had wasn't enough.

Mrs. Holt   Blame my parents, then. Blame their parents!

Mr. Holt   I wish I'd given my boy a different mother!

Mrs. Holt   And I wish you'd flushed your seed down the toilet!

Infuriated, they are on the verge of striking each other when a barrage of flashbulbs goes off and a **Reporter***'s voice is heard.*

Reporter   Mr. and Mrs. Holt: do you have a statement for the press?

The same gesture that would have been a blow becomes an embrace as they face the press.

Mr. Holt   Yes. We love and support our son—

Mrs. Holt   —during this terrible ordeal and we will do everything—

Mr. Holt   —we will do everything in our power—

Mrs. and Mrs. Holt   —to help him.

They stand erect and close. Dozens of flashbulbs snap their united front.

Freeze on the **Holts** *in bright light.*

Then blackout.

End of Act One.

Act Two

Lights come up on a coffin being carried in procession, followed by **Mrs. Diamond** *and the* **Newscaster** *addressing the nation.*

Newscaster   All flags in the state were lowered to half-mast today in mourning for the late Governor Philip Diamond. After funeral services, the governor's mother and a small group of relatives accompanied the coffin to the family burial plot. Camera Nine was permitted a brief interview with Mrs. Diamond.

He intercepts the procession and turns to **Mrs. Diamond.**

Newscaster   Do you have anything to tell the public on this sad occasion?

Mrs. Diamond   When a person is found to have a cancer, the growth is cut out. When a society becomes malignant, the tumors must be removed. Donald Holt is a tumor of the most virulent sort.

Newscaster   We seem to be living through an epidemic of violence, almost a plague.

Mrs. Diamond   Then the carriers should be burned.

Newscaster   You want Donald Holt executed?

Mrs. Diamond   If there were justice. But there isn't. The practice, even the ideal of justice, has been driven out of this century.

Newscaster   As you know, our state does have the death penalty.

Mrs. Diamond   Having it and using it are two different things.

Newscaster   It's a great tragedy, Mrs. Diamond, for all—

Mrs. Diamond   Nonsense. For the world it's not a tragedy at all. It's gossip!

Newscaster   For the world, it's the loss of a great statesman.

Mrs. Diamond   The world didn't sing lullabies to its great statesman, and rock him to sleep, and wipe his tears.

She draws herself up.

Good day, sir.

She motions the cortege on.

Lights up on **Mrs. Holt** *at home, sitting with* **Milly**, *who is visibly pregnant.* **Mrs. Holt** *is polishing silver.*

Milly   . . . they stuck a long needle and syringe right here, near the navel, and drew up some amniotic fluid. Now they're studying the cells.

Mrs. Holt *winces;* **Milly** *gets flustered.*

Milly   Cells with genetic material, that kind of cell, not . . .! . . . Giving birth at my age, you know, I'm high risk for having a child with Down's syndrome.

Mrs. Holt   They can isolate a criminal chromosome, too. An extra Y. What if you found out your baby had it, Milly? Would you abort?

Milly   Well, who can say? I mean, we don't even know the sex yet . . .

Mrs. Holt   Pray for a girl. Only boys can have the extra Y. But if it is a boy, Milly, and if you knew in advance that—

Milly   It's taken me forever to get pregnant, Carol. The doctor said this was the last fling of my uterus. Really, I don't want to think about—

Mrs. Holt   If Donald had it and I'd known, would I have aborted? Should I have? Could I have? That's how my mind spins, Milly. Night after night.

Milly   It takes time, you'll make your peace with—

Mrs. Holt   He was such a sweet baby . . . You thought so, too, didn't you, Milly? Did you ever see anything wrong? With him? Or how we raised him? You can tell me the truth.

Milly   Everything looked good to me.

Mrs. Holt   But it wasn't. It wasn't good.

Milly   I never dreamed . . .

Mrs. Holt   Nightmare, Milly. Nightmare is the right word . . . Want a drink?

Gets a bottle of scotch.

Milly   No, no thank you . . . It's only three o'clock, Carol.

Mrs. Holt (*drinks*)   Three, five, eleven: it's all the same to me.

Milly   Maybe you should get some help.

Mrs. Holt   Liquor helps.

Pours another.

Lights up on **Mr. Holt** *addressing his class.*

Mr. Holt   . . . but since that day in 1945 when we dropped an atomic bomb on the Japanese city of Hiroshima, our image of that country has turned upside down. Yes, class, we've learned to admire and envy Japan, not only for its brilliant technology but for its ethic, which is the exact opposite of ours. Now I always believed our American democracy was just about perfect—but the Japanese, well, they think our stress on individualism makes kids feel they have to be bigger and better than the next guy, that they have to tear themselves out of the community and stand above it. And the result is they rip the social fabric to shreds! Think about that, class! I sure am.

In **Mrs. Holt**'s *home:*

Mrs. Holt   How do you explain what's happened? When you talk to your friends— or to yourself? How do you explain it?

Milly I don't try.

Mrs. Holt Not even now, when—People are calling for—Oh Milly, he could be put to death!

Milly God forbid!

Mrs. Holt God doesn't forbid anything. Haven't the last hundred years taught us that?

Milly You mustn't blame God, Carol, you mustn't.

Mrs. Holt I don't. But you should. You believe in Him.

Milly It's not God's fault that Donald . . . did . . . what he did.

Mrs. Holt Of course not. It's mine. Everyone knows that. How silly of me to try and pass the buck, especially to the Divine Unmoved Mover.

Milly Don't talk that way. You're torturing yourself. Honestly, Carol, I don't know where you're going to find your comfort; I don't know how you're going to get through this.

Mrs. Holt Lloyd is lucky; he has his job. Me, I sit at home, polish the silver—and think silver . . . bullets . . . guns . . . death.

In the classroom:

Mr. Holt . . . And right from day one, you kids get the idea you have to be stupendous, you have to be stars, or superstars, and if you don't cut the mustard, well then, you're a nothing, a big fat zero. But the Japanese, they don't grow to be six feet tall and they don't tower over everyone else—they don't even want to. They create the bonsai and the netsuke and the haiku, miniatures. Half the time they don't even put their names on the things! They don't need to be famous or make a billion; they're team players! What a difference from us, huh?

*In **Mrs. Holt**'s home:*

Mrs. Holt Well, you won't need to buy a crib, Milly. I've kept Donald's. All these years

Milly Oh no, no, thank you very much, but I couldn't . . .

Mrs. Holt It's in perfect condition. A gorgeous crib, solid wood, white, with little animals embossed on it. Donald only used it till he was two.

Milly I'm sure it's very nice but . . . I think . . . well . . . I think we'd rather have a new crib. Thanks, anyway.

Mrs. Holt But they're so expensive. Why not—

She understands; fighting back tears, bitterly.

Oh. Oh. I see . . . You could fumigate the mattress.

Milly Oh, Carol, it's not . . . It's just . . .

Mrs. Holt (*pouring another glass*)   Well, Milly, I want to toast to a perfect amnio! I'll pray for a girl—but girl or boy, I hope your baby will be a joy to you from birth to—to—

She can't continue without weeping. **Milly** *comforts her and, before leaving, gently empties the filled glass and the bottle.*

Lights up on **Donald** *in his cell, reading a letter, and on* **Linda**, *arranging tiger lilies into a bouquet.*

Linda

> My Dearest Donald: I heard what you said at your trial today, about an assassin being just a freelance soldier, and I agree with you 100 percent. It's the army's fault for rejecting you. Serves them right! Sometimes I think when I read about you on the net that you're the action part of me: stuff I think about, you say and do. I'm sending you some flowers to brighten up your cell. When I was in the hospital for pneumonia— boorring!— I loved it when I got flowers. The reason I'm choosing tiger lilies is because they remind me of you: wild as a tiger and sensitive, too, like the lily. It's the perfect combination. I hope you'll stay smiling now. Love always, Linda.

Donald (*calling through the bars*)   Guard. Guard! I'll be getting some flowers. Bring them as they come so they won't die.

Smiles as **Linda** *has instructed and kisses the letter.*

In **Mrs. Holt**'s *home: Alone now, she has curled up with a book.*

In **Mr. Holt**'s *classroom:*

Mr. Holt   . . . So I've been looking into it, class, and what I see is that every country has its own brand of violence. Maybe it's not random like it is here because there's no disputing that America is number one in the world when it comes to serial killers and mass murderers and boys who'll shoot you . . . shoot you dead 'cause they don't like your smile. But—and this is a big but—we don't torture our people for speaking against the government like in China, and we don't stone boys and girls for holding hands like in Pakistan or Iran; we don't destroy our own people or turn them into suicide bombers, but, well, I just don't know. I don't know what soil is best for raising kids. . . . What do the experts say? What do *you* say? I want a five-page essay on that. By Monday.

Lights follow him from the classroom to **Donald** *in his cell.*

At the same time, **Mrs. Holt** *adjusts the lamp for better reading light.*

Donald   Hey, Dad.

Mr. Holt   Hey, son.

Donald   You weren't going to come till next week. What's up?

Mr. Holt (*awkwardly fishing a letter out of his pocket; whispering*)   This. Shhh.

Sneaks it to **Donald**.

Mr. Holt   The police went through everything—your computer, your closet, desk—but . . . well . . . seems like they missed this.

Donald (*reading it*)   Oh yeah. I wrote to thank the company for building me the semi—they did a great job, especially with the custom grip—and they wrote back to thank me for thanking them. Very courteous guys.

Mr. Holt   The letter's dated four months before—It shows premeditation, you know.

Donald   If I didn't pre-meditate, Dad, it wouldn't have happened.

Mr. Holt   But why? And why Diamond? I just can't grasp it, son. You never raised your hand against another human being. And Diamond was a terrific governor. You thought so, too. You couldn't wait to vote that first time because it was for him. I don't get it, I just don't.

Donald   It's like in tennis, Dad. You always want to play a guy who's better than you are. It makes *you* better.

Mr. Holt   "Play"?

Donald   Hey, hey, don't get stressed. You know, my head makes these funny connections.

Mr. Holt   Nothing funny about where you are today.

Donald   Dad, c'mon.

Mr. Holt *tries to hide his tearfulness, but can't.*

Donald   C'mon! I'm being a man about this, you be a man, too!

Mr. Holt   Should I burn the letter?

Donald   Destroy evidence? You?

Mr. Holt   Well, like Emerson says, "A foolish consistency is the—

Donald *completes the quotation with him; a moment of connection.*

Mr. Holt/Donald   —hobgoblin of little minds."

Donald   . . . Yeah, but . . . Don't mess with the letter, Dad. Turn it in. For Mom's sake. If you get into trouble, too, she'll be all alone.

In **Mrs. Holt**'s *home: the lamp suddenly glares like an inquisitor's spotlight into her face.*

Mrs. Holt   My name is Carol Holt. I swear to tell the truth, the whole truth, and nothing but the truth.

Donald (*partially to his father; now and then only to himself*)   She's not taking care of herself. She looks bad. I bet she's not sleeping. She'll go to the doctor, get some pills. But not too many, Dad. Don't let her take too many.

Mrs. Holt (*as before*)   My name is Carol Holt. It was Carol Bristol before I married.

Donald   She'll be on the news, television, all over the net. She'll try not to cry but she will. Because of me. People will see how smart she is. She'll get a major book contract. She'll get thin, or maybe she'll get fat, she'll worry her heart out. Because of me.

Mr. Holt   You should have thought of all that before.

Snatches the letter from **Donald***'s hand and exits.*

Donald   But she'll get stronger. She'll get to start over. She'll have a new life. Because of me.

Lights remain dimly on him watching her through the bars of his cell.

In two distinct voices, she unsparingly interrogates herself:

Mrs. Holt   My name is Carol Bristol Holt. When I was a child, they called me Carly.
  Irrelevant!

My name is Carol Holt. I married Lloyd Holt in 19—
  Get to the point.

My name is Carol Holt. I am the mother of Donald Holt.
  Aha! She admits it!

Admits what? I'm not accused.
  Aren't you?

I'm not on trial.
  Aren't you?

I labored for sixteen hours. I refused an epidural. I didn't want to be numb; I wanted to feel his birth,
  Any animal in the fields could do a better job than you did.

I am not on trial!
  Aren't you?

Why? Why? He was wanted, he was loved . . .
  Maybe you loved him too much.

How much is too much?
  No? Then maybe you didn't love him enough.

I loved him better than my life.
  What life, Mrs. Holt?

I'm not on trial!
  Aren't you?

I was as good as any other mother.
  You're a cold woman.

Not cold. Reserved. That is not a crime.
  For a mother? Isn't it?

Mothers come in all tones and temperatures.
Did you hold him, play with him? Did you coo? Did you tickle?

I did. Yes, I did.
You didn't give him a bottle at night.

The doctor advised against it.
He cried for hours.

The doctor said to let him cry.
Who knew better, the doctor or the mother?

I don't know. Leave me alone. I'm not on trial.
Aren't you?

Maybe I was too close to him. So close I couldn't see—
Maybe, she says!

Maybe I didn't read the signs. Or maybe the signs were unreadable.
Everyone can read them now, Mrs. Holt.

I didn't know what he was hiding in his heart!
A child hides, a parent seeks!

I didn't know he was lost.
Why? Why didn't you know? Why? Why? Why?

I tried, I did. He was a locked room!
Then why didn't you break down the door, Mrs. Holt? Why? Why?

Agonized, she turns toward **Donald** *in his cell.*

Mrs. Holt   Why didn't you open the door, Donald? Why didn't you let me in?

Donald   I didn't have the key, Mom.

Mrs. Holt   If I'd only known that, Donald! If I'd only known!

Donald   Don't beat yourself up. You're not God.

Mrs. Holt   I'm your mother. Mothers should know what God can't.

Mr. Holt *quietly enters his home. He takes the letter from his pocket and silently burns it to ash.*

Mrs. Holt   If I'd grabbed your sleeve that morning . . . If I'd spilled coffee on your pants . . . you wouldn't have gotten there in time. If I questioned you about your suit, why you paid so much money for it, why it was so important you have it . . . If I'd followed you . . .

Donald   Give yourself a break, Mom. There's no way you could have stopped it!

Mrs. Holt   I'd give my life if I could. That morning. That awful morning!

Donald *leaves his cell, enters the kitchen, sits down at the table, puts a slice of bread in the toaster.*

Mrs. Holt   How could he toast his bread like he always does?

Mr. Holt takes the chair next to **Donald**.

Mrs. Holt   How could he look you in the eye and smile?

Mr. Holt   'Morning, son. Glad to see you up so early.

Donald   "The early bird catches the worm," Dad, even I know that.

Mr. Holt   Well, I'm glad to see I've taught you something.

Donald   A real student can learn from everything. Pass the butter, please.

Mr. Holt   I'm having scrambled eggs. Your mother can make you some, too. You know, if I don't eat a good breakfast, I get to feeling faint.

Donald   I won't feel faint.

Mrs. Holt   So how about telling us a little something about this job interview—

Donald   Hey. Let's see how it works out, okay?

Mrs. Holt   It must be pretty important to justify that suit.

Mr. Holt   Good shave, son, good shave.

Donald   Yeah, I want to look my best.

Takes his father's hand, presses it to his cheek.

Feel. Not one bristle. A man couldn't get a closer shave.

Mr. Holt   You get any closer, you'll take off your skin.

Donald   I'll be okay, don't worry . . . Gotta go now. 'Bye, Mom.

Big hug; he kisses her.

Mrs. Holt   Donald! You haven't kissed me since you were— . . . Why did he kiss me then? Did he want me to taste it on his lips? Was he saying goodbye . . .?

Mr. Holt   Carol. We couldn't read his mind.

Mrs. Holt   Why not? He's our son. We should have!

*Pulls **Donald** back into the bear hug; he kisses her as before.*

Mrs. Holt   Donald. You haven't kissed me since you were nine years old.

Pause.

Why today?

No response.

What does it mean?

Ditto.

Talk to me. Tell me. Why are you up so early, why did you tell me not to worry, why did you kiss me when you left?

Shakes him; he remains unresponsive.

Something terrible is going to happen. Save yourself, darling. Save us. Let me stop.

it, Donald. Please. Let me stop you.

Donald   That sourdough really makes good toast.

Exits slowly—and into cell.

Mrs. Holt *runs after him;* **Mr. Holt** *grabs her back.*

Mr. Holt   It's over, Carol. Finished.

Mrs. Holt   How can I live with it? Today, tomorrow, all the years of all my life? When I'm sixty? Seventy?

Mr. Holt   You'll lean on me. And I'll lean on you.

Exit both.

Lights come up on **Donald** *in his cell and on* **Linda**, *getting dressed in her prettiest dress.* **Donald** *is reading her letter.*

Linda

> Dearest Donald: Your folks sound fantastic, so supportive! Mine don't understand one single thing I think or do, so I just behave the way they want me to behave on the outside, and inside I'm *outrageous*. Needless to say, they'd go nuts if I said I wanted to visit a guy in prison so I lied and told them I was invited to be a bridesmaid at my friend's wedding in Toledo, and since they're awfully sentimental about weddings they said okay and paid for my ticket. I'm pretty nervous about seeing you. Maybe you won't think I'm your soul mate when I'm right there in the flesh. But probably you will. Do you think we'll be able to hold hands? I saw a movie where a girl came to see her boyfriend in jail but there was glass between them at visiting so they couldn't touch each other, not even once! God, that'd kill me! I'm dying to hold your hand that was so courageous and true. By the time you get this letter, I'll be strutting down the ramp of the airplane . . .

That's what she's doing; walking down the ramp toward his cell, fluffing her hair.

> I'm so psyched! I can't believe it. Me and you. It's like the most romantic story ever told. I mean, people write books and make movies about shit like this. And we're living it. Diamond was a lump of coal: you're the real jewel. Love ya, Linda.

Meets **Donald** *at his cell. A chair awaits her outside it.*

Linda   Well, hello, Donald Holt! Yeah! I like those eyes.

Donald   You look like a kid.

Linda   Uh-huh. Jailbait. I'll get you in trouble.

Realizes that she is barred from him by bars or plexi-glass.

Not today, I guess. What did they think I was going to do? Jump you? These prison people: all they think about is sex, sex, sex.

Donald   Let me see your hands.

Linda   I wish I had a present for you but . . . okay.

Holds up her hands.

Here they are: my empty hands.

Donald   They're very small. Do you really play the piano?

Linda   Do I?!

Holding her hands in the air, she begins playing an imaginary keyboard: the second movement of the Kreutzer Sonata, *and soon starts humming the melody.* **Donald** *picks up an imaginary violin and bow to play in concert with her, the violin part of the sonata. The duet builds and builds and builds until, by silent mutual consent, it ends at an orgasmic crescendo.*

Linda   We did it, Donald, we did it! From the minute I saw you, I said: There he is, my twin, my soul mate, the violin part of me. Just turn me inside out—and there you are, Donald Holt! Run away with me, Donald. Escape.

Donald   You really *are* trouble.

Linda   I'll bring you a blowtorch, a saw, an uzi, a bomb. I'll pretend I'm pregnant— the guards can't x-ray pregnant women—and I'll make an arsenal of my belly,

Donald   You're the girl from *Omaha*?

Linda   We'll sprout wings, stick nuclear physics in our tails, and take off like rockets.

Donald   Yeah! Yeah! We'll hijack a plane from a private field and up we'll go, me at the controls.

He's up on his chair now, piloting the plane.

We're swooping and gliding and shooting through clouds and sometimes the sun smiles down on us and sometimes the moon winks us a blessing, and we fly and we fly and we're flying high . . . and then what? Then what?

Suddenly lost, he looks at her.

Linda   We'll land, we'll have to land, right?

Donald   Right! So I'll bring the plane down, gently, keeping the pressure equal, and and and—then what?

Linda   Then we'll be somewhere else, somewhere like like like Bamanututi or Transendencia, faraway places with unfuckingbelievable beauty, where no one ever heard of Donald Holt. And we'll bring out our instruments and people will flip when they hear our music. We'll play Beethoven—

Donald   —and Schubert and Brahms; we'll play every duet in history, we'll be the most famous husband-and-wife duo—

Linda (*mouth dropping*)   Husband-and— . . .?

Donald   Wife, yeah, because we'll be married by then—

Linda (*tries to throw her arms around him, kiss him, but . . .*)   Well, well, yeah! I accept! I'll marry you! Oh, I can't wait to tell my parents. I'll just say you're—Ohhh. Do you think they'll make us have the wedding here? Euuu. That would be pretty—

Catches herself when she sees his expression.

—pretty *amazing*, huh? We *want* something unusual because *we're* unusual, right? I mean, who needs eight bridesmaids all wearing the same dress—and a receiving line—and a chocolate fountain—I saw these crazy designs in Bridal Fantasies—and I *love* chocolate but if I'm wearing white and I get some on my dress—no, I'm not taking that risk!

Donald   I love chocolate, too.

Linda   We really have so much in common, don't we? But the big thing is *music*.

Donald   Nothing bigger or better that that!

Linda   So for the wedding, let's put together our favorite duets—it will be so symbolic, you know, like how we're putting our lives together.

Donald   Sounds good, yeah.

Linda   You'll put your arms around me and we'll dance the first dance . . . I bet you're a fabulous dancer.

Donald   Well . . . no . . . not really.

P.A. Voice   All visitors must leave immediately, all visitors must leave.

Linda   Donald. Did you hear? I have to go.

Donald   Don't! Please! Not yet.

Linda   I'll come back tomorrow. And the day after that. If you want.

Donald   I want, yes, yes, I want.

P.A. Voice   All visitors must leave immediately, all visitors must leave NOW.

Linda   From now on, we'll be everything to each other. You'll be the tiger and I'll be the lily, or vice-versa, it doesn't matter, they can't live without each other, they're the same flower.

Donald   That's a very cool way of putting it.

Linda   Well, yeah! I'm a very cool girl!

Bends over to show him her underpants, patterned with bright tiger lilies.

Except when I'm hot.

Blows him a seductive kiss.

So kiss yourself for me. And I'll kiss myself for you. 'Bye, sweetie. Bye-bye. Love ya!

Lights remain on **Donald** *peering from his cell as* **Linda** *leaves and come up on* **Jordan** *with* **Mr.** *and* **Mrs. Holt.**

Jordan   Here's how I think we should pitch it:

Dramatically, as is his wont.

Sole gunman. No conspiracy, no coercion. Conducted his due diligence at shooting ranges, fairground games, video arcades. At home—on his computer. Went to gun shows and pawn shops and ammunition stores. Everyone had advice and firearms to offer. He bought a semi with a sixteen-round cartridge online. Had it customized— replaced the vinyl grip with leather. Easy as pie.

Mr. Holt   Hold on there. I'm a Second Amendment guy. . . . I always *was*, anyway. You know:

Donald *echoes from his cell.*

Mr. Holt   A gun can't shoot itself. A man's needed to shoot it.

Mrs. Holt   A man can't shoot a gun if there's no gun to shoot. Donald could not have shot seven people *without* a gun. Get rid of them, I say. Get rid of every gun and bullet in the country. The world.

Mr. Holt   That's not going to happen, Carol.

Mrs. Holt   It should. It could. Boycott every company that makes or sells guns. Picket the men who profit from them, day and night. Carry legal weapons into the White House or the Senate or the NRA—

Jordan   He needed more than a gun. He also needed a computer and $1100 bucks.

Mr. Holt   For the gun?! Where did he get that kind of money?

Jordan   From his mother's wallet.

Mrs. Holt *(stunned)*   He did?

Donald   Sorry, Mom.

Jordan   He took it out little by little, over months.

Mrs. Holt   He planned it then, he really planned it . . .

Jordan   You can call it planning but it's not the way you and I plan. Donald's mind thinks to a different drummer. Something like this:

Drums in a bizarre rhythm; acts out the scenario of his summation.

One day Donald Holt is ambling down the street and he sees a big poster, an enormous poster of an enormous personality—a movie star, the president, a hero, a saint, someone like that—and suddenly a thought floats into his mind: Wouldn't it be cool to take that guy down? Not so unusual, a thought, even a murderous one, that flits into consciousness and flits right out—but in Donald, the thought did not fly away, it stuck, lodged in a brain cell, and spread till it became malignant, repeating— take him down, how cool, take him down, take him down. And this idea stalked him, it came back again and again. And he said no to it again and again, no, no—but how many times can a person say no? So one day, he said yes, and the act was inevitable.

Mr. Holt   Well, maybe not. Maybe . . . I oughta tell you . . . it was sort of . . . my fault.

Donald   Dad . . . don't—

Mr. Holt   I . . . I smoked pot with him, see . . . I knew it was wrong and illegal, too, but . . . I did it for love. To be pals with him, you know. Do you think . . . well, maybe that's what set him off? Because of me, because of my example, I mean . . . maybe he started thinking drugs were . . . okay. I mean, a boy's father smokes dope, the kid can do it, too, right?

Mrs. Holt   You did that, Lloyd?!

Mr. Holt   Yeah, I did. . . . You think maybe it could be a mitigating factor in his defense?

Mrs. Holt   But if the school hears that you used—

Mr. Holt   What do I care about that?

Donald (*directly now; through the bars*)   You'd throw away your job, Dad, your reputation? For me?

Mr. Holt   To keep you from hell? You bet I would!

Donald   He smoked once with me. Once. And this is a man who r*eally* doesn't know how to inhale!

(*To* **Jordan**.) I hope you'll buy yourself a new suit for the trial. A decent pair of shoes. You look like a nothing.

Jordan (*looking down at his shoes*)   What's wrong with my shoes?

Donald   There will be photos of you in all the media. You represent me, you look like shit, they'll think I'm shit.

Jordan   They already think you're shit, Donald. You may look like your normal, average—

Donald   Average? I don't think so.

Jordan   Some people I interviewed said you were less than average. You know what I mean.

Donald *snorts*.

Jordan   And they say you're a virgin.

Donald   What do they know?

Jordan   I didn't find anyone with whom you'd been intimate.

Donald   Respect their privacy, okay, man? And mine. Just don't say I'm a virgin. You'll embarrass me. And no insanity defense. I may be a piece of shit but I knew exactly what I was doing.

Jordan   That's not the opinion of the psychiatrist.

Donald   How does he know? I didn't open my mind to him.

Jordan   He studied it all the same.

Donald   And what did he study it with? Right. With *his* mind.

Lights up on **Doctor Loeb** *on the witness stand.*

Doctor Loeb   The prosecution is trying to establish motive. But there is no motive, at least not one that makes sense to us: jealousy, revenge, money, even deep political conviction . . . In the most profound meaning of the word, the killing was "senseless"—a word attached every week, it seems, to some inexplicable act of violence. And yet Donald went about his preparations deliberately and with forethought. As he told me:

Reads from his notes: **Donald** *talks with him, in unison or at specific phrases.*

Doctor Loeb/Donald   "I set things up to get alerts whenever he was going to make an appearance. First I thought of catching him in Philly—that would have been easy, too—but Cleveland, well, what could be better? Open carry. An easy drive from home. It was one of those town meeting type things. He was scheduled for 11 o'clock. I had a fake press card on me. That eased me in, that and my suit. I could have been a major campaign donor for all anyone knew. The guard glanced into my laptop bag and waved me in. I counted on that. They never really look unless you're a total weirdo or black or Arab. The place was jammed. I couldn't get a seat up close but I was ready. The minute he stepped onto the podium and I had a good view I took out the gun and stood up—"

Doctor Loeb   But why? Why Governor Diamond?

Donald   You're asking *me*? I was busy doing it; you experts are supposed to handle the interpretations.

Doctor Loeb   You admired the governor.

Donald   Well, sure. Why would a man want to sacrifice his future for someone he didn't admire? That's the whole point.

Doctor Loeb   The governor didn't know you.

Donald   For an instant he did. That bullet had my name on it. For an instant he knew me and had me inside him. *That*'s the whole point.

Doctor Loeb   What Donald Holt did was not wrong to him. It wasn't right.

Doctor Loeb/Donald   It was necessary. To fulfill something.

Doctor Loeb   What something? I don't know. How fulfill? I don't know that either. But I am certain that Donald had no consciousness of the pain and suffering his act would cause—not the governor's or the "collaterals," their families, his own family . . . And not because he is cold-blooded or vicious, which he is not, but because other people are not real to him. And why is that? I think that Donald Holt is not real to himself. He has a deep, life-long void in the very place that makes us human. Does this constitute mental defect? You must be the judge of that. Murder is as old as Cain but psychology was only born with Freud. We are a long way from understanding why one child grows up to build a skyscraper and another to bomb it. Or why one young man, abused, neglected, without a single advantage in the world, becomes a fine human being and Donald Loeb turns into—this!

Gestures to **Donald**, *who erupts in scornful laughter.*

Donald   Donald *Loeb*?

His mockery reverberates harshly. Everyone backs away from the discordant sound except for **Mrs. Holt**. *She and* **Donald** *are left alone.*

Mrs. Holt   How can you laugh? He's been working to understand you. He was feeling empathy, Donald, empathy—an emotion you've never experienced, it seems.

Donald   I feel empathy, Mom. I feel it right now. For you.

Mrs. Holt   You feel it for yourself. For everyone else, you have contempt.

Donald   No. We live in a democracy. Everyone deserves credit—the lawyer, the shrink, the guards. On their gravestones it will say:

In mock-heroic tones.

"Here lies a man who rose from the first step—to the second!"

Mrs. Holt (*staring at him*)   And what will it say on your gravestone?

Donald   What are you doing, Mom?

Mrs. Holt   Just looking. Looking at you.

Donald   What for? You know everything about me.

Mrs. Holt   Do I?

Donald   Come on. Don't stare at me like that.

Mrs. Holt   Why not?

Donald   I don't know. It's like you're trying to drill holes in me . . . Stop, Mom, it makes me want to run away from you.

Mrs. Holt   What about the people you put holes in? The people who ran away from you?

Donald   Drop it, Mom. It's over.

Mrs. Holt   It will never be over. Not for them, not for you *or* for me.

Donald   I'm sorry, Mom, okay?

Mrs. Holt   Are you, Donald? Are you sorry?

Donald   . . . Yeah . . . I think so . . .

Mrs. Holt   You think? What does that mean?

Donald   What does "sorry" feel like?

Mrs. Holt *is shocked.*

Donald   Tell me. Then I'll know if I feel it.

Mrs. Holt   It feels like . . . shame. Shame and sadness mixed together. You want to take back the bad thing you did. You think about it continually, it interferes with your coffee and your pleasure—

Donald   No, no, I wouldn't like that. So I don't know if I'm sorry or . . . what.

She reacts

Well, you want me to tell you the truth, don't you?

Mrs. Holt   I do—yes, and I don't . . .

Donald   What can I do about it, Mom? If I don't feel what I'm supposed to feel? I'm not making excuses. I knew I shouldn't take a life.

Mrs. Holt   Lives.

Donald   Lives, okay. Don't rub it in. But you know—you want the truth, right?—it was good for me. It made me feel better.

Mrs. Holt   Better?

Donald   Yeah. Like . . . relieved.

Mrs. Holt   Relieved? People died so you could feel relief?!

Donald   You want me to say I did something terrible? Okay, I did. I broke a commandment! . . . I broke your heart, too, probably. And Dad's. So I guess you're not going to forgive me. . . . Right?

Mrs. Holt   Obviously I'm not very good at predicting the future.

Donald   Can you get them to give me my violin, Mom? I don't know how I can live here without my music.

Mrs. Holt   Think positively. Maybe they'll send you to Sing Sing.

Donald   Mom!

Mrs. Holt   Listen for the creak of that woman's wheelchair. The children crying for their mother, the mother crying for her baby. The governor gasping for breath. That's your music.

Donald   Forget it, Mom. Go home.

Mrs. Holt   I need to see you.

Donald   You've seen me all your life.

Mrs. Holt   I haven't. That's what I see. I look back on all those years, on things that seemed so innocent, and every memory I have is changed by what's happened. I didn't know you. I was afraid to know you.

Donald   I'm the image of you, Mom. Flesh of your flesh and blood of your blood—

Mrs. Holt   How can you even speak those words—*flesh, blood*—

Donald   You see me every time you look in the mirror. We have the same eyes and eyebrows and cheekbones and—

Mrs. Holt   No, Donald. We're not the same. A mother is not her son. Nothing can change what you've done. And nothing will change that I'm your mother. But I'm getting to know you now: a boy who's almost a man. A boy who played music and dreamt about murder. I didn't kill anyone. You did. You.

Donald   Stop! Get out of my eyes, Mom!

Puts his hands over his eyes.

Mrs. Holt   You can't hide anymore. I'm getting a good look at you, Donald. A mother is looking at her child. A mother is seeing her son.

Lights fade there and come up on the courtroom: **Jordan** *is giving his dramatic summation, a piñata handing above.*

Jordan   . . . Why this piñata? A lot more colorful than PowerPoint! We all become kids when we see one of these, don't we? What's inside, what's inside, we want to know. Because it could be anything—candies, rose petals, butterflies, worms . . . So—in this one? Ready? Here goes!

Swats it; swats it more; breaks it open. Nothing falls out.

Hey, hey! What a cheat! There's nothing inside! Same as with my client. He is as empty as that piñata—a shell, a kind of computer animation. On the surface, he seems like anyone else, like you, like me—but does he have a heart? Everyone has a heart. But does Donald's heart thrill with love? Move in sympathy? Weep in shame? It does not. He has a soul, or so we are led to believe, but does that soul fall on its knees and cry out for guidance and grace? I have not seen it. He is so immersed in his narrow inner world that he is incapable of understanding the consequences of his behavior. It must be clear to you already that several big screws are not just loose in this man but altogether missing. The law does not want you to convict someone who is not responsible for his actions just as it would not condemn a cat for eating a mouse. Rise above the desire for vengeance and declare him innocent by reason of mental defect.

A gavel. Lights change.

Judge (*offstage voice*)   The jury has reached a verdict. Donald Holt, please rise and face the bench.

Donald *and* **Jordan** *do so.*

Elsewhere in the courtroom are the **Holts**, **Mrs. Diamond**, **Linda**, *maybe others.*

Judge   On the several counts of murder and attempted murder, this court finds you guilty!

Donald   Yesss! I always said I wasn't crazy. And now twelve people of the people have agreed with me.

Mrs. Diamond   Guilty. Good. I have some justice.

Mrs. Holt   I hope it gives you comfort.

Mrs. Diamond   Cold comfort, I assure you. Very very cold.

Jordan   Sorry, kid. I did my best.

Donald   Not your fault, man.

They shake hands.

By the way, that suit is awesome.

Jordan *is pleased.*

Donald   But *blue* socks?

Jordan *glances down at his socks, sees that it is so, nods sheepishly.*

Mrs. Holt   Don't worry, it's not over, we won't give up, we'll appeal, we'll—

Donald   Hey, don't sweat it. I'm okay.

Mr. Holt   Forgive us, son, if we somehow . . . trespassed against you. We didn't mean to.

Donald   Don't take it on yourselves, you and Mom. It was all me. I don't know why things turned out like this. It just . . . happened. It's just . . . me.

Gesturing to where **Linda** *is sitting alone.*

Donald   I want you to meet someone. Come on, don't be shy.

Linda *hesitantly walks over.*

Donald   This is Linda.

She is very flustered and curtsies.

Linda   I know that was a stupid thing to do, Mr. and Mrs. Holt but, I mean, what's a good way to show how . . . I mean, well, you're his *parents*!

Mrs. Holt   . . . Hello, Linda.

Mr. Holt   Pleased to meet you.

Linda   I know how wonderful you've been through all this and I want you to rest assured I'll take good care of Donald. I may look flibberty-gibbet but I'm a wonderful support system.

Donald   Excuse me, folks. I only have a few more visiting minutes and . . . you know.

Linda   Please say come to the wedding. It will be very controversial, a prison wedding; we'll be all over YouTube. I'm going to wear a veil—it's really cool to look old-fashioned this year. And I'll carry big bouquets of tiger lilies. And the music, the music will be ours.

Donald   See you soon, okay?

Mr. Holt   Oh, sure, okay, son.

Mrs. Holt *moves as if to kiss* **Donald** *goodbye but* **Linda** *interposes herself between them and lifts up her face to be kissed.*

Mrs. Holt *does so.*

Mr. Holt *puts his arm around his wife as they exit.*

Lights fade in the courtroom and follow **Mr.** *and* **Mrs. Holt** *as they walk toward home, leaning on each other. The voices of* **Linda** *and* **Donald** *follow them, too.*

Linda's Voice   Do you think they liked me?

Donald's Voice   Oh yeah. And when they get to know you, they'll love you.

Linda's Voice   And when the babies come? They won't be able to resist. We'll be making them grandparents! My folks, too. They'll forgive us anything. Especially by the second or third.

Donald's Voice   Hey, hey, one step at a time, okay?

The **Holts** *get into bed, in the same position as in the Prologue, and fall asleep right away.*

Linda's Voice   Okay. But you should know, triplets run in my family.

Donald's Voice   You're kidding!

Linda's Voice   Yup.

They laugh.

Mrs. Holt *startles upright in bed.*

Donald's Voice   I bet my mom will cry at the wedding.

Linda's Voice   Well, duhhhh. It's a tradition. Mothers always cry at their child's wedding.

In the **Holts'** *home, a new door now becomes visible.*

Mrs. Holt *gets out of bed, puts on a black coat and walks toward it with infinitely slow movements, as in the Prologue. She raises her hand to the ornate knocker, hesitates.*

Donald's Voice   . . . What if I get the death penalty?

Linda's Voice   The death—? No, no way. That's not going to happen.

Donald's Voice   If the jury recommends it, yeah, it could.

Linda's Voice   Omigod, omigod. That would be a nightmare. A real nightmare!

Mrs. Holt *knocks.*

The door opens. **Mrs. Diamond**, *leaning on a cane, also dressed in black, stands there. In tense silence, they confront each other.*

Mrs. Diamond   And why are you dressed in black, Mrs. Holt?

Mrs. Holt   I too have lost a son, Mrs. Diamond.

Mrs. Diamond   Will you come in?

Mrs. Holt   Thank you.

Enters the house. They are both encompassed in a single bright light.

It's very kind of you to see me.

Mrs. Diamond   I see you.

Mrs. Holt   You look at me the way I look at myself.

Mrs. Diamond   We both have our afflictions.

Mrs. Holt   You make it very difficult, Mrs. Diamond. But I had to come—to tell you in person how sorry—

Mrs. Diamond   How original of you, Mrs. Holt.

Mrs. Holt   —more than sorry! Pained, anguished, heartsick—poor words, I know, to describe these feelings, but . . . what else do we have?

Mrs. Diamond   We?! Please. Don't include me in your generalizations.

Mrs. Holt   No one knows better than I what you must be suffering.

Mrs. Diamond   If you want absolution, go to your priest.

Mrs. Holt   I don't have a priest, Mrs. Diamond. All I have is hell. And you're there with me, I know you are. I feel you breathing next to me as we walk under that hail of fire. I think of *my* boy—and I weep for yours. I listen again and again to the sounds of my baby's laughter, that sweet music, and I hear your boy's laughter, too—and it goes on, ringing in my ears, night after night, like a death bell pealing for both of them, for both of us.

Mrs. Diamond   Spare me your odious comparisons.

Mrs. Holt   I can't. Our sons are linked together, now and forever. Yours is the martyr, mine is the animal that killed him. Yours is the hero, mine the scum. You have that, at least.

Mrs. Diamond   I didn't want the least, Mrs. Holt. My son was the best this country had to offer. The best!

Mrs Holt   He was, he was an excellent man . . . I know. But what can I—

Mrs. Diamond   It's too late for all that. You should have ripped that creature out of you with a coat hanger!

Mrs. Holt   No!

Mrs. Diamond   You dare say "no"?

Mrs. Holt   I do say it, I do. Look.

Pulling photographs from her purse.

I beg you to look.

She forces them in front of **Mrs. Diamond**'s *eyes.*

Mrs. Holt   Here's Donald at six months, with his three new teeth. Here he is at a year, taking his first steps. This is Donald at two. He could recite every nursery rhyme in his book. Don't look away. I want you to see. This is the boy you hate. The boy you want to execute. He cast his first vote for your son. When the governor spoke on television, Donald was watching. His wall was covered with pictures of movie stars and athletes and musicians—and your Philip.

Mrs. Diamond   Stop it! Do you hear? Don't tell me any more about your son's perversities!

She raises her cane and brings it down on the frame of the sofa, near **Mrs. Holt**. *A framed photograph of Philip falls to the floor with a loud metallic sound.*

Mrs. Diamond   There! Now you've destroyed something else! How dare you walk into my house with your excuses! How dare you ask that I forgive you! Live with your torment, Mrs. Holt, as I live with mine. Have some dignity, at least.

Mrs. Holt   You think your son's photograph is worth more than mine? Your memories more than mine? Yes, that's how it is with the rich. Even your grief is superior to ours. So. Tell me, Mrs. Diamond: do you save your . . . excrement for your archives?

Mrs. Diamond *slaps her.* **Mrs. Holt** *traps the hand against her cheek.*

Mrs. Holt   Feel, Mrs. Diamond, feel. Skin. Flesh. Wrinkles, like yours. Blood underneath, like yours.

Pulls the hand to her breast.

Breasts that gave milk to my child.

To her belly.

A womb that grew full. A stomach scarred with stretch marks.

Between her legs.

A vagina, like yours. Remember? This is where his head pushed out!

Releases **Mrs. Diamond**'s *hand.*

Mrs. Holt   I loved my son. I'll love him forever. That's what fate has forced on me. That's my dignity, Mrs. Diamond.

She stoops to pick up the photo of Philip and hands it to **Mrs. Diamond**.

The door collapses. Behind it, **Linda** *is revealed in bridal attire.*

Linda   We rushed it, I'm so so sorry, Mrs. Holt, but who knows what his sentence will be? And it was so awful. They wouldn't let me stay for our conjugal rights, I was sure they would, they made me leave right after the judge said "husband and wife" and then it was over . . . no tiger lilies, no music, no dancing. Girls always get to dance at their wedding. It's her first dance as a couple, the most important one in a girl's life.

Mrs. Holt   . . . Come here, Mrs. Holt. I'll dance with you.

She holds out her arms. They dance, until lights fade out.

End of Play.

Introduction to Ntozake Shange

Wesley Brown

Born Paulette Williams in Trenton, New Jersey, in 1948, Ntozake Shange (Ntozake is Zulu for "she who comes with her own things" and Shange translates as "one who walks with lions") received a BA from Barnard College and a Master's in American Studies from the University of Southern California. Shange became active in the poetry, music, and performance scene in San Francisco before coming to New York in the mid-1970s, and began performing in bars and theater venues such as Woodie King, Jr.'s New Federal Theater. King suggested to Joseph Papp at the Public Theater that he go see her show. Papp decided to produce Shange's series of narrative poems in the voices of several black women. The groundswell of audience and critical attention led to the piece called *for colored girls who have considered suicide/when the rainbow is enuf* opening on Broadway in 1975.

Not surprisingly, Shange, who used music and dance as an integral part of the performance of the written word, was more than a little wary of the constraints of the well-made play in particular and the theater establishment of Broadway more generally. While *for colored girls . . .* received an Obie Award for its Off-Broadway production, it garnered neither of Broadway's highest honors: the Tony Award or the New York Drama Critics' Circle Award. However, Trazana Beverley (one of the seven women in *for colored girls . . .*) did receive a Tony Award for Best Featured Actress in a play.

While Broadway's highest honors did not come to Shange's choreopoem, controversy surely did. The play was hailed by many for its unflinching dramatizations of black women's lives. However, panels and forums were organized where black male critics, for the most part, took issue with what they believed were negative portrayals of black men in the narratives of black women in Shange's play which was responsible for its success on and off Broadway. Other mainstream critics argued that Shange's writing was too self-conscious and bent on destroying the English language. She agreed that there was truth in these comments and wrote in her collection of essays, *See No Evil*: "i can't count the number of times i have viscerally wanted to attack deform n maim the language that i waz taught to hate myself in/ . . . being an afro-american writer is something to be self-conscious abt/& yes/in order to think n communicate/i haveta fix my tool to my needs/i have to take it apart to the bone/so that the malignancies/ fall away/leaving us space to literally create our own image."

Shange followed *for colored girls . . .* with *A Photograph: Lovers in Motion* (1977), *Where the Mississippi Meets the Delta* (1977), and *Boogie Woogie Landscapes* (1979). In *Spell #7* (1979), the cringe-inducing presence of a huge minstrel mask hovered above the stage. In responding to the presence of the minstrel mask, Shange explained that "the minstrel may be banned as racist/but the minstrel is more powerful in his deformities than our alleged rejection of him." She goes on to say that "in everything i have ever written & everything I hope to write/I have made use of what Frantz Fanon called 'combat breath' . . . my people have lived with cut-off lives n limbs [and] are in throes of pain n sensation experienced by my characters . . . [who are] responding to the involuntary constrictions n amputations of their humanity/in the context of combat breathing."

A group of black women and men appear on stage wearing minstrel masks. After taking them off, a self-anointed magician/interlocutor presides over the gathering of actors/performers in a bar who commiserate with one another, individually, in pairs or collectively regarding the demeaning stereotypes they must perform either on stage or in their daily lives in order to survive. Moving seamlessly from one sequence to the next, they enact scathing and painful parodies of themselves that reveal how they are implicated in the cruelties they visit upon one another.

In one scene, a black woman portrays a stereotypical image of a white woman with nothing much on her mind but the hair on her head that she flings about. It should be noted that many whites in the audiences during the first previews of *Spell #7* objected to this parody of the willful ignorance of a certain spectrum of white women, prompting Joseph Papp to demand that Shange remove the scene from the play before the official opening at the Public Theater. Apparently, it was fine for the blacks on stage to parody themselves, but it was unthinkable that the power of the minstrel mask could hold dominion over the representations of whites as well. Nonetheless, *Spell #7* is a trenchant and disturbing examination of the self-denying roles that women and men are groomed for by various American incarnations of the minstrel mask.

In 1980, Shange received an Obie Award for her adaptation of Brecht's *Mother Courage and Her Children*, focusing on a black family in the American Southwest during the post-Civil War period. Shange published works of fiction: *Sassafrass, Cypress and Indigo* (1982); *Betsey Brown* (1985); *Liliane: Resurrection of the Daughter* (1994); and *Some Sing, Some Cry* (2010 with Ifa Bayeza).

In 2011, after suffering two strokes, Shange was diagnosed with a neurological disorder characterized by progressive weakness and impaired sensory function in the arms and legs. Undaunted by these challenges, Shange reemerged into the artistic world in 2017 with a solo show, backed up by a musical ensemble at the Blue Note Jazz Club in New York City. She also published *Wild Beauty*, her first book of poetry in ten years, and Barnard College acquired her archive. As she approached seventy, Shange reflected on having come full circle: "in one way, I've gone back to my beginnings because I am working in nightclubs with musicians reading my poetry, which is how I started. That is how *for colored girls* . . . started." Ntozake Shange passed away on October 27, 2018.

Spell #7

Ntozake Shange

this show is dedicated to my great-aunt marie, aunt lizzie, aunt jane and my grandma,
viola benzena, and her buddy, aunt effie, and the lunar year.

Characters (*in order of appearance*)

Lou, *a practicing magician*
Alec, *a frustrated, angry actor's actor*
Dahlia, *a young gypsy (singer/dancer)*
Eli, *a bartender who is also a poet*
Bettina, *Dahlia's co-worker in a chorus*
Lily, *an unemployed actress working as a barmaid*
Natalie, *a not-too-successful performer*
Ross, *a guitarist-singer with Natalie*
Maxine, *an experienced actress*

Spell #7 was originally produced by Joseph Papp's New York Shakespeare Festival in New York City, 1979, with the following personnel: Oz Scott, Director. Dianne McIntyre, Choreographer. Original Music by David Murray and Butch Morris. Scenery by Robert Yodice. Costumes by Grace Williams. Lighting by Victor En Yu Tan. Production Stage Manager, Jacqueline Yancey.

With: Mary Alice, Avery Brooks, Laurie Carlos, Dyane Harvey, Larry Marshall, Reyno, LaTanya Richardson, Beth Shorter, and Ellis Williams. Jay Fernandez, Samuel L. Jackson, and Jack Landron also appeared during the run.

Act One

There is a huge black face mask hanging from the ceiling of the theater as the audience enters. In a way the show has already begun, for the members of the audience must integrate this grotesque, larger than life misrepresentation of life into their pre-show chatter. Slowly the house lights fade, but the mask looms even larger in the darkness.

Once the mask is all that can be seen, **Lou,** *the magician, enters. He is dressed in the traditional costume of Mr. Interlocutor: tuxedo, bow-tie, top hat festooned with all kinds of whatnots that are obviously meant for good luck. He does a few catchy "soft shoe" steps and begins singing a traditional version of a black play-song.*

Lou (*singing*)
10 lil picaninnies all in bed
one fell out and the other nine said:
i sees yr hiney
all black & shiney
i see yr hiney
all black & shiney/ shiney

As a greeting.

yes/ yes/ yes/ isnt life wonderful

Confidentially.

my father is a retired magician
which accounts for my irregular behavior
everything comes outta magic hats
or bottles wit no bottoms & parakeets
are as easy to get as a couple a rabbits
or 3 fifty-cent pieces/ 1958
my daddy retired from magic & took
up another trade cuz this friend a mine
from the 3rd grade/ asked to be made white
on the spot
what cd any self-respectin colored american magician
do wit such an outlandish request/ cept
put all them razzamatazz hocus pocus zippity-doo-dah
thingamajigs away   cuz
colored chirren believin in magic
waz becomin politically dangerous for the race
& waznt nobody gonna be made white
on the spot just
from a clap of my daddy's hands
& the reason i'm so peculiar's
cuz i been studyin up on my daddy's technique

& everything i do is magic these days
& it's very colored/ very now you see it/ now you
dont mess wit me

Boastfully.

i come from a family of retired sorcerers/ active houngans & pennyante fortune tellers
wit 41 million spirits/ critturs & celestial bodies on our side
   i'll listen to yr problems
   help wit yr career/ yr lover/ yr wanderin spouse
   make yr grandma's stay in heaven more gratifyin
   ease yr mother thru menopause & show yr son
   how to clean his room

While **Lou** *has been easing the audience into acceptance of his appearance and the
mask, the rest of the* **Company** *enters in field-hand garb, blackface, and the
countenance of stephan fetchit when he was frightened.*

YES YES YES 3 wishes is all you get
   scarlet ribbons for yr hair
   a farm in mississippi
   someone to love you madly
all things are possible
but aint no colored magician in his right mind
gonna make you   white
i mean
   this is blk magic
you lookin at
& i'm fixin you up good/ fixin you up good & colored
& you gonna be colored all yr life
& you gonna love it/ bein colored/ all yr life/ colored   & love it
love it/ bein colored SPELL #7!

Lou *claps his hands and the* **Company**, *which had been absolutely still til this
moment/ jumps up. With a rhythm set on a washboard carried by one of them, they
begin a series of steps that identify every period of afro-american entertainment:
aerobats, tap dancers, calindy dancers, cotton club choruses, appolo theater doo-wop
groups, til they reach a frenzy in the midst of "hambone, hambone where ya been"/ &
then take a bow in eddie cantor style. The lights bump up abruptly.* **Lou** *walks thru
the black faced figures in their kneeling poses, arms outstretched as if they were going
to sing "mammy."*

Lou   why dont you go on & integrate a german-american school in st. louis mo./
1955/ better yet why dont ya go on & be a red niggah in a blk school 1954/ i got it/
try & make one friend at camp in the ozarks in 1957/ crawl thru one a jesse james'
caves wit a class of white kids waitin outside to see the whites of yr eyes/ why
dontcha invade a clique of working class italians trying to be protestant in a jewish
community/ & come up a spade/ be a lil too dark/ lips a lil too full/ hair entirely too
nappy/ to be beautiful be a smart child trying to be dumb/ you go meet somebody
who wants/ always/ a lil less/ be cool when yr body says hot/ & more/ be a mistake in

racial integrity/ an error in white folks' most absurd fantasies/ be a blk kid in 1954/ who's not blk enuf to lovingly ignore/ not beautiful enuf to leave alone/ not smart enuf to move outta the way/ not bitter enuf to die at an early age/ why dontchu c'mon & live my life for me/ since the dreams aint enuf/ go on & live my life for me/ i didnt want certain moments at all/ i'd give em to anybody awright.   alec.

When he hears his name **Alec** *gives his minstrel mask to* **Lou** *and rises. The rest of the* **Company** *move away from him, or move in place as if in mourning.*

Alec   st. louis/ such a colored town/ a whiskey black space of history & neighborhood/ forever ours to lawrenceville/ where the only road open to me waz cleared by colonial slaves/ whose children never moved/ never seems like mended the torments of the Depression or the stains of demented spittle/ dropped from the lips of crystal women/ still makin independence flags/ st. louis/ on a halloween's eve to the veiled prophet/ usurpin the mystery of mardi gras/ i made it mine tho the queen waz always fair/ that parade of pagan floats & tamborines/ commemmorates me/ unlike the lonely walks wit liberal trick or treaters/ back to my front door/ bag half empty/ my face enuf to scare anyone i passed/ gee/ a colored kid/ whatta gas. Here/ a tree/ wanderin the horizon/ dipped in blues/ untended bones/ usedta hugs drawls rhythm & decency here a tree/ waitin to be hanged sumner high school/ squat & pale on the corner/ like our vision waz to be vague/ our memory of the war/ that made us free/ to be forgotten/ becomin paler/ linear movement from sous carolina to missouri/ freedmen/ landin in jackie wilson's yelp/ daughters of the manumitted swimmin in tina turner's grinds/ this is chuck berry's town disavowin miscega-nation/ in any situation/ & they let us be/ electric blues & bo didley's/ rockin pneumonia & boogie-woogie flu/ the slop & short fried heads/ runnin always to the river chambersburg/ lil italy/ i passed everyday at the sweet shoppe/ & waz afraid/ the cops raided truants/ regularly/ & after dark i wd not be seen wit any other colored/ sane & lovin my life

Loud shouts and cries of a white mob are heard. The still black faced **Company** *tries to move away from the menacing voices.*

Voices   hey niggah/ over here

Alec   behind the truck lay five hands claspin chains

Voices   hey niggah/ over here

Alec   round the trees/ 4 more sucklin steel

Voices   hey niggah/ over here

Alec   this is the borderline

Voices   hey niggah/ over here

Alec   a territorial dispute

Voices   hey niggah/ over here

Alec (*crouched on floor*)   cars loaded with families/ fellas from the factory/ one or two practical nurses/ become our trenches/ some dig into cement wit elbows/ under engines/ do not be seen in yr hometown after sunset/ we suck up our shadows

The **Company** *has been moved to shed their masks. They exit with their true faces bared to the audience, except* **Dahlia**, *who has also shed her overalls and wig, revealing a finely laced unitard and the body of a modern dancer. She throws her mask to* **Alec**, *who tosses it offstage.* **Dahlia** *begins a lyrical but pained dance solo as* **Alec** *speaks for them.*

Alec   we will stand here
our shoulders embrace an enormous spirit
my dreams waddle in my lap
run round to miz bertha's
where lil richard gets his process
run backward to the rosebushes
& a drunk man lyin
down the block to the nuns
in pink habits/ prayin in a pink chapel
my dreams run to meet aunt marie
my dreams haunt me like the little geechee river
our dreams draw blood from old sores
this is our space
we are not movin

Dahlia *finishes her movement/* **Alec** *is seen reaching for her. Lights out. Lights up on* **Lou**, *who bitterly repeats his challenge to the audience.*

Lou   why dontchu go on & live my life for me i didnt want certain moments at all
i'd give them to anybody

Lou *waves his hand, and the minstrel mask disappears. He signals to his left, and lights up on the interior of a lower manhattan bar and its bartender,* **Eli**, *setting up for the night.* **Eli** *greets* **Lou**/ *continues to set up tables, chairs, etc.* **Lou** *moves to the jukebox, taps it with his cane, and "we are family" by sister sledge begins to play.* **Lou** *starts to tell us where we are, but* **Eli** *interrupts. Throughout* **Eli**'s *poem, the members of the* **Company** *enter the bar in street clothes, not minstrel clothes, identifying themselves as former minstrels by doing dance steps reminiscent of their earlier solos. They continue to dance, individually or in couples, as* **Eli** *speaks.*

Lou   this is

Eli   (*interrupting*)
MY kingdom.
there shall be no tresspassers/ no marauders
no tourists in my land
you nurture these gardens   or   be shot on sight
carelessness & other priorities
are not permitted within these walls
i am mantling an array of strength & beauty
no one shall interfere with this
the construction of my self
my city   my theatre
my bar   come to my poems

but understand we speak english carefully
& perfect antillean french
our toilets are disinfected
the plants here sing to me each morning
come to my kitchen my parlor even my bed
i sleep on satin   surrounded by hand made
infants who bring me good luck & warmth
come even to my door
the burglar alarm/ armed guards vault from the east side
if i am in danger   a siren shouts
you are welcome
to my kingdom   my city   my self
but yr presence must not disturb these inhabitants
leave nothing out of place/ push no dust under my rugs
leave not a crack in my wine glasses
no finger prints
clean up after yrself in the bathroom
there are no maids here   no days off
for healing   no insurance policies
for dislocation of the psyche
aliens/ foreigners/ are granted resident status
we give them a little green card
as they prove themselves non-injurious
to the joy of my nation
i sustain no intrusions/ no double-entendre romance
no soliciting of sadness   in my life
are those who love me well
the rest are denied their visas
is everyone ready to boogie?

When **Eli** *calls for a boogie, the* **Company** *does a dance that indicates they have worked and played together for a long time. As the dance ends, the* **Company** *disperses, sitting and chatting at the bar and tables.* **Lily,** *the waitress, is continually moving about the bar, taking orders for drinks and generally staying on top of things.*

Alec (*to* **Lily**)   gimme a triple bourbon/ & a glass of angel dust. these thursday nite audiences are abt to kill me

Eli *moves behind bar to make drinks.*

Dahlia   why do i drink so much?

Bettina, Lily, Natalie (*in unison*)   who cares?

Dahlia   but i'm an actress. i have to ask myself these questions

Lily   that's a good reason to drink

Dahlia   no/ i mean the character. alec, you're a director/ give me some motivation

Alec   motivation/ if you didn't drink you wd remember that you're not workin

Lily   i wish i cd get just one decent part

Lou   say as lady macbeth or mother courage?

Eli   how the hell is she gonna play lady macbeth and macbeth's a white dude?

Lily   ross & natalie/ why are you countin pennies like that?

Natalie   we had to wait on our money again

Ross   and then we didn't get it

Bettina   maybe they think we still accept beads & ribbons.

Natalie   i had to go around wit my tambourine just to get subway fare

Eli   don't worry abt it/ have one on me

Natalie   thank you eli

Bettina (*falling out of her chair*)   OH . . .

Alec   cut her off eli/ don't give her no more

Lily   what's the matter bettina/ is yr show closin?

Bettina (*gets up, resets chair*)   no/ my show is not closin/ but if that director asks me to play it any blacker/ i'm gonna have to do it in a mammy dress

Lou   you know/ countin pennies/ lookin for parts/ breakin tambourines/ we must be outta our minds for doin this

Bettina   no we're not outta our minds/ we're just sorta outta our minds

Lily   no/ we're not outta our minds/ we've been doing this shit a long time/ ross/ captain theophilis conneau/ in *a slaver's logbook/* says that "youths of both sexes wear rings in the nose and lower lip and stick porcupine quills thru the cartilage of the ear." ross/ when ringlin' bros. comes to madison square garden/ dontcha know the white people just go

Ross   in their cb radios

Dahlia   in their mcdonald's hats

Eli   with their save america t-shirts & those chirren who score higher on IQ tests for the white chirren who speak english

Alec   when the hockey games absorb all america's attention in winter/ they go with their fists clenched & their tongues battering their women who dont know a puck from a 3-yr-old harness racer

Bettina   they go & sweat in fierce anger

Ross   these factories

Natalie   these middle management positions

Ross   make madison square garden

Bettina   the temple of the primal scream

Lily *gets money from cash register and heads toward jukebox.*

Lily   oh how they love blood

Natalie   & how they dont even dress for the occasion/ all inconspicuous & pink

Eli   now if willie colon come there

Bettina   if/ we say/ the fania all stars gonna be there/ in that nasty fantasy of the city council

Ross   where the hot dogs are not even hebrew national

Lily   and the bread is stale

Ross   even in such a place where dance is an obscure notion

Bettina   where one's joy is good cause for a boring chat with the pinkerton guard

Dahlia   where the halls lead nowhere

Eli   & "back to yr seat/ folks"

Lily   when all one's budget for cruisin

Lou   one's budget for that special dinner with you know who

Lily   the one you wd like to love you

Bettina   when yr whole reasonable allowance for leisure activity/ buys you a seat where what's goin on dont matter

Dahlia   cuz you so high up/ you might be in seattle

Lily   even in such a tawdry space

Eli   where vorster & his pals wd spit & expect black folks to lick it up

Ross (*stands on chair*)   in such a place i've seen miracles

All   oh yeah/ aw/ ross

Ross   the miracles

"Music for the love of it" by butch morris comes up on the jukebox/ catchy and up-tempo. The **Company** *begins a dance that highlights their ease with one another and their familiarity with the latest dance steps.*

Lily   the commodores

Dahlia   muhammad ali

Natalie   bob marley

Alec   & these folks who upset alla 7th avenue with their glow/ how the gold in their braids is new in this world of hard hats & men with the grace of wounded buffalo/

how these folks in silk & satin/ in bodies reekin of good love comin/ these pretty muthafuckahs

Dahlia   make this barn

Lily   this insult to good taste

Bettina   a foray into paradise

Dahlia, Lily, Alec, Natalie, and Ross (*in unison*)   we dress up

Bettina, Eli, and Lou (*in unison*)   we dress up

Dahlia   cuz we got good manners

Ross   cd you really ask dr. funkenstein to come all that way & greet him in the clothes you sweep yr kitchen in?

All   NO!

Bettina   cd you say to muhammad ali/ well/ i just didnt have a chance to change/ you see i have a job / & then i went jogging & well/ you know its just madison square garden

Lou   my dear/ you know that wont do

Natalie   we honor our guests/ if it costs us all we got

Dahlia   when stevie wonder sings/ he dont want us lookin like we ain't got no common sense/ he wants us to be as lovely as we really are/ so we strut & reggae

Eli   i seen some doing the jump up/ i myself just got happy/ but i'm tellin you one thing for sure

Lily   we fill up where we at

Bettina   no police

Natalie   no cheap beer

Dahlia   no nasty smellin banyo

Ross   no hallways fulla derelicts & hustlers

Natalie   gonna interfere wit alla this beauty

Alec   if it wasnt for us/ in our latino chic/ our rastafare/ our outer space funk suits & all the rest i have never seen

Bettina   tho my daddy cd tell you bout them fox furs & stacked heels/ the diamonds & marie antoinette wigs

Eli   it's not cuz we got money

Natalie   it's not cuz if we had money we wd spend it on luxury

Lily   it's just when you gotta audience with the pope/ you look yr best

Bettina   when you gonna see the queen of england/ you polish yr nails

Natalie   when you gonna see one of them/ & you know who i mean

Alec   they gotta really know

Bettina   we gotta make em feel

Eli   we dont do this for any old body

Lou   we're doin this for you

Natalie   we dress up

Alec   is our way of sayin/ you gettin the very best

Dahlia   we cant do less/ we love too much to be stingy

Ross   they love us too much to be loved ordinary

Lily   we simply have good manners

Ross   & an addiction to joy

Female Cast Members (*in unison*)   WHEE!

Dahlia   we dress up

Male Cast Members (*in unison*)   HEY!

Bettina   we gotta show the world/ we gotta corner on the color

Ross   happiness just jumped right outta us/ & we are lookin good

Maxine *enters, taking on an exaggerated "femme-fatale" character to bring the* **Company** *to attention. They freeze, half in respect/half in parody.*

Maxine (*after long pause*)   cognac!

The **Company** *relaxes, goes to tables or the bar.* **Ross** *crosses to* **Maxine** *at her table & begins an improvisation.*

Ross   she left the front gate open/ not quite knowing she wanted someone to walk on thru the wrought iron fence/ scrambled in whiskey bottles broken round old bike spokes/ some nice brown man to wind up in her bed/ she really didnt know/ the sombrero that enveloped her face waz a lil too much for an april nite on the bowery/ & the silver halter dug out from summer cookouts near riis beach/ didnt sparkle with the intensity of her promise to have one good time/ before the children came back from carolina, brooklyn cd be sucha drag. every street cept flatbush & nostrand/ reminiscent of europe during the plague/ seems like nobody but sickness wax out walkin/ drivels & hypes/ a few youngsters looking for more than they cd handle/ & then there waz fay/

Maxine *rises, begins acting out the story.*

Ross   waitin for a cab. anyone of the cars inchin along the boulevard cd see fay waznt no whore/ just a good clean woman out for the nite/ & tho her left titty jumped out from under her silver halter/ she didnt notice cuz she waz lookin for a cab. the dank air fondled her long saggin bosom like a possible companion/ she felt good. she stuck her tin-ringed hand on her waist & watched her own ankles dance in the nite. she waz gonna have a good time tonite/ she waz awright/ a whole lotta woman/ wit that special brooklyn bottom strut. knowing she waznt comin in til dawn/ fay covered herself/ sorta/ wit a light kacky jacket that just kept her titties from rompin in the wind/ & she pulled it closer to her/ the winds was comin/ from nowhere jabbin/ & there waznt no cabs/ the winds waz beatin her behind/ whisperin/ gigglin/ you aint goin noplace/ you an ol bitch/ shd be at home wit yr kids. fay beat off the voices/ & an EBONY-TRUE-TO-YOU cab climbed the curb to get her. (*As cabdriver.*) hope you aint plannin on stayin in brooklyn/ after 8.00 you dead in brooklyn. (*As narrator.*) She let her titty shake like she thot her mouth oughtta bubble like/ wd she take off her panties/ i'd take her anywhere

Maxine (*as if in cab*)   i'm into havin a good time/ yr arms/ veins burstin/ like you usedta lift tobacco onto trucks or cut cane/ i want you to be happy/ long as we dont haveta stay in brooklyn

Ross   & she made like she waz gypsy rose lee/ or the hotsy totsy girls in the carnival round from waycross/ when it waz segregated

Maxine   what's yr name?

Ross   my name is raphael

Maxine   oh that's nice

Ross   & fay moved where i cd see her out the rear view mirror/ waz tellin me all bout her children & big eddie who waz away/ while we crossed the manhattan bridge/ i kept smilin. (*As cabdriver.*) where exactly you goin?

Maxine   i dont really know. i just want to have a good time, take me where i can see famous people/ & act bizarre like sinatra at the kennedy's/ maybe even go round & beat up folks like jim brown/ throw somebody offa balcony/ you know/ for a good time

Ross   the only place i knew/ i took her/ after i kisst the spaces she'd been layin open to me. fay had alla her $17 cuz i hadnt charged her nothin/ turned the meter off/ said it waz wonderful to pick up a lady like her on atlantic avenue/ i saw nobody but those goddamn whores & fay

Maxine *moves in to* **Ross** *and gives him a long, passionate kiss.*

Ross   now fay waz a gd clean woman/ & she waz burstin with pride & enthusiasm when she walked into the place where i swore/ all the actresses & actors hung out

The **Company** *joins in* **Ross's** *story, responding to* **Maxine** *as tho she waz entering their bar.*

Ross   oh yes/ there were actresses in braids & lipstick/ wigs & winged tip pumps/ fay assumed the posture of someone she'd always admired/ etta james/ the waitress asked her to leave cuz she waz high/ & fay knew better than that

Maxine (*as* **Lily** *pantomimes throwing her out*)   i aint high/ i'm enthusiastic/ and i'm gonna have me a gooooood/ ol time

Ross   she waz all dressed up/ she came all the way from brooklyn/ she must look high cuz i/ the taxi-man/ well i got her a lil excited/ that waz all/ but she was gonna cool out/ cuz she was gonna meet her friends/ at this place/ yes. she knew that/ & she pushed a bunch of rhododendrum/ outta her way so she cd get over to that table/ & stood over the man with the biggest niggah eyes & warmest smellin mouth

Maxine   please/ let me join you/ i come all the way from brooklyn/ to have a good time/ you dont think i'm high do ya/ cd i please join ya/ i just wanna have a good ol time

Ross (*as* **Bettina** *turns from* **Maxine**)   the woman sipped chablis & looked out the window hopin to see one of the bowery drunks fall down somewhere/ fay's voice hoverin/ flirtin wit hope

Lou (*turning to face* **Maxine**)   why dont you go downstairs & put yr titty in yr shirt/ you cant have no good time lookin like that/ now go on down & then come up & join us

As **Maxine** *turns away*, **Bettina** *and* **Lou** *get up and move to another table*

Ross   fay tried to shove her flesh anywhere/ she took off her hat/ bummed a kool/ swallowed somebody's cognac/ & sat down/ waitin/ for a gd time

Maxine (*rises and hugs* **Ross**)   aw ross/ when am i gonna get a chance to feel somethin like that/ i got into this business cuz i wanted to feel things all the time/ & all they want me to do is put my leg in my face/ smile/ &

Lily   you better knock on some wood/ maxine/ at least yr workin

Bettina   & at least yr not playin a whore/ if some other woman comes in here & tells me she's playin a whore/ i think i might kill her

Eli   you'd kill her so you cd say/ oh dahlia died & i know all her lines

Bettina   aw hush up eli/ dont you know what i mean?

Eli   no miss/ i dont/ are you in the theater?

Bettina   mr. bartender/ poet sir/ i am theater

Dahlia   well miss theater/ that's a surprise/ especially since you fell all over the damn stage in the middle of my solo

Lily   she did/ did she?

Eli   miss theater herself fell down?

Dahlia   yeah/ she cant figure out how to get attention without makin somebody else look bad

Maxine   now dahlia/ it waznt that bad/ i hardly noticed her

Dahlia   it waz my solo/ vou werent sposed to notice her at all!

Bettina   you know dahlia/ i didnt do it on purpose/ i cda hurt myself

Dahlia   that wd be unfortunate for you

Bettina   well miss thing with those big ass hips you got/ i dont know why you think you can do the ballet anyway

The **Company** *breaks; they're expecting a fight.*

Dahlia (*crossing to* **Bettina**)   i got this (*Demonstrates her leg extension.*) & alla this (**Dahlia** *turns her back to* **Bettina** *and slaps her own backside.* **Bettina** *grabs her, turns her around, and they begin a series of finger snaps.* **Eli** *crosses to break up the impending fight.*)

Eli (*separating them*)   ladies ladies ladies. people keep tellin me to put my feet on the ground i get mad & scream/ there is no ground only shit pieces from dogs horses & men who dont live anywhere/ they tell me think straight & make myself somethin/ i shout & sigh/ i am a poet/ i write poems i make words cartwheel & somersault down pages outta my mouth come visions distilled like bootleg whiskey/ i am like a radio but i am a channel of my own i keep sayin i write poems/ & people keep askin me what do i do/ what in the hell is going on? people keep tellin me these are hard times/ what are you gonna be doin ten years from now/ what in the hell do you think/ i am gonna be writin poems i will have poems inchin up the walls of the lincoln tunnel/ i am gonna feed my children poems on rye bread with horseradish/ i am gonna send my mailman off with a poem for his wagon/ give my doctor a poem for his heart/ i am a poet/ i am not a part-time poet/ i am not a amateur poet/ i dont even know what that person cd be/ whoever that is authorizing poetry as an avocation/ is a fraud/ put yr own feet on the ground

Bettina   i'm sorry eli/ i just dont want to be a gypsy all my life

The bar returns to normal activity. Lights change to focus on **Lily**. *Only* **Bettina** *is aware that* **Lily** *is voicing her private thoughts, and she joins her as a partner in fantasy, not as a voyeur.*

Lily   i'm simply gonna brush my hair. rapunsel pull yr tresses back into the tower. & lady godiva give up horseback riding. i'm gonna alter my social & professional life dramatically. i will brush 100 strokes in the morning/ 100 strokes midday & 100 strokes before retiring. i will have a very busy schedule. between the local trains & the express/ i'm gonna brush. i brush between telephone calls. at the disco i'm gonna brush on the slow songs/ i dont slow dance with strangers. i'ma brush my hair before making love & after. i'll brush my hair in taxis. while windowshopping. when i have visitors over the kitchen table/ i'ma brush. i brush my hair while thinking abt anything. mostly i think abt how it will be when i get my full heada hair. like lifting my head in the morning will become a chore. i'll try to turn my cheek & my hair will weigh me down (**Lily** *falls to the floor.* **Bettina** *helps lift her to her knees, then begins to dance and mime as* **Lily** *speaks.*) i dream of chaka khan/ chocolate from graham central station with all seven wigs/ & medusa. i brush & brush. i use olive oil /hair food/ & posner's vitamin E. but mostly i brush & brush, i may lose contact with most of my friends. i cd lose my job/ but i'm on unemployment & brush while waiting on line for my check. i'm sure i get good recommendations from my social worker: such a fastidious woman/ that lily/ always brushing her hair. nothing in my dreams suggests that hair brushing/ per se/ has anything to do with my particular heada hair. a therapist might say that the head fulla hair has to do with something else/ like: a symbol of lily's unconscious desires. but i have no therapist (*She takes imaginary pen from* **Bettina**, *who was pretending to be a therapist, and sits down at table across from her.*) my dreams mean things to me/ like if you dreamed abt tobias/ then something has happened to tobias/ or he is gonna show up. if you dream abt yr grandma who's dead/ then you must be doing something she doesnt like/ or she wdnta gone to all the trouble to leave heaven like that. if you dream something red/ you shd stop. if you dream something green/ you shd keep doing it. if a blue person appears in yr dreams/ then that person is yr true friend & that's how i see my dreams. & this head fulla hair i have in my dreams is lavender & nappy as a 3-yr-old's in a apple tree. i can fry an egg & see the white of the egg spreadin in the grease like my hair is gonna spread in the air/ but i'm not egg-yolk yellow/ i am brown & the egg white isnt white at all/ it is my actual hair/ & it wd go on & on forever/ irregular like a rastaman's hair. irregular/ gargantuan & lavender. nestled on blue satin pillows/ pillows like the sky. & so i fry my eggs. i buy daisies dyed lavender & laced lavender tablemats & lavender nail polish. though i never admit it/ i really do believe in magic/ & can do strange things when something comes over me. soon everything around me will be lavender/ fluffy & consuming. i will know not a moment of bitterness/ through all the wrist aching & tennis elbow from brushing/ i'll smile. no regrets/ "je ne regrette rien" i'll sing like edith piaf. when my friends want me to go see tina turner or pacheco/ i'll croon "sorry/ i have to brush my hair."

i'll find ambrosia. my hair'll grow pomegranates & soil/ rich as round the aswan/ i wake in my bed to bananas/ avocados/ collard greens/ the trammps' latest disco hit/ fresh croissant/ pouilly fuisse/ ishamel reed's essays/ charlotte carter's stories/ all stream from my hair.

& with the bricks that plop from where a 9-year-old's top braid wd be/ i will brush myself a house with running water & a bidet. i'll have a closet full of clean bed linen & the lil girl from the castro convertible commercial will come & open the bed repeatedly & stay on as a helper to brush my hair. lily is the only person i know whose every word leaves a purple haze on the tip of yr tongue. when this happens i says clouds are forming/ & i has to close the windows. violet rain is hard to remove from blue satin pillows

Lou *gets up and points to* **Lily** *who is sitting very still.*

Lou   you have to come with me/ to this place where magic is/ to hear my song/ some times i forget & leave my tune in the corner of the closet under all the dirty clothes/ in this place/ magic asks me where i've been/ how i've been singin/ lately i leave myself in all the wrong hands/ if you were to come with me/ to this place where magic is involved in undoin our masks/ i wd be able to smile & answer. in this place where magic always asks for me i discovered a lot of other people who talk without mouths who listen to what you say/ by watchin yr jewelry dance & in this place where magic stays you can let yrself in or out but when you leave yrself at home/ burglars & daylight thieves pounce on you & sell yr skin/ at cut-rates on tenth avenue

Ross *had been playing an acoustic guitar softly as* **Lou** *spoke.* **Alec** *picks up on the train of* **Lou's** *thoughts and begins a story. Slowly,* **Natalie** *becomes the woman* **Alec** *describes.*

Alec   she had always wanted a baby/ never a family/ never a man/ she had always wanted a baby/ who wd suckle & sleep/ a baby boy who wd wet/ & cry/ & smile/ suckle & sleep.

when she sat in bars/ on the stool/ near the door/ & cross from the juke box/ with her legs straddled & revealin red lace pants/ & lil hair smashed under the stockings/ she wd think how she wanted this baby & how she wd call the baby "myself" & as she thot/ bout this lil brown thing/ she ordered another bourbon/ double & tilted her head as if to cuddle some infant/ not present. the men in the bar never imagined her as someone's mother/ she rarely tended her own self carefully

Natalie *slowly rises from her chair and sits astride on the floor.*

Alec   just enough to exude a languid sexuality that teased the men off work/ & the bartender/ ray who waz her only friend. women didnt take with her/ so she spent her afternoons with ray/ in the bar round the corner from her lil house/ that shook winsomely in a hard wind/ surrounded by three weepin willows

Natalie   my name is sue-jean & i grew here/ a ordinary colored girl with no claims to any thing/ or anyone. i drink now/ bourbon/ in harder times/ beer/ but i always wanted to have a baby/ a lil boy/named myself

Alec   one time/ she made it with ray

Natalie   & there waznt nothin special there/ only a hot rough bangin/ a brusque barrelin throwin of torso/ legs & sweat/ ray wanted to kiss me/ but i screamed/ cuz i didnt like kissin/ only fuckin/ & we rolled round/ i waz a peculiar sorta woman/ wantin no kisses/ no caresses/ just power/ heat & no easiness of thrust. ray pulled himself outta me/ with no particular exclamation/ he smacked me on my behind. i waz grinnin/ & he took that as a indication of his skill/ he believed he waz a good lover/ & a woman like me/ didnt never want nothin but a hard dick/ & everyone believed that/ tho no one in town really knew

Alec   so ray/ went on behind the bar cuz he had got his

Natalie   & i lay in the corner laughin/ with my drawers/ twisted round my ankles & my hair standin every which way/ i waz laughin/ knowin i wd have this child/ myself/ & no one wd ever claim him/ cept me cuz i waz a low-down thing/ layin in sawdust & whiskey stains. i laughed & had a good time masturbatin in the shadows

Alec   sue-jean ate starch for good luck

Natalie   like mama kareena/ tol me

Alec   & she planted five okras/ five collards/ & five tomatoes

Natalie   for good luck too/ i waz gonna have this baby. i even went over to the hospital to learn prenatal care/ & i kept myself clean

Alec   sue-jean's lanky body got ta spreadin & her stomach waz taut & round high in her chest/ a high pregnancy is sure to be a boy/ & she smiled

Natalie   i stopped goin to the bar

Alec   started cannin food

Natalie   knittin lil booties

Alec   even goin to church wit the late nite radio evangelist

Natalie   i gotta prayer cloth for the boy/ myself waz gonna be safe from all that his mama/ waz prey to

Alec   sure/ sue-jean waz a scandal/ but that waz to be expected/ cuz she waz always a po' criterish chile

Natalie   & wont no man bout step my way/ ever/ just cuz i hadda bad omen on me/ from the very womb/ i waz bewitched is what the ol women usedta say

Alec   sue-jean waz born on a full moon/ the year of the flood/ the night the river raised her skirts & sat over alla the towns & settlements for 30 miles in each direction/ the nite the river waz in labor/ gruntin & groanin/ splittin trees & families/ spillin cupboards over the ground/ waz the nite sue-jean waz born

Natalie   & my mother died/ drownin/ holdin me up over the mud crawlin in her mouth

Alec   somebody took her & she lived to be the town's no one. now with the boy achin & dancin in her belly/ sue-jean was a gay & gracious woman/ she baked cakes & left them on the stoop of the church she had never entered just cuz she wanted/ & she grew plants & swept her floors/ she waz someone she had never known/ she waz herself with child/ & she waz a wonderful bulbous thing

Natalie   the nite/ myself waz born/ ol mama kareena from the hills came down to see bout me. i hollered & breathed/ i did exactly like mama kareena said/ & i pushed & i pushed & there waz a earthquake up in my womb/ i wanted to sit up & pull the tons of logs trapped in my crotch out/ so i cd sleep/ but it wdnt go way/ i pushed & thot i saw 19 horses runnin in my pussy/ i waz sure there waz a locomotive stalled up in there burnin coal & steamin & pushin gainst a mountain

Alec   finally the child's head waz within reach & mama kareena/ brought the boy into this world

Natalie   & he waz awright/ with alla his toes & his fingers/ his lil dick & eyes/ elbows that bent/ & legs/ straight. i wanted a big glassa bourbon/ & mama kareena brought it/ right away, we sat drinkin the bourbon/ & lookin at the child whose name waz myself/ like i had wanted/ & the two of us ate placenta stew/ i waznt really sure

Alec   sue jean you werent really sure you wanted myself to wake up/ you always wanted him to sleep/ or at most to nurse/ the nites yr dreams were disturbed by his cryin

Natalie   i had no one to help me

Alec   so you were always with him/ & you didnt mind/ you knew this waz yr baby/ myself/ & you cuddled him/ carried him all over the house with you all day/ no matter/ what

Natalie   everythin waz goin awright til/ myself wanted to crawl

Alec (*moving closer to* **Natalie**)   & discover a world of his own/ then you became despondent/ & yr tits began to dry & you lost the fullness of yr womb/ where myself/ had lived

Natalie   i wanted that back

Alec   you wanted back the milk

Natalie   & the tight gourd stomach i had when myself waz bein in me

Alec   so you slit his wrists

Natalie   he waz sleepin

Alec   sucked the blood back into yrself/ & waited. myself shriveled up in his crib

Natalie   a dank lil blk thing/ i never touched him again

Alec   you were always holdin yr womb/ feelin him kick & sing to you bout love/ & you wd hold yr tit in yr hand

Natalie   like i always did when i fed him

Alec   & you waited & waited/ for a new myself. tho there were labor pains

Natalie   i screamed in my bed

Alec   yr legs pinnin to the air

Natalie   spinnin sometimes like a ferris wheel/ i cd get no child to fall from me

Alec   & she forgot abt the child bein born/ & waz heavy & full all her life/ with "myself"

Natalie   who'll be out/ any day now

Eli *moves from behind the bar, confused about whether he should help* **Natalie** *or clean tables. He stops suddenly.*

Eli   aint that a goddamn shame/ aint that a way to come into the world/sometimes i really cant write sometimes i cant even talk

The minstrel mask comes down slowly. Blackout, except for lights on the mask, which remains visible through intermission.

Intermission.

Act Two

Lights up on the **Company,** *frozen on stage.* **Lou** *waves the minstrel mask away. As it flies up, he begins.*

Lou   in this place where magic stays you can let yrself in or out

Lou *waves his hand. A samba comes over the jukebox and activity is begun in the bar again.* **Dahlia, Natalie,** *and* **Lily** *enter, apparently from the ladies room.*

Natalie   i swear we went to that audition in good faith/ & that man asked us where we learned to speak english so well/ i swear this foreigner/ asked us/ from the city of new york/ where we learned to speak english

Lily   all i did was say "bom dia/ como vai"/ & the englishman got red in the face

Lou *(as the Englishman)*   yr from the states/ arent you?

Lily   "sim"/ i said/ in good portuguese

Lou   but you speak portuguese

Lily   "sim"/ i said/ in good portuguese

Lou   how did you pick that up?

Lily   i hadda answer so simple/ i cdnt say i learned it/ cuz niggahs cant learn & that wda been too hard on the man/ so i said/ in good english: i held my ear to the ground & listened to the samba from belim

Dahlia   you shd have said: i make a lotta phone calls to cascais, portugao

Bettina   i gotta bahiano boyfriend

Natalie   how abt: i waz an angolan freedom fighter

Maxine   no/ lily/ tell him: i'm a great admirer of zeza motto leci brandao

Lily   when the japanese red army invaded san juan/ they poisoned the papaya with portuguese. i eat a lotta papaya. last week/ i developed a strange schizophrenic condition/ with 4 manifest personalities: one spoke english & understood nothing/ one spoke french & had access to the world/ one spoke spanish & voted against statehood for puerto rico/ one spoke portuguese. "eu nao falo ingles entao y voce"/ i dont speak english anymore/ & you?

All the women in the **Company** *had been doing samba steps as they spoke. Now they all dance around a table in their own ritual.* **Alec** *and* **Lou** *try to join in. The women scatter to different tables, leaving the two interlopers alone.*

Alec   not only waz she without a tan, but she held her purse close to her hip like a new yorker. someone who rode the paris metro or listened to mariachis in plaza santa cecilia. she waz not from here *(He sits at a table.)*

Lou *(following suit)*   but from there

Alec   some there where colored/ mulattoes/ negroes/ blacks cd make a living big enough to leave there to come here/ where no one went there much any more for all sorts of reasons

Lou   the big reasons being immigration restrictions & unemployment. nowadays, immigration restrictions of every kind apply to any non-european persons who want to go there from here

Alec   some who want to go there from here risk fetching trouble with the customs authority there

Lou   or later with the police, who can tell who's not from there cuz the shoes are pointed & laced strange

Alec   the pants be for august & yet it's january

Lou   the accent is patterned for petionville, but working in crown heights

Alec   what makes a person comfortably ordinary here cd make him dangerously conspicuous there

Lou   so some go to london or amsterdam or paris/ where they are so abounding no one tries to tell who is from where

Alec   still the far right wing of every there prints lil pamphlets that say everyone from there shd leave & go back where they came from

Lou   this is manifest legally thru immigration restrictions & personally thru unemployment

Alec   anyway the yng woman waz from there/ & she waz alone. that waz good. cuz if a person had no big brother in gronigen/ no aunt in rouen

Lou   no sponsor in chicago

Alec   this brown woman from there might be a good idea. everybody in the world/ european & non-european alike/ everybody knows that rich white girls are hard to find. some of them joined the weather underground/ some the baader-meinhof gang

Lou   a whole bunch of them gave up men entirely

Alec   so the exotic lover in the sun routine becomes more difficult to swing/ if she wants to talk abt plastic explosives & the resistance of the black masses to socialism/ instead of giving head as the tide slips in or lending money

Lou   just for the next few days

Alec   is hard to find a rich white girl who is so dumb/ too

Lou   anyway. the whole world knows/ european & non-european alike/ the whole world knows that nobody loves the black woman like they love farrah fawcett-majors. the whole world dont turn out for a dead black woman like they did for marilyn monroe

Alec (*contradicting*)   actually/ the demise of josephine baker waz an international event

Lou   but she waz also a war hero. the worldwide unbeloved black woman is a good idea/ if she is from there & one is a young man with gd looks/ piercing eyes/ & knowledge of several romantic languages

Throughout this conversation **Alec** *and* **Lou** *make attempts to seduce, cajole, and woo the women of the* **Company** *as their narrative indicates. The women play the roles as described.*

Alec   the best dancing spots/ the hill where one can see the entire bay at twilight

Lou   the beach where the seals & pelicans run free/ the hidden "local" restaurants

Alec   "aw babee/ you so pretty" begins often in the lobby of hotels where the bright handsome yng men wd be loiterers

Lou   were they not needed to tend the needs of the black women from there

Alec   tourists are usually white people or asians who didnt come all this way to meet a black woman who isnt even foreign

Lou   so hotel managers wink an eye at the yng men in the lobby or by the bar who wd be loitering/ but are gonna help her have a gd time

Alec   maybe help themselves too

Lou   everybody in the world/ european & non european alike/ everybody knows the black woman from there is not treated as a princess/ as a jewel/ a cherished lover

Alec   that's not how sapphire got her reputation/ nor how mrs. jefferson perceives the world

Lou   you know/ babee/ you dont act like them. aw babee/ you so pretty

Alec   the yng man in the hotel watches the yng black woman sit & sit & sit/ while the european tourists dance with each other/ & the dapper local fellas mambo frenetically with secretaries from arizona/ in search of the missing rich white girl. our girl sits &

Female Cast Members (*in unison*)   sits & sits & sits

Alec (*to* **Dahlia** *and* **Natalie,** *who move to the music*)   maybe she is courageous & taps her foot, maybe she is bold & enjoys the music/ smiling/ shaking shoulders. let her sit & let her know she is unwanted

Lou   she is not white & she is not from here

Alec   let her know she is not pretty enuf to dance the next meringue. then appear/ mysteriously/ in the corner of the bar. stare at her. just stare. when stevie wonder's song/ "isnt she lovely"/ blares thru the red-tinted light/ ask her to dance & hold her as tyrone power wda. hold her & stare

Ross *and* **Eli** *sing the chorus to "Isn't She Lovely" by Stevie Wonder.*

Lou   dance yr ass off. she has been discovered by the non-european fred astaire

Alec (*dancing with* **Dahlia**)   let her know she is a surprise/ an event. by the look on yr face you've never seen anyone like this black woman from there. you say: "aw/

you are not from here?"/ totally astonished. she murmers that she is from there. as if to apologize for her unfortunate place of birth.

Lou   you say

Alec   aw babee/ you so pretty. & it's all over (*He tosses* **Dahlia** *aside.* **Lou** *grabs her to illustrate his narrative.*)

Lou   a night in a pension near the sorbonne. pick her up from the mattress. throw her gainst the wall in a show of exotic temper & passion: "maintenant/ tu es ma femme. mous nous sommes maries." unions of this sort are common wherever the yng black women travel alone. a woman traveling alone is an affront to the non-european man who is known the world over/ to european & non-european alike/ for his way with women

Alec   his sense of romance/ how he can say:

Lou   aw babee/ you so pretty . . . and even a beautiful woman will believe no one else ever recognized her lovliness

Eli (*approaching* **Bettina**)   or else/ he comes to a cafe in willemstad in the height of the sunset. an ablebodied/ sinewy yng man who wants to buy one beer for the yng woman, after the first round/ he discovers he has run out of money/ so she must buy the next round/ when he discovers/ what beautiful legs you have/ how yr mouth is like the breath of tiger lilies. we shall make love in the/ how you call it/ yes in the earth/ in the dirt/ i will have you in the soil. probably under the stars & smelling of wine/ an unforgettable international affair can be consummated

The **Company** *sings "Tara's Theme" as* **Eli** *ends his speech.* **Eli** *and* **Bettina** *take a tango walk to the bar.* **Maxine** *pretends to photograph them as they sail off into the sunset.*

Maxine   at 11:30 one evening i waz at the port authority/ new york/ united states/ myself. now i waz there & i spoke english & waz holding approximately $7 american currency/ when a yng man from there came up to me from the front of the line of people waiting for the princeton new jersey united states local bus. i mean to say/ he gave up his chance for a good seat to come say to me:

Ross   i never saw a black woman reading nietzsche

Maxine   i waz demure enuf/ i said i have to for a philosophy class. but as the nite went on i noticed this yng man waz so much like the other yng men from here/ who use their bodies as bait & their smiles as passport alternatives. anyway the nite did go on. we were snuggled together in the rear of the bus going down the jersey turnpike. he told me in english/ that he had spoken all his life in st. louis/ where he waz raised:

Ross   i've wanted all my life to meet someone like you. i want you to meet my family/ who havent seen me in a long time/ since i left missouri looking for opportunity (*He is lost for words.*)

Lou (*stage whisper*)   opportunity to sculpt

Ross   thank you/ opportunity to sculpt

Maxine   he had been everyplace/ he said

Ross   you arent like any black woman i've ever met anywhere

Maxine   here or there

Ross   i had to come back to new york cuz of immigration restrictions & high unemployment among black american sculptors abroad

Maxine   just as we got to princeton/ he picked my face up from his shoulder & said:

Ross   aw babee/ you so pretty

Maxine   aw babee/ you so pretty. i believe that nite i must have looked beautiful for a black woman from there/ though i cd be asked at any moment to tour the universe/ to climb a 6-story walkup with a brilliant starving painter/ to share kadushi/ to meet mama/ to getta kiss each time the swing falls toward the willow branch/ to imagine where he say he from/ & more. i cd/ i cd have all of it/ but i cd not be taken/ long as i dont let a stranger be the first to say:

Lou   aw babee/ you so pretty

Maxine   after all/ immigration restrictions & unemployment cd drive a man to drink or to lie (*She breaks away from* **Ross**.) so if you know yr beautiful & bright & cherishable awready/ when he say/ in whatever language:

Alec (*to* **Natalie**)   aw babee/ you so pretty

Maxine   you cd say:

Natalie   i know. thank you

Maxine   then he'll smile/ & you'll smile. he'll say:

Eli (*stroking* **Bettina**'s *thigh*)   what nice legs you have

Maxine   you can say:

Bettina (*removing his hand*)   yes. they run in the family

Maxine   oh! what a universe of beautiful & well traveled women!

Male Cast Members (*in unison*)   aw babee/ i've never met anyone like you

Female Cast Members (*in unison, pulling away from men to stage edges*)   that's strange/ there are millions of us!

After unsuccessful attempts to get their women to talk, male **Company** *clusters center stage. They decide to serenade the women.* **Ross** *takes first verse of "Ooo Baby Baby" by Smokey Robinson. Others sing backup.*

Ross (*singing*)   i did you wrong/ my heart went out to play/ but in the game i lost you/ what a price to pay/ i'm cryin

Male Cast Members (*singing*)   oo oo oo/ baby baby/ oo oo oo/ baby baby

This brings no response from the women. **Eli** *is elected to take the second verse.*

Eli   mistakes i know i've made a few/ but i'm only human/ you've made mistakes too/ i'm cryin

Male Cast Members (*singing*)   oo oo oo/ baby baby/ oo oo oo/ baby baby

Female **Company** *slowly return to men. They dance as they continue to sing chorus.* **Lily** *is alone. She walks awkwardly about the room of couples.*

Male Cast Members and Lily (*singing*)   i'm just about at the end of my rope/ but i cant stop trying/ i cant give up hope/ cause i/ i believe one day/ i'll hold you near/ whisper i love you/ until that day is here/ i'm cryin/ oo oo oo/ baby baby

The **Company** *continues to sing.*

Lily   unfortunately the most beautiful man in the world is unavailable that's what he told me i saw him wandering abt/ said well this is one of a kind & i might be able to help him out so alone & pretty in all this ganja & bodies melting he danced with me & i cd become that a certain way to be held that's considered in advance a way a thoughtful man wd kiss a woman who cd be offended easily/ but waznt cuz of course the most beautiful man in the world knows exactly what to do with someone who knows that's who he is/ these dreads fallin thru my dress so my nipples just stood up these hands playin the guitar on my back the lips somewhere between my neck & my forehead talking bout ocho rios & how i really must go marcus garvey cda come in the door & we/ we wd still be dancin that dance the motion that was more to do with kinetic energy than shootin stars/ more to do with the impossibility of all this/ & how it waz awready bein too much our reason failed we tried to go away & be just together aside from the silence that weeped with greed/ we didnt need/ anything/ but one another for tonite just he is the most beautiful man in the world says he's unavailable & this man whose eyes made me half-naked & still & brazen/ waz singin with me since we cd not talk/ we sang

Male **Company** *end their chorus with a flourish.*

Lily   we sang with bob marley this man/ surely the most beautiful man in the world/ & i sang/ "i wanna love you & treat you right/

Company *begins to reggae dance.*

Lily   i wanna love you every day & every nite"

Company (*dancing and singing*)   we'll be together with the roof right over our heads we'll share the shelter of my single bed/ we'll share the same room/ jah provide the bread

Dahlia (*stops dancing with* **Lou**)   i tell you it's not just the part that makes me love you so much

Lou   what is it/ wait/ i know/ you like my legs

Dahlia   yes/ uh huh/ yr legs & yr arms/ &

Lou   but that's just my body/ you started off saying you loved me/ now i see it's just my body

Dahlia   oh/ i didnt mean that/ it's just i dont know you/ except as the character i'm sposed to love/ & well/ i know rehearsal is over/ but i'm still in love with you

They go to the bar to get drinks, then sit at a table.

Ross (*to* **Natalie**)   but baby/ you have to go on the road. we need the money

Natalie   i'm not going on the road so you can fuck all these aspiring actresses

Ross   aw/ just some of them/ baby

Natalie   that's why i'm not going

Ross   if you dont go on the road i'll still be fuckin em/ but you & me/ we'll be in trouble/ you understand?

Natalie (*stops dancing*)   no i dont understand

Ross   well let me break it down to you

Natalie   please/ break it down to me

Bettina (*stops dancing with* **Alec**)   hey/ natalie/ why dont you make him go on the road/ they always want us to be so goddamned conscientious

Alec (*stops dancing*)   dont you think you shd mind yr own bizness?

Natalie   yeah bettina/ mind yr own bizness (*She pulls* **Ross** *to a table with her.*)

Bettina (*to* **Alec**)   no/ i'm tired of having to take any & every old job to support us/ & you get to have artistic integrity & refuse parts that are beneath you

Alec   thats right/ i'm not playing the fool or the black buck pimp circus/ i'm an actor not a stereotype/ i've been trained. you know i'm a classically trained actor

Bettina   & just what do you think we are?

Maxine   well/ i got offered another whore part downtown

Eli   you gonna take it?

Maxine   yeah

Lily   if you dont/ i know someone who will

Alec (*to* **Bettina**)   i told you/ we arent gonna get anyplace/ by doin every bit part for a niggah that someone waves in fronta my face

Bettina   & we arent gonna live long on nothin/ either/ cuz i'm quittin my job

Alec   be in the real world for once & try to understand me

Bettina   you mean/ i shd understand that you are the great artist & i'm the trouper

Alec   i'm not sayin that we cant be gigglin & laughin all the time dancin around/ but i cant stay in these "hate whitey" shows/ cuz they arent true

Bettina   a failure of imagination on yr part/ i take it

Alec   no/ an insult to my person

Bettina   oh i see/ you wanna give the people some more make-believe

Alec   i cd always black up again & do minstrel work/ wd that make you happy?

Bettina   there is nothin niggerly abt a decent job. Work is honorable/ work!

Alec   well/ i got a problem. i got lots of problems/ but i got one i want you to fix & if you can fix it/ i'll do anything you say. Last spring this niggah from the mid-west asked for president carter to say he waz sorry for that forgettable phenomenon/ slavery/ which brought us all together. i never did get it/ none of us ever got no apology from no white folks abt not bein considered human beings/ that makes me mad & tired. someone told me "roots" waz the way white folks worked out their guilt/ the success of "roots" is the way white folks assuaged their consciences/ i dont know this/ this is what i waz told. i dont get any pleasure from nobody watchin me trying to be a slave i once waz/ who got away/ when we all know they had an emancipation proclamation/ that the civil war waz not fought over us. We all know that we/ actually dont exist unless we play football or basketball or baseball or soccer/ pele/ see they still import a strong niggah to earn money. art here/ isnt like in the old country/ where we had some spare time & did what we liked to do/ i dont know this either/ this is also something i've been told. i just want to find out why no one has even been able to sound a gong & all the reporters recite that the gong is ringin/ while we watch all the white people/ immigrants & invaders/ conquistadors & relatives of london debtors from georgia/ kneel & apologize to us/ just for three or four minutes. now/ this is not impossible/ & someone shd make a day where a few minutes of the pain of our lives is acknowledged. i have never been very interested in what white people did/ cuz i waz able/ like most of us/ to have very lil to do with them/ but if i become a success that means i have to talk to white folks more than in high school/ they are everywhere/ you know how they talk abt a neighborhood changin/ we suddenly become all over the place/ they are now all over my life/ & i dont like it. I am not talkin abt poets & painters/ not abt women & lovers of beauty/ i am talkin abt that proverbial white person who is usually a man who just/ turns yr body around/ looks at yr teeth & yr ass/ who feels yr calves & back/ & agrees on a price. we are/ you see/ now able to sell ourselves/ & i am still a person who is tired/ a person who is not into his demise/ just three minutes for our lives/ just three minutes of silence & a gong in st. louis/ Oakland/ in los angeles

The **Company** *looks at him as if he's crazy.* **Alec** *tries to leave the bar.* **Bettina** *stops him.*

Bettina   yr still outta yr mind. ain't no apologies keeping us alive

Lou   what are you gonna do with white folks kneeling all over the country anywan/ man? (**Lou** *signals everyone to kneel.*)

Lily   they say i'm too light to work/ but when i asked him what he meant/ he said i didnt actually look black. but/ i said/ my mama knows i'm black & my daddy/ damn sure knows i'm black/ & he is the only one who has a problem thinkin i'm black/ i said so let me play a white girl/ i'm a classically trained actress & i need the work & i

can do it/ he said that wdnt be very ethical of him. Can you imagine that shit/ not
ethical

Natalie (*jocularly*)   as a red-blooded white woman/ i cant allow you all to go on like
that cuz today i'm gonna be a white girl/ i'll retroactively wake myself up/ ah low &
behold/ a white girl in my bed/ but first i'll haveta call a white girl i know to have
some more accurate information. what's the first thing white girls think in the
morning/ do they get up being glad they aint niggahs/ do they remember mama/ or
worry abt gettin to work/ do they work? do they play isadora & wrap themselves in
sheets & go tip-toeing to the kitchen to make maxwell house coffee/ oh i know/ the
first thing a white girl does in the morning is fling her hair.

so now i'm done with that/ i'm gonna water my plants/ but am i a po' white trash
white girl with a old jelly-jar/ or am i a sophisticated & protestant suburbanite with 2
Valiums slugged awready & a porcelain water carrier leading me up the stairs strewn
with heads of dolls & nasty smellin white husband person's underwear? if i waz really
protected from the niggahs/ i might go to early morning mass & pick up a tomato pie
on the way home/ so i cd eat it during/ the *young & the restless.* in Williams arizona
as a white girl/ i cd push the navaho women outta my way in the supermarket & push
my nose in the air so i wdnt haveta smell them. coming from bay ridge on the train &
cd smile at all the black & puerto rican people/ & hope they cant tell i want them to
go back where they came from/ or at least be invisible.

i'm still in my kitchen/ so i guess i'll just have to fling my hair again & sit down. i shd
pinch my cheeks to bring the color back/ i wonder why the colored lady hasnt arrived to
clean my house yet/ so i cd go to the beauty parlor & sit under a sunlamp to get some
more color back/ it's terrible how god gave those colored women such clear complexions/
it takes em years to develop wrinkles/ but beauty can be bought & flattered into the world.

as a white girl on the street/ i can assume since i am a white girl on the streets/ that
everyone notices how beautiful i am/ especially lil black & Caribbean boys/ they love
to look at me/ i'm exotic/ no one in their families looks like me/ poor things. if i waz
one of those white girls who loves one of those grown black fellas/ i cd say with my
eyes wide open/ totally sincere/ oh i didnt know that/ i cd say i didnt know/ i cant/ i
dont know how/ cuz i'ma white girl & i dont have to do much of anything.

all of this is the fault of the white man's sexism/ oh how i loathe tight-assed thin-lipped
pink white men/ even the football players lack a certain relaxed virility. that's why my
heroes are either just like my father/ who while he still cdnt speak english knew enough
to tell me how the niggers shd go bach where they came from/ or my heroes are
psychotic faggots who are white/ or else they are/ oh/ you know/ colored men.

being a white girl by dint of my will is much more complicated that i thought it wd
be/ but i wanted to try it cuz so many men like white girls/ white men/ black men/
latin men/ jewish men/ asians/ everybody. so i thought if i waz a white girl for a day i
might understand this better/ after all gertrude stein wanted to know abt the black
women/ alice adams wrote *thinking abt billie/* joyce carol oates has three different
black characters all with the same name/ i guess cuz we are underdeveloped
individuals or cuz we are all the same/ at any rate i'm gonna call this "thinkin abt

white girls"/ cuz helmut newton's awready gotta book called *white women*/ see what i mean/ that's a best seller/ one store i passed/ hadda sign said:

> **WHITE WOMEN**
> **SOLD OUT**

it's this kinda pressure that forces us white girls to be so absolutely pathological abt the other women in the world/ who now that they're not all servants or peasants want to be considered beautiful too. We simply crinkle our hair/ learn to dance the woogie dances/ slant our eyes with make-up or surgery/ learn spanish or claim argentinian background/ or as a real trump card/ show up looking like a real white girl. you know all western civilization depends on us.

i still havent left my house. i think i'll fling my hair once more/ bnt this time with a pout/ cuz i think i havent been fair to the sisterhood/ women's movement faction of white girls/ although/ they always ask what do you people really want. as if the colored woman of the world was a strange sort of neutered workhorse/ which isnt too far from reality/ since i'm still waiting for my cleaning lady & the lady who accepts quarters at the bathroom in sardi's. Those poor creatures shd be sterilized/ no one shd have to live such a life. cd you hand me a towel/ thank you Caroline. i've left all of maxime's last winter clothes in a pile for you by the back door. they have to be cleaned/ but i hope yr girls can make good use of them.

oh/ i'm still not being fair/ all the white women in the world dont wake up glad they aint niggahs/ only some of them/ the ones who dont/ wake up thinking how can i survive another day of this culturally condoned incompetence. i know i'll play a tenor horn & tell all the colored artists i meet/ that now i'm just like them/ i'm colored i'll say cuz i have a struggle too. Or i cd punish this white beleagered body of mine with the advances of a thousand ebony bodies/ all built like franco harris or peter tosh/ a thousand of them may take me & do what they want/ cuz i'm so sorry/ yes i'm sorry they were born niggahs. But then if i cant punish myself to death for being white/ i certainly cant in good conscience keep waiting for the cleaning lady/ & everytime i attempt even the smallest venture into the world someone comes to help me/ like if i do anything/ anything at all i'm extending myself as a white girl/ cuz part of being a white girl is being absent/ like those women who are just with a man but whose names the black people never remember/ they just say oh yeah his white girl waz with him/ or a white gin got beat & killed today/ why someone will say/ cuz me niggah told her to give him her money & she said no/ cuz she thought he realized that she waz a white girl/ & he did know but he didnt care/ so he killed her & took the money/ but the cops knew she waz a white girl & cdnt be killed by a niggah especially/ when she had awready said no. The niggah was sposed to hop round the corner backwards/ you dig/ so the cops/ found the culprit within 24 hours/ cuz just like emmett till/ niggahs do not kill white girls.

i'm still in my house/ having flung my hair-do for the last time/ what with having to take 20 valium a day/ to consider the ERA/ & all the men in the world/ & my ignorance of the world/ it is overwhelming. i'm so glad i'm colored. boy i cd wake up in the morning & think abt anything. i can remember emmett till & not haveta smile at anybody.

Maxine (*compelled to speak by* **Natalie**'s *pain*)   whenever these things happened to me/ & i waz young/ i wd eat a lot/ or buy new fancy underwear with rhinestones & lace/ or go to the movies/ maybe call a friend/ talk to made-up boyfriends til dawn/ this waz when i waz under my parents' roof/ & trees that grew into my room had to be cut back once a year/ this waz when the birds sometimes flew thru the halls of the house as if the ceilings were sky & i/ simply another winged creature. yet no one around me noticed me especially. no one around saw anything but a precocious brown girl with peculiar ideas. like during the polio epidemic/ i wanted to have a celebration/ which nobody cd understand since iron lungs & not going swimming waznt nothing to celebrate. but i explained that i waz celebrating the bounty of the lord/ which more people didnt understand/ til i went on to say that/ ot was obvious that god had protected the colored folks from polio/ nobody understood that. i did/ if god had made colored people susceptible to polio/ then we wd be on the pictures & the television with the white children. i knew only white folks cd get that particular disease/ & i celebrated. That's how come i always commemorated anything that affected me or the colored people. according to my history of the colored race/ not enough attention waz paid to small victories or small personal defeats of the colored. i celebrated the colored trolley driver/ the colored basketball team/ the colored blues singer/ & the colored light heavy weight champion of the world. then too/ i had a baptist child's version of high mass for the slaves in new orleans whom i had read abt/ & i tried to grow watermelons & rice for the dead slaves from the east. as a child i took on the burden of easing the ghostcolored-folks' souls & trying hard to keep up with the affairs of my own colored world.

when i became a woman/ my world got smaller. my grandma closed up the windows/ so the birds wdnt fly in the house any more. waz bad luck for a girl so yng & in my condition to have the shadows of flying creatures over my head. i didnt celebrate the trolley driver anymore/ cuz he might know i waz in this condition. i didnt celebrate the basketball team anymore/ cuz they were yng & handsome/ & yng & handsome cd mean trouble. but trouble waz when white kids called you names or beat you up cuz you had no older brother/ trouble waz when someone died/ or the tornado hit yr house/ now trouble meant something abt yng & handsome/ & white or colored. if he waz yng & handsome that meant trouble. seemed like every one who didnt have this condition/ so birds cdnt fly over yr head/ waz trouble. as i understood it/ my mama & my grandma were sending me out to be with trouble/ but not to get into trouble. the yng & the handsome cd dance with me & call for sunday supper/ the yng & handsome cd write my name on their notebooks/ cd carry my ribbons on the field for gd luck/ the uncles cd hug me & chat for hours abt my growing up. So i counted all 492 times this condition wd make me victim to this trouble/ before i wd be immune to it/ the way colored folks were immune to polio.

i had discovered innumerable manifestations of trouble: jealousy/ fear/ indignation & recurring fits of vulnerability that lead me right back to the contradiction i had never understood/ even as a child/ how half the world's population cd be bad news/ by yng & handsome/ & later/ eligible & interested/ & trouble.

plus/ according to my own version of the history of the colored people/ only white people hurt little colored girls or grown colored women/ my mama told me only white people had social disease & molested children/ & my grandma told me only white

people committed unnatural acts. that's how come i knew only white folks got polio/
muscular dystrophy/ sclerosis/ & mental illness/ this was all verified by the television.
but i found out that the colored folks knew abt the same vicious & disease ridden
passions that the white folks knew.

the pain i succumbed to each time a colored person did something that i believed only
white people did waz staggering. my entire life seems to be worthless/ if my own
folks arent better than white folks/ then surely the sagas of slavery & the jim crow
hadnt convinced anyone that we were better than them. i commenced to buying pieces
of gold/ 14 carat/ 24 carat/ 18 carat gold/ every time some black person did something
that waz beneath him as a black person & more like a white person. i bought gold cuz
it came from the earth/ & more likely it came from south africa/ where the black
people are humiliated & oppressed like in slavery. i wear all these things at once/ to
remind the black people that it cost a lot for us to be here/ our value/ can be known
instinctively/ but since so many black people are having a hard time not being like
white folks/ i wear these gold pieces to protest their ignorance/ their disconnect from
history. i buy gold with a vengeance/ each time someone appropriates my space or my
time without permission/ each time someone is discourteous or actually cruel to me/
if my mind is not respected/ my body toyed with/ i buy gold/ & weep. i weep as i fix
the chains round my neck/ my wrists/ my ankles. i weep cuz all my childhood
ceremonies for the ghost-slaves have been in vain. colored people can get polio &
mental illness. slavery is not unfamiliar to me. No one on this planet knows/ what i
know abt gold/ abt anything hard to get & beautiful/ anything lasting/ wrought from
pain. no one understands that surviving the impossible is sposed to accentuate the
positive aspects of a people.

Alec *crosses immediately to* **Maxine.** *As he reaches her,* **Lou,** *in full magician's
regalia, freezes the* **Company.**

Lou   yes yes yes 3 wishes is all you get
   scarlet ribbons for yr hair
   a farm in mississippi
   someone to love you madly

all things are possible but aint no colored magician in his right mind gonna make you
white cuz this is blk magic you lookin at & i'm fixin you up good/ fixin you up good
& colored & you gonna be colored all yr life & you gonna love it/ being colored/ all
yr life colored & love it/ love it/ bein colored

Lou *beckons the* **Company** *to join him in the chant "colored & love it." It becomes a
serious celebration.* **Lou** *suddenly freezes them.*

Lou   crackers are born with the right to be alive/ i'm making ours up right here in yr
face/ & we gonna be

Company *continues to sing "colored & love it/ love it/ bein colored." Minstrel mask
comes down. Blackout except for mask.* **Company** *sings "colored & love it" as
audience exits.*

Finis.

Introduction to Beth Henley

Aimée K. Michel

Elizabeth "Beth" Becker Henley was born in Jackson, Mississippi, in 1952 into a segregated South. She was the second of four daughters of attorney Charles Boyce and Elizabeth Josephine Henley, an actress in local theaters. Her relationship to her sisters particularly and her family life in general provided rich material for her plays. Henley attributes her love of theater and early introduction to its magic to her mother. In Ben Hodges' book *The Play that Changed My Life*, Henley describes her first experience of theater when her mother picked her up for kindergarten carpool dressed as a green beanstalk for her current part in *Jack and the Beanstalk*. Her teachers and fellow classmates were in awe and Henley was transfixed by the transformation of her mother into a being in which "she had eclipsed species and gender." This initiation into the transformative nature of theater was followed with an understanding of its power. She goes on to describe attending a strike of the set for the play *A Hatful of Rain*, in which her mother starred. She was astonished by the anguish with which her mother watched the set disappear and was intrigued that her mother seemed to take the theater more seriously than life.

While she was in public high school in Jackson, court-ordered desegregation began and she remembers those years as confusing and chaotic. Mississippi, at the heart of the Deep South, fought desegregation fiercely and violently. Lynching, fire bombing, and riots were prevalent and culminated in the infamous Battle of Oxford, the Ole Miss riot of 1962 when violence erupted on the Oxford campus of the University of Mississippi in response to the enrollment of a black military veteran, James Meredith, in the university as its first black student. President Kennedy called in the US army and the Mississippi National Guard to quell the rioting students and citizens. In the end, Meredith enrolled and graduated, but the state continued its resistance to desegregation into the twenty-first century.

Southerners who grew up in this charged atmosphere lived in a dichotomous world where whites were privileged to live in relative safety and blacks lived daily in fear of death and destruction. In the Oxford Research Encyclopedia's section on Southern Gothic Literature, Thomas Ærvold Bjerre writes:

> The Southern Gothic brings to light the extent to which the idyllic vision of the pastoral, agrarian South rests on massive repressions of the region's historical realities: slavery, racism, and patriarchy. Southern Gothic texts also mark a Freudian return of the repressed: the region's historical realities take concrete forms in the shape of ghosts that highlight all that has been unsaid in the official version of southern history.

Henley's plays speak directly from the Southern Gothic tradition. Bjerre writes, "Characteristics of Southern Gothic include the presence of irrational, horrific, and transgressive thoughts, desires, and impulses; grotesque characters; dark humor, and an overall angst-ridden sense of alienation."

Though her work has been compared to William Faulkner, Tennessee Williams, Flannery O'Connor, and Carson McCullers, all Southern Gothic writers, Henley carves new ground and brings the form into the present. Hers is the perspective of one who lived through the beginnings of the end of white male dominance in the South, as desegregation, the Civil Rights movement and the Women's Liberation movement challenged the patriarchy. Her Southern women are dominant, powerful and upend all expectations. As daughters of the South, they are implicated in its past. However, Henley's women are claiming their voices, confronting the patriarchy, and writing their own lives.

In *Interviews with Contemporary Women Playwrights*, by Kathleen Betsko and Rachel Koenig, Henley asserts, "I like to write characters who do horrible things, but whom you can still like . . . because of their human needs and struggles. . . . I try to understand that ugliness is in everybody. . . . we are filled with dark, bloody, primitive urges and desires."

"I've always been attracted to split images," she continues. "The grotesque combined with the innocent, a child walking with a cane; a kitten with a swollen head; a hunchback drinking a cup of fruit punch. Somehow these images are a metaphor for my view of life; they're colorful. Part of that is being brought up in the South; southerners always bring out the grisly details in any event." Henley's comedy comes from this very distinct Southern point of view. "The way my family dealt with hardships was to see the humor or the ironic point of view in the midst of tragedy. And that's just how my mind works."

Knowing she wanted to study theater and become an actress, Henley left Mississippi for Dallas, Texas, and Southern Methodist University where her first play, *Am I Blue*, was performed in the Margo Jones Theater, named for the woman who launched the American regional theater movement. After receiving a BFA in theater in 1974, she attended the University of Illinois Urbana for a year before moving to Los Angeles.

While pursuing acting jobs, she continued writing and completed *Crimes of the Heart* in 1978. At the recommendation of a friend, she submitted it to the Actors Theater of Louisville's Great American Play contest in 1979 and it was co-winner of the prize, receiving a production at ATL and a nomination for a Susan Smith Blackburn Award. At twenty-seven years old, Henley was suddenly in the limelight. *Crimes* was developed through several productions, eventually winning the 1981 Pulitzer Prize for Drama and arriving on Broadway in the same year, where it was awarded the Best American Play by the New York Drama Critics' Circle.

Henley followed this success with *The Wake of Jamey Foster*, *The Miss Firecracker Contest*, *The Debutante Ball*, and *The Lucky Spot*, all taking place in Mississippi and Louisiana. Henley's Southern point of view defines these early plays, which are filled with characters who are trying to fit into a society with which they are at odds. At the same time, she was writing screenplays. Her screenplay for *Crimes of the Heart* was nominated for an Oscar for Best Adapted Screenplay and she adapted her 1984 play *Miss Firecracker Contest* into the 1989 film *Miss Firecracker*.

In the 1990s Henley moved the geographical locations of her plays West, beginning with *Abundance*, set in Wyoming and Missouri, and moving to Los Angeles with *Signature* and *Control Freaks* and to Wisconsin with *Revelers*. Her off beat *L-play* has no distinct setting, and she ends the decade with *Impossible Marriage* set somewhere outside of Savannah, Georgia. Plays in the first decade of the twenty-first century include *Family Week, Ridiculous Fraud*, and *Laugh*. Henley's newest play *Lightning (or The Unbuttoning)* premiered at the Powerhouse Theater in Poughkeepsie, New York, in summer 2019. In all of these plays, Henley masterfully experiments with style and abstraction of form while continuing to hone her strong comic voice.

In 2012 she premiered *The Jacksonian*, a play about which she has said, "It's taken me my whole career to be able to write this play—to be able to look at how dark that time was with enough distance to turn it into a play." First produced at the Audrey Skirball-Kenis Theater at the Geffen Playhouse in Los Angeles and directed by Robert Falls, it opened in New York City in 2013 at the Acorn Theater.

Though she has written many plays set in Mississippi, this is the first set in her hometown of Jackson, and, in an interview with Rob Weinert-Kendt for the *New York Times* article "Southern Without the Comfort," Henley confesses that it includes many autobiographical elements. The narrator of the play, sixteen-year-old Rosy Perch, is helplessly watching her parents' marriage disintegrate. Henley's own parents divorced when she was about that age. Her father, also, went to live in a hotel and, like Rosy, she brought him a Christmas tree to try to make things better. The charged political environment in the play is reminiscent of her teenage years when the KKK was radically active. In 1968, when she was sixteen, Henley was intimately exposed to the violence of the segregated South when her sister's fifth-grade teacher was killed by the police as she participated in a KKK bombing of the home of a Jewish leader. Apparently she was wearing hot pants when killed and the grotesque comedy of that image stayed with the playwright.

The darkness of the era is articulated in Henley's description of the setting in her stage directions: "The motel exists as a haunting memory, a sort of purgatory that was Jackson, circa 1964". The time frame is March to December, but the scenes are not linear or chronologically played. She writes: "Rosy's terror and her will quake the landscape of time, space and memory."

Rosy is the Chorus and she announces the murder, guiding us forward and backward in time, hoping she can stop it from happening: "I need to stop an accident at the motel." But it is clear that she can't. From the first scene at the bar we are in film noir territory, and the sinister air reeks of decay. Fred, the bartender, says, "The heart is a muscle and mine is decayed," speaking for every character in the play. Despite themselves, they are all implicated in the toxic violence around them.

Knowing that there will be a murder, we are left wondering which character will be killed. However, murder has already happened. A female cashier at the Texaco station has been brutally murdered by Fred, and an innocent black worker at the station has been framed and faces execution. A dental patient of Bill's took part in the bombing of a Negro church in Meridien, murdering more innocent people. Hate and death permeate their lives.

In the midst of it, Bill preaches his dental religion. He can render everyone pain free. He can drug them into oblivion. "Come to me and you'll feel no pain," he promises. But the pain around him cannot be drugged away. Rosy knows:

> They say things happen for *reasons*. But the *reasons* are not real. It's just the swamp you're living on that pulls you under.
> Under weeds, wet grass, mud. Lifetimes of rot and blood, lynched blood, buried in Mississippi soil.

Racism is one of the swamps in the South, pulling it under, but the other one is misogyny. Both Bill and Fred commit violence on women. Rosy shares that Bill hit her mother. Susan accuses him of sterilizing her against her will. Fred has brutally killed a woman and threatens to kill Eva. He sexually exposes himself to Rosy. The white patriarchy is threatened from all sides and the men strike back, violently.

In the play's climax Henley gives Susan a powerful voice as she drapes a sheet over her derelict husband: "Here's your sheet! Join the lynching! Be like your daddy! Join the KKK! . . . Kill, bomb, tie an engine block to a body and throw it in a swamp! Let the terror—the terror." Bill's response is to shut her up for good, brutally murdering her.

In the last scene, Rosy tries to make sense of what happened, "I knew my father was in trouble and my mother was not well," but in the end, there is no sense to be made. The double terrors of racism and misogyny continue to distort and derange. Henley ends with a final flashback when Rosy had a good day with her daddy. She remembers Bill risking his life to save her hat, the knight in shining armor who can make anything all right. He's not so sure it happened . . . not in the world as he knows it, but Rosy longs for that safe feeling she had as a child, "I remember—back when I was little," back in an idyllic South that never truly existed.

The Jacksonian

Beth Henley

Scene One

Lights up on an ice machine at the Jacksonian Motel.

Time: The night of the murder, December 17, 1964.

Lights up on **Rosy Perch**, *sixteen. She wears pajamas and is wrapped in a blanket.*

Rosy   There's been an accident there's going to be I need to stop an accident at the motel. The Jacksonian Motel.

She watches as **Bill Perch** *enters and goes to the ice machine. He has blood on his hands and shirt. He violently digs an ice bucket into the ice. Ice crashes! He holds the ice in the bucket and stares out for no more than a moment. He exits.*

Rosy   We need to leave.

We need to leave in time.

The time is. What time is.

The following lines overlap **Fred** *and* **Eva**'s *entrances into the bar.*

Rosy   It's not Christmas. It's near around before—before Christmas.

There is a Christmas tree at the motel. But it is not the real tree.

The real tree is at home.

And it is before—

Before a time that makes the time of murder.

A bar/restaurant at the Jacksonian Motel.

Time: The night of the murder, December 17, 1964.

There is a manger scene and a string of Christmas lights.

Eva White *is staring coldly across space.*

Fred Weber *is smoking a cigarette with a burning tip. A sinister silence.*

Eva   I know what it is.

Fred   What?

Eva   What ya got me in my stocking.

Fred   No.

Eva   It's a surprise.

Fred   No.

Eva   I like Christmas. Jesus was born. He likes me. Jesus loves all the little children. Want to know what I got you? It's easy to guess. You wear it on *this* finger. I'm saving it for Christmas. Like we said.

Fred   I never said.

Eva   You said you're my *fiancé*. Fred, my *fiancé*.

Fred   Don't say it like that.

Eva   I know you don't think you deserve me. But I won't let you throw away your one chance at happiness. There's not many chances people get. I'm your one and only chance. You think life is nothing but sorrow and misery is a blessing from God. But you deserve happiness, you deserve me. I got my shoes dyed bone ivory to match the bridal dress. We might as well think about having children. Some kids would be nice.

Fred   It's not going to work out like everybody hoped.

Eva   It's going to work out like I hoped. Right after Christmas we're going to the justice of the peace and tying the knot.

Fred   Eva, I didn't wanna bother you with this and cause you to have a nervous breakdown.

Eva   What?

Fred   There's a muscular constriction. My heart's hard. It's not pumping as much blood as it should. It'll kill me. Two or three months. Could be days. The heart is a muscle and mine is decayed.

Eva   I don't believe you have such a heart like that. A decayed heart.

Fred   It's the way it is with my heart.

They look at each other steadily.

I won't make a widow out of you. Wouldn't be right. I can't let a young woman marry a terminal man.

God would strike me down for selfish pride. You don't wanna make me look bad in the eyes of the Lord? Would you?

Eva   No. Not that.

Fred   Not more of that. Keep me out of hell, Eva. The dentist is single.

Eva   He's married.

Fred   Separated. A long time. For good.

Eva   Maybe not.

Fred   Wife's filing for divorce. Got a big-time lawyer. She's serving papers after Christmas.

Eva   How do you know?

Fred   She let it slip after some scotch.

Eva   Fred, we're engaged.

Fred   That was before my heart's muscular constriction.

Eva   It's sworn between us.

Fred   Set your sights on the living.

Eva   Remember back in April? The filling-station lady?

Fred   Wasn't that a terrible tragic thing.

Eva   It sure was sad at the funeral visitation. Seeing her in a coffin. One of her kids, a little girl, was crawling up on the coffin like she never realized her mama was dead.

Fred   You already told me the whole story.

Eva   Everyone could see her underpants. Pink. The little girl's underpants. It was a funny sight.

Fred   "A funny sight."

Eva   Her daddy had to carry her off that corpse. Crying all the way. He was the widower. Manager of the Texaco station. To his everlasting regret he was not there the night his wife got shot and killed.

Fred   You'll get the money. The running-away money. I won't need it dead.

Eva   When do I get it?

Fred   I'll give it to you on Christmas. In a wrapped package.

Eva   How much of it do I get?

Fred   Pretty much all.

Eva   Your heart's fine.

Fred   I don't lie.

Eva   That's not true. Both of us . . . You know I lie. On the Bible and under God. Tell me for real about your heart.

Fred   I'm dying, Eva! You like hearing it? I'll say it again. I am a dead man. Terminal. A corpse.

Eva   You're scaring me.

Fred   Boo!

Eva   I've been waiting. Here waiting for everything to be that is not going to be.

Fred   I'm the one who is dying.

Eva   At least you're going somewhere.

Eva *exits as* **Fred** *draws on the cigarette and lights come up on* **Bill Perch** *'s motel room.*

Scene Two

Bill Perch *'s motel room at the Jacksonian Motel.*

Time: The night of the murder, December 17, 1964.

Perch *stands by the bed wearing a suit and tie. He clips his fingernails carefully with nail scissors. Silence.*

He goes to the phone and picks up the receiver. He dials the rotary phone. He waits while it rings.

Perch   Hello, Mama . . . We're doing fine. How're you? . . . Not a thing to worry about. It's a lull, a lull is circular, it's round, in the end it's not a lull . . . I don't know, it could be people are taking better care of their teeth, fluoride, dental floss. It's never one thing; it's an amalgam, to use a dental analogy . . . Uh huh, I know . . . The fact is, unfortunately, we can't come Christmas Day . . . Susan doesn't want to make the drive. She wants to stay home. Have Christmas at home . . . Tell Daddy I'll come hunt with him on the weekend . . . Mama, I do not need any more of your unsolicited advice. You don't seem to take it into consideration that I'm a member of the American Dental Association, I've given the lieutenant governor Novocain . . . I am not getting "huffy" . . . Yes, I deposited the check . . . Tell Daddy I won't need any more. Things will start up after the first of the year. It's just a—

Knocking at the door.

Lull. Someone's knocking at the door . . . I don't know who? I have to go see . . . Susan's here. She's in the bathroom . . . Mama, people go to the goddamn bathroom . . .

More hesitant knocking at the door.

I'm not being rude. There's someone knocking at the door. Mama, I have to go answer my front door.

He hangs up the phone and goes to answer the door.

Rosy *stands at the door holding a small Christmas tree and a box of ornaments.* **Rosy** *is a strange girl with acne on her face. She wears a coat that she does not take off.*

Perch   Rosy.

Rosy   Hi.

Perch   What's that?

Rosy   A Christmas tree.

Perch   Where's your mother?

Rosy   She left. She'll come back to pick me up.

Perch   Where'd she go?

Rosy   I don't know. She wants me to decorate this tree with you.

Perch   I don't want a tree in here.

Rosy   Yes, sir.

She moves to take the tree away.

Perch   Bring it in. We don't want to upset your mother.

She brings in the tree.

Perch   Your mother is crazy. You know that?

Rosy   Yes, sir.

Perch   When is she coming back?

Rosy   She said she wanted us to decorate the tree and have supper in the restaurant.

Perch   I'll buy you a steak. A fillet.

Rosy   I just want the fish sticks.

Perch   You need to eat a substantial meal. A fillet or T-bone steak. Something to work your jaw.

Rosy   Yes, sir.

(*About the ornaments.*) Should I put these on?

Perch   Yes. Let's not upset your mother.

She starts to put ornaments on the tree.

Perch   What do you want for Christmas?

Rosy   A wicker wheelchair. I saw one in an antique store on Capitol Street. If I got it I wouldn't have to walk. I could just roll around.

Perch   I'm not getting you a goddamn wheelchair.

Rosy   Yes, sir.

Perch   Did you try out for the Murrah Miss drill team?

Rosy   They didn't pick me. I didn't try my hardest so they didn't pick me.

Perch   Always try your hardest.

Rosy   Yes, sir. I just didn't this once.

Perch   You won't get anywhere unless you try your hardest, even then you could end up in a ditch like your Uncle Jim. He just drove off the road and it was over. Don't speed on roads that curve.

Rosy   I won't. I didn't get my driver's license. I failed the test.

Perch   You failed the test?

Rosy   Yes, sir.

Perch   Why?

Rosy   I couldn't parallel park.

Perch   Didn't your mother teach you?

Rosy   She doesn't know how.

Perch   I'll teach you. We'll go out to the parking lot at the football coliseum and I'll teach you. We'll go some Sunday when it's empty.

Rosy   Yes, sir.

Perch (*about an ornament*)   What's that?

Rosy   The glass slipper.

Perch   Don't put it on this tree. It's your mother's favorite. Put it on the tree at home. I'll see it there.

Rosy   Mama says you won't listen to her.

Perch   I listen to your mother.

Rosy   She says I need to be the go-between and tell you she doesn't want you to come home for Christmas.

Slight but sharply painful beat.

Perch   You want me, don't you?

Rosy   Yes, sir.

Perch   I found a psychiatrist in New Orleans to take your mother to. No one here would ever know that we went. You could come with us and help explain your mother's problems. Tell how she threw hot coffee and locks herself in the bathroom. Sits in the tub all day without water. I need a witness. Would you do that? Be my witness? Your mother likes to lie. I don't want to put you on the spot. Your skin's broken out. That happens in adolescence. Open your mouth. Smile. Those teeth are good. You have good teeth.

Rosy   Yes, sir.

Perch   Let's get some supper. Go wash your hands. You can have a Shirley Temple and a baked Alaska.

Rosy   Yes, sir.

She goes into the bathroom and washes her hands. Sound of water rushing.

Perch   Did you bring your toothbrush?

Rosy (*offstage*)   Yes, sir.

Perch   I want you to brush after every meal.

Rosy *enters from the bathroom.*

Rosy   I do.

Perch   Better wash my hands. And we'll go.

He exits to the bathroom. Sound of water rushing.

Rosy *looks at the small Christmas tree for a moment.*

She turns to the audience.

The end of Scene Two flows directly into Scene Three.

Scene Three

Jacksonian bar/restaurant.

Time: May, 1964, afternoon.

Perch *meets* **Fred** *and* **Eva**.

Fred *is behind the bar.*

Rosy *steps through space and speaks to the audience.*

Rosy   The separation. My parents' separation.

It was a temporary measure. A limited arrangement.

May.

My father moved out of our house in May. My birthday month. I turned sixteen. It was after my parents fought and he hurt her—worse than always.

Perch *enters and goes to sit at the bar.*

Rosy   Daddy moved to the Jacksonian Motel. Just for a time. A short time. A temporary measure.

She exits.

Perch *is drinking a scotch.* **Fred** *is behind the bar.*

Fred   Another drink?

Perch   Well . . .

He downs his drink.

Good timing.

Fred   My peripheral vision is keen.

Perch   Nice to hear a man speak up for himself. Don't bury it with false pride.

Fred   I can sense what people want.

Perch   Give people what they want, in case they've forgotten.

Fred (*giving* **Perch** *a drink*)   Nice smile. Many men don't have nice smiles. You have got one.

Perch   I'm a dentist.

Fred   I'm impressed.

Perch   Dr. Bill Perch.

Fred   Fred Weber.

Perch   Do you take care of your teeth, Fred?

Fred   My teeth are very important to me.

Perch   Many people don't realize the correlation between oral conditions and general health. To say it is profound is not to overstate it. If you would like to make an appointment, I have a business card.

Fred   Alright.

Perch   I don't like to advertise myself but will not stand on false pride concerning your teeth.

Fred (*looking at the card*)   You work here in Jackson?

Perch   Medical Arts Building on North State Street.

Fred   How long are you visiting us?

Perch   Not long . . . A day or two here in May.

Fred   May's a pretty month.

Perch   I'm known as the "Painless Dentist." Come to me and you'll feel no pain. It's not like the old days. There's a whole new era of sterility. I use disposable needles. X-ray machines are much improved. I have the high-speed drills with water coolant, not the belt driven. Reclining motorized dental chair. Music. I let patients select the radio channel they prefer. It gives them a sense of ease and distraction. Much of it is in the manner. You hypnotize the fear with a steady manner. Of course I do use anesthesia when needed. Many options there, Fred: nitrous oxide, Novocain, lidocaine, Sodium Pentothal, chloroform. I can fix it to where you don't feel a thing.

Fred   I'll make an appointment.

Perch   We all need regular oral examinations.

Ice machine.

Eva *enters by the ice machine dressed in her finest.*

Eva *opens the heavy lid. She picks up a piece of ice and rubs her forehead and wrists.*

Eva   Dear Jesus. Forgive me, Jesus. Forgive me for everything I swore on that courtroom Bible.

She slams down the lid of the ice machine.

Bar/restaurant.

Fred *gives* **Perch** *a fresh drink.*

Perch   I usually don't. I'm very disciplined. But this morning's paper—nothing to make you turn down a drink.

Fred   Yeah.

Perch   The Negro church in Meridian—

Fred   What?

Perch   Another fire bomb.

Fred   Had not heard

Perch   Third one this month.

Eva *enters.*

Eva   Fred, I'm back.

Fred *goes to her.*

Fred   How'd it go?

Eva   Good. They recorded me on a machine. All the lawyers were there, pro and con and prosecution. I swore to them every detail and they believed me. I want to buy a sensible wedding dress. Not like in the fairy tales. I'm not sixteen. I never was sixteen.

Fred   Eva.

Eva   I like it when you say my name.

Fred   Eva. Eva?

Eva   Yeah?

Fred   I have to take the ring back. I borrowed it from a friend and it has to be returned.

Eva   I know.

Fred   Here's a drink.

Eva   Thanks.

(*About the ring.*) It looks good on me. Could I keep it for tonight?

Fred   No.

Eva   It's still true though. It's in the public record. We're engaged. You're my fiancé. That's what I said in the room on the recording machine. I swore it on a courtroom Bible.

Fred   Eva, the ring.

Eva   Will you get me another?

Fred   I told you I would.

Eva   Swear on a stack of Bibles?

Fred   I swear on every Bible there is in creation.

She hands him the ring.

Eva   Get me one just like this.

Fred   Won't be no comparison.

He exits with the ring.

Eva   He's so sweet. We're engaged. Fred is my fiancé. I was just downtown giving alibi evidence against the colored man who killed the cashier lady at Texaco. Don't you think he should be lynched?

Perch   I do not.

Eva   He will be.

Perch   The man hasn't been arraigned.

Eva   He'll be found guilty and sentenced to execution.

Perch   There's no evidence I know of.

Eva   The paper says he's the prime suspect 'cause he worked right there on the premises.

Perch   I use that Texaco station. Louis Wright is seventy something years old, has glaucoma.

Eva   He was the only colored employed at the station. And he knew the system.

Perch   I think folks need to stop jumping to conclusions and wait for some actual facts.

Eva   Are you some sort of outside agitator?

Perch   No, ma'am.

Eva   Where're you from?

Perch   Here. Jackson.

Eva   Where in Jackson?

Perch   In Eastover.

Eva (*impressed*)   You have a house in Eastover?

Perch   Yes, ma'am.

Eva   That's a real wealthy area. Big fancy houses and yards.
What's your occupation?

Perch   I'm a dentist.

Eva   A dentist? You don't mind putting your fingers in people's mouths? Touching their tongues?

Perch   You grow accustomed to it. Easily.

Eva   I wouldn't. All the slobber and blood and you could get bit. You need strong hands to be a dentist. Yours look strong. Look at the hair on your knuckles. Wouldn't want that tickling in my mouth.

Perch   You'd be surprised how painless a trip to the dentist can be.

Eva   I don't think I would. You know why? 'Cause I don't even have a dentist. My mouth is sweet. Naturally kissable. I see you're married. Maybe you can help Fred pick out my ring. Introduce him to a fine jeweler.

Perch   I don't know a lot about jewelry. My specialties are gum disease and anesthesia.

Eva   Why are you staying here? At the Jacksonian if you live in Eastover?

Perch   We're painting our house. We're having the house painted.

Eva   What color?

Perch *shrugs his shoulders in a distracted manner.*

Eva   Don't you know? Bet your wife knows.

Perch   Yes. Susan. I have a wife, Susan.

Eva   Any kids?

Perch   A daughter.

Eva   Where are they?

Perch   Shopping.

Eva   All women like to shop. Especially if they have money. To get pretty things.

Perch   Alright. Very nice talking to you.

Eva   Does that mean you're going?

Perch   I need to retire to my room.

Eva   It's early. It's afternoon.

Perch   Yes, I believe it is. Good day, Miss . . .

Eva   White. Eva White.

Perch   Dr. Bill Perch.

Eva   The dentist.

Perch   Yes, ma'am.

He exits. **Eva** *raises her hand and gazes at her ring finger.*

Scene Four

Bar/restaurant.

Time: The night of the murder, December 17, 1964.

Rosy *sits alone at a table picking at her baked Alaska.*

Fred *wipes off the bar.*

Fred   Are you enjoying your baked Alaska?

Rosy   It's big

Perch *enters. He is returning from the bathroom.*

Perch (*to* **Rosy**)   What time did your mother say she was coming back?

Rosy   She didn't tell me.

Perch   I don't understand people who cannot grasp time. The importance of time. Go on and finish your dessert.

Rosy   Yes, sir.

Perch   My wife does not adhere to time. She doesn't see that things can only happen in time. Without time where are we? I'll look for her car—out on the highway.

He exits. **Fred** *walks to* **Rosy**'s *table and points at the baked Alaska.*

Eva *enters and watches* **Fred.**

Fred   You don't want to finish it?

Rosy   No.

Fred   I'll take it.

He takes the baked Alaska. **Eva** *sits down at* **Rosy**'s *table.*

Eva   What do you think about Fred? Have you looked at him?

Rosy   Yeah.

Eva Does he look sick to you? Like he's on death's door?

Rosy Don't know.

Eva I don't wanna marry a dead man. I have my dreams. You want to see my shoes? They match the bridal dress.

Rosy I saw them. You showed me.

Fred *exits behind the bar.*

Eva Where's your homework?

Rosy I'm out of school for Christmas.

Eva I'm glad I don't go to school now. With them.

Rosy You mean Negroes?

Eva How many you got all together?

Rosy Five.

Eva Five. I never had any, they didn't let 'em in.

Rosy I got two in English and three in PE.

Eva How many Jews?

Rosy Don't know.

Eva Good thing you're doing it and not me.

Rosy Did you ever even finish high school?

Eva (*a lie*) Yeah. I did.

Rosy What year?

Eva When are your parents divorcing?

Rosy My parents don't believe in divorce.

Eva Your daddy's been living here at the Jacksonian since May. He's our longest-staying customer.

Rosy My parents will never divorce. People who are nice don't do that. Only trashy people do that, or movie stars who are rich trashy people.

Eva Takes care of his own laundry. His shirts. Underwear and shirts. I never knew a married man to do his own laundry.

Rosy Everything in our family is fine.

Fred *enters.*

Eva Fred has me an engagement ring for my Christmas stocking. But I can't afford a funeral. I look old in black.

Rosy   Eva.

Eva   What?

Rosy   No one is ever going to marry you.

Eva   Why do you say that? What is wrong with you? It's not true. I'm getting married. If it's not Fred it will be another man. One who is right close by.

Rosy   My daddy is never going to associate with you in real society.

Eva   You got no idea about grown-up behavior. They will fool you every time.

Rosy   It would be beneath him.

Perch *enters.* **Fred** *serves him a scotch.*

Perch   Yes, sir, Fred, your peripheral vision is keen.

Fred   Why, thank you, Dr. Perch.

Eva   What are those things on your face?

Rosy   Nothing.

Eva   Red puss-y things? Makes you look uglier than you are.

Rosy   Good.

Eva   Why would you want to be ugly?

Rosy   For the good of humankind.

Eva   What do you mean?

Rosy   Other people can help themselves to feeling better than me. Knowing they don't have a face like mine makes them smirk and sigh with relief. I don't want to clear these up; I prefer to keep them aflame. For humanity.

Eva   If you was my stepdaughter I'd thrash you with rawhide till you washed that face.

Rosy   Hardy, har, har.

Susan Perch *enters. She brings Christmas gifts. Apples covered with cloves, decorated with cinnamon sticks and velvet ribbon. They are uniquely beautiful.*

Susan   Merry Christmas! Merry Chrissy!

Perch   Susan!

Susan   I've brought y'all presents. Here, Eva, just a little happy. And here's one for you, Fred.

Fred   Thanks.

Eva   Yeah.

Susan   Homemade Christmas sachet. Rosy and I pressed hundreds of cloves into each apple, one by one by one 'til all our fingers were worn out and blistered. The cinnamon stick and velvet ribbons remind me of an old-fashioned Christmas.

Perch   Rosy had dinner. A T-bone steak. I made her eat it without ketchup.

Susan   Did she have steak sauce?

Perch   Only a dab. Right, Rosy?

Rosy   Yes, sir.

Perch   It was a good meal. T-bone is a fine cut of beef. Tell your mother.

Rosy   It was good.

Susan   She hardly eats anything I cook.

Rosy   Yes I do.

Perch   Don't contradict your mother.

Rosy   Yes, sir.

Perch   We don't have to go to Mama's and Daddy's for Christmas.

Susan   They love to see you. I bought gifts you can take from us. A negligee for your mother and an engraved sterling ashtray for your father. Did you get your Christmas tree?

Perch   Yes.

Susan   Good. Did you decorate it?

Perch   Looks good. You want to come see it?

Susan   Well, alright. Rosy?

Perch   She already saw it.

Susan   She can see it again.

Perch   Rosy, do you want to see the tree again?

Rosy   I don't know. No.

Perch   Alright. Let's go see it.

He and **Susan** *exit.*

Fred (*to* **Eva**)   You need to clean three and seven. Carla went home. Swollen kneecaps. Like somebody hit her with a baseball bat.

Eva   She's just lazy.

Fred   Go on.

Eva   Later I'll go on. (*To* **Rosy** *who is holding the baby Jesus figure from the manger scene.*) Don't touch that. Don't play with his swaddling. That's Christ Baby Jesus, not a doll! Put him back.

Rosy   You put him back. I have to brush my teeth.

She exits to the bathroom with her purse.

Eva   I know what is going on here. I can smell it burning. You don't want to marry me and you're making up lies. Just remember, they have not gassed that nigger for killing the Texaco woman; so don't try to pull one. Not on me. I will go to jail for perjury to get you gassed.

Fred   Do you know who you are talking to, Eva? You are talking to a murderer. And I have few qualms left. Really no qualms. Whatsoever.

Eva   I'll go to the dentist. I'll go entangle him but understand you are the one I love but for hating you entirely.

She exits.

Motel room.

Susan *and* **Perch** *enter. She looks at the forlorn tree. She goes to it.*

He watches as she rearranges ornaments on the tree. She has a good eye and improves the look of the tree.

Bar/restaurant.

Rosy *enters from the bathroom wearing dark lipstick.*

Fred   Did you put on lipstick?

Rosy   No.

Fred   Would you like another Cherry Coke?

Rosy   Yeah. Why not.

Fred   I like you so I'll add extra cherries.

Rosy   Fred?

Fred   Yeah?

Rosy   Are you dying?

Fred   No. That's a lie to get her out of my hair. I can't marry Eva. She smells like broken-up crayons in a dirty room.

Rosy   Yeah. All the colors you don't want to use.

Scene Five

Motel room.

Time: The night of the murder, December 17, 1964.

Susan *stands back and appraises the tree.*

Susan   It needs lights. Lights make the tree. I'll send Rosy with some lights.

Perch   I don't need lights. Anyway . . . Coming home. I've been at the Jacksonian for a time. Need to take charge of my family. Be with my family.

Susan   No.

Perch   There is a psychiatrist in New Orleans we could go see.

Susan   What for?

Perch   I need you to understand everything isn't all my fault.

Susan   I think it is.

Perch   All my fault? Susan, you have moods. You swear at me and threaten. Get hysterical.

Susan   There are medical reasons for that. They take things out of you and you are not the same. You're different. Very changed. There's no money in my checking account.

Perch   I'm working on that.

Susan   I had an ovarian cyst. The size of a pea the doctor told me. I went under anesthesia and you let them take out every woman part of me!

Perch   It was/ a medical necessity, Dr. Carpenter—Susan, you're getting—don't get—

Susan (*overlapping from/*)   I would never have given consent! They gutted me! You let them cut out my womb. You let them do it! You son of a bitch! I could kill you!

She claws him deep and hard on the face.

He feels the marks on his face.

She holds her hand, looking at the flesh that is under her nails.

Perch   For God's sake. Susan. Please. Dr. Carpenter advised—

She goes into the bathroom.

Perch   My God. I didn't want to lose you. I'm sorry. My God. I'm sorry. My God.

She returns with a wet towel and gives it to him to soothe his face.

Susan   Bill. Here.

Perch   I don't know. Things keep going downhill. I try to stop them but they keep sliding and . . .

Susan   What?

Perch   In the end things will be okay. It's a lull.

A silence. She turns away. He looks at her. She breathes. He breathes.

Susan   I took an arrangement of cauliflowers and irises to the garden club. I thought it was revolutionary. But it went unappreciated and was mocked.

Perch   I think it's because you're an artist. You have artistic feelings.

Susan   I'm not an artist. I'm a wife and mother. I'm nothing. A nonentity.

Perch   Everyone thinks—you're a lovely lady.

Susan   People talk about me behind my back. I don't tell them but they know you're living here. They know you hit me.

Perch   I never would. Never again.

Susan   I can't kill myself. I would never kill myself. If I did it wouldn't be in a violent fashion. Not a gun or wrists cut; cut wrists. No blood. Blood is private. It would never be at home. Not where Rosy could find me. I'd come here to the Jacksonian, bring pills and gin. That would be the way. To float away. With a nice brand of gin, morphine, Novocain, ether. I could get it. I could borrow it from you. But I never would kill myself, no matter how good of an idea I thought it was, because even if I did, nothing would change. Nothing would be lost or gained even by that. My nose is all wrong.

Perch   No, it isn't.

Susan   They have surgery now. Surgery that could give me a classical nose.

Perch   You don't need surgery.

Susan   Clearly, clearly, cleariy I do.

Perch   Susan, I want to try.

Susan   I know you do. This place is depressing. The carpet is the color of despair. You should look for a nice apartment. I keep telling you that.

Perch   I like it here because it's temporary. And we came here one time together before we were married.

Susan   I remember.

Perch   Same time of year.

Susan   It was at my instigation. I didn't want to be a virgin on my wedding day. I thought it was sappy—a virgin bride.

Perch   You came disguised as something. Incognito.

Susan   I wore a hat with a veil so I wouldn't be recognized. I turned my engagement ring around to make it look like a wedding band.

Perch   You were the most beautiful girl in the world.

Susan   I thought no one was ever going to marry me because my nose was all wrong. But you did not seem to mind it. You saw other things.

Perch   All along, I wanted you. Susan Stanford. I only wanted you.

Susan   You brought me here and I demurred. Clinging to a worn-out innocence. I was a virgin until the day I got married. What a silly thing.

Perch   It wasn't silly.

Susan   You were gallant.

Perch   I wanted to do what you wanted.

Susan   You did.

Perch   Good.

Susan   I let you feel under my skirt. You're a dentist. Your hands are always clean. Your fingers are agile. They understand how to manipulate with precision in small cavities.

Perch   Let me touch you there. I want to. Pretty girl.

Susan   Rosy is waiting.

Perch   She likes it here. She's made friends. Pretty, pretty girl.

Susan   I need a scotch. With ice.

Perch   I'll get ice.

He exits.

Susan *smells the perfume on the pulse of her wrist.*

Rosy *appears on stage wearing her coat and holding schoolbooks. She goes to* **Susan** *and smells her perfume.*

Rosy   Ice, blood, ice.

Rosy is waiting. She likes it here. She's made friends.

October. *Tu es un cochon.* I have to study French.

She leaves the motel room and steps through time into the bar, sits at a table and opens her book.

Susan *exits.*

Scene Six

Bar/restaurant.

Time: October 1964.

Rosy *and* **Fred** *have a strange interaction.*

Rosy *is sitting at a table in the bar wearing her coat. A schoolbook is laid in front of her. She holds a pencil and stares out at nothing.*

Fred *appears at the ice machine smoking. Something is disturbing him. He fills a silver ice bucket and walks into the bar.*

Fred   Rosy. Where's your daddy?

Rosy   Gone. Mama's late.

Fred   Aren't you hot in that coat?

Rosy   I don't know.

Fred   You don't know? Why not?

Rosy   I can't tell if it's hot or cold. I don't feel the weather.

Fred   It's warm. For October.

Rosy   I don't feel weather.

Fred   Want a Cherry Coke? On the house?

Rosy   No.

Fred   Are you wearing lipstick?

She is not.

Rosy   No.

Fred   Looks like you are. Pretty lips. Rosy.

Rosy   I have to study.

Fred   What are you studying?

Rosy   French.

Fred   I don't know French.

Rosy (*not necessarily to him*)   *Tu es un cochon.*

Fred   What's that?

Rosy   It means, you are a pig.

Fred   Me? No. Why me?

Rosy   What you did. To that woman. You know.

Fred   I know I'm not a pig. You don't like me. Do you? You don't call me "Sir." Most of the girls, the ladies find me to be a man with appeal. But you don't see the allure. That's why I like you, Rosy. That is why I am drawn to you. You're a good judge of character. You see deep into the pit of the human soul. And that is how I look at you.

I see how pretty you are both inside and out. You are pulsing with sweetness. Inside and out. You know what I mean?

She starts writing with the pencil, ignoring him.

Fred   I got something I can do most people can't. I swallow swords. I am a sword swallower. Not a fake trick. The real feat.

She stops writing and looks at him.

Rosy   How's it feel?

Fred   It never feels pleasant or comfortable. You have to learn to relax muscles that are not under your voluntary control. Learning to ignore an involuntary reaction to a natural bodily function takes a tremendous amount of will and practice. Over and over. Deliberately activating the gag reflex. Over and over. Causing vomiting, choking, gagging.

Rosy   That's sickening.

Fred   Yeah, but eventually you are able to remove a natural and involuntary process that protects you from harm.

Rosy   Why would ya?

Fred   Glory! Southern defiance pride and glory. It's the most dangerous job in the world. Swallowing steel.

Rosy   What's the longest sword you ever swallowed?

Fred   Twenty-nine-inch solid-steel blade. Thirty-three inches is the world record.

Rosy (*holding up a stainless-steel knife*)   Swallow this.

Fred   That's cutlery.

Rosy   It's not long. It's short. Should be easy.

Fred   Thing is, Rosy, I had to give up the practice of sword swallowing. Lacerated some blood vessels in the trachea. Blood shot out of my mouth in a gush. A ruby fountain. That was my final performance.

Rosy   You made it up.

Fred   No. I would not lie to you. I would not.

Rosy   I have to study French.

Fred   Take off your coat.

Rosy   I'm not hot. I don't feel weather.

Fred   Watch me.

She looks at him.

He drinks a glass of water.

Fred   Watch what I do.

He takes the stainless-steel knife and thrusts it down his throat.

He gags and coughs. He pulls out the knife. The blade has blood on it. He is still choking.

She stands up.

Rosy   Are you hurt?

Fred (*still coughing*)   I did that for you 'cause I think you're pretty. Inside and out.

Rosy   Don't do that for me.

Fred   You've cast a spell.

Rosy   I know you're no good.

Fred   But I am. I am good.

She gathers her book.

Rosy   I'm sorry you bled. I'm leaving. I'll go wait for my mother. I'm sorry you bled. Don't bleed for me. Don't ever.

She exits.

Fred *wipes the blood off his mouth.*

Scene Seven

Motel room.

Time: The night of the murder, December 17, 1964.

Flashback to the end of Scene Five.

Perch   Let me touch you there. I want to. Pretty girl.

Susan   Rosy is waiting.

Perch   She likes it here. She's made friends. Pretty, pretty girl.

Susan   I need a scotch. With ice.

Perch   I'll get ice.

He exits.

Susan *smells the perfume on the pulse of her wrist.*

Ice machine.

Time: The night of the murder, December 17, 1964.

Eva *stands at the ice machine drinking a Coke.*

Perch *enters carrying a metal ice bucket.*

Eva   Hi.

Perch   Miss Eva.

Eva   I was just changing some bedsheets.

Perch   Uh huh.

Eva   You need yours changed?

Perch   They're fine.

Eva   Haven't been wrinkled?

Perch   No. Not yet.

Eva   All clean?

Perch *scoops ice into the bucket.*

Eva   How are things with your wife?

Perch   Fine.

Eva   Do you expect to get back with her?

Perch   If she will have me.

Eva   I think she won't.

Perch   Why not?

Eva   I heard—

Perch   What?

She takes a piece of ice from his bucket and sensually glides it across her mouth.

Eva   Different things, on different occasions. Over periods of time.

Perch   Such as?

Eva   Mrs. Perch is filing divorce papers on you.

Perch   Who said?

Eva   Rosy.

Perch   Rosy?

Eva   She thought you knew.

Perch   No. I did not know.

Eva   You need fresh towels? I could give you extra.

He walks away with the ice.

Eva *slings the ice cube back into the ice machine.*

She exits.

Motel room.

Susan *sits on the edge of the bed charged with sensuality.* **Perch** *enters with the ice.*

Perch   Ice.

Susan   Yes.

Perch *puts ice in a glass and pours in the scotch. He hands her a glass.*

Susan   Thank you.

She takes a sip and looks at him with flirtatious nervousness.

I don't think I should stay. I feel . . . Maybe I should go? How silly. I'm demurring once again.

Perch   Alright. Have your drink and go home.

Susan   Well. Merry Christmas.

Perch   I've thought it over. Given it thought. I'm better off here. I can't make it work. The marriage. I'm not made for marriage. That is the bold and naked truth.

Susan   You told me it would work out.

Perch   I had that wrong.

Susan   You fooled me.

Perch   Fooled myself.

Susan   What are we going to do?

Perch   Aren't you filing for divorce?

A moment between them.

Susan   I spoke with an attorney.

Perch   What attorney?

Susan   Tom Royals.

Perch   Tom Royals. He's first-rate. So what did you tell Tom Royals about me? About our lives?

Susan   Nothing. I just wanted some information.

Perch   What information?

Susan   He said you'd have to support us. Provide for us.

Perch   Haven't I done that? Christ, I've always provided for my family! You don't have to go to Tom Royals to find that out! Did you file papers? Huh?

Susan   . . .

Perch   I believed things could work out but they can't.

Susan   Do you love me?

Perch   Does it matter? It doesn't matter.

Susan   We're leaving. I'll get Rosy and we're going home.

Perch   Tell Rosy Merry Christmas.

Susan   Son of a fucking bitch.

She exits.

Perch *goes to a drawer, pulls out a brown bottle of morphine, and drinks from it. He exits into the bathroom.*

Bar/restaurant.

Rosy *is playing with the figures in the manger scene.* **Fred** *is smoking and watching her.*

Susan *enters.*

Susan (*continued*)   Rosy, we're leaving.

Rosy   Yes, ma'am.

Susan   I'm divorcing your father.

Rosy   Don't. She doesn't mean it. Please don't! Mama, please don't get divorced!

Susan   Poor Rosy. Poor Rosy. I hope sometimes she'll die young of something so she won't have to be in this world. It's not her world. It's a world some people do well in because somehow they imagine to think they are doing something, something, something. Climb a mountain because it's there. Kneel down and pray to a victim of torture nailed to a cross along with others. Not even on his own, along with others.

Handing **Rosy** *her bag.*

Susan   You drive. I can't drive.

Rosy   Please, don't get divorced! Mama, please don't! Please! / I beg you, Mama! Please!

Susan (*overlapping from /*)   STOP IT! STOP IT RIGHT NOW. ROSY, STOP!

Rosy   Yes, ma'am.

Susan   Please. Let's don't take ourselves so seriously.

Susan *and* **Rosy** *exit.*

Motel room.

Perch *enters from the bathroom with a tank of nitrous oxide and a mask.*

He inhales the gas. This is not his first hit.

He laughs and reels around.

Perch (*singing, perhaps*)   Rudolph too red nosed rain beer. Very shiny nose. Shiny red nose. Nose shiny red. Shiny, shiny. Nose. Red *all* red.

Eva *knocks on the motel room door.*

Eva   Dr. Perch?

Perch   Miss Eva?

Eva   I brought you some extra towels.

Perch   Whatever you got! Bring it in! I need it. Whatever you got.

Eva *enters with towels. Aghast she drops the towels.*

Rosy *appears on stage wearing her coat. She addresses the audience.*

Rosy   My parents did things they should not have done.

There were no reasons.

They say things happen for *reasons*. But the *reasons* are not real. It's just the swamp you're living on that pulls you under.

Under weeds, wet grass, mud. Lifetimes of rot and blood, lynched blood, buried in Mississippi soil.

How it pulls through the nerves in my mouth. I keep my mouth closed and push it back down.

September. Algebra. I'll try out for the drill team.

Sound of running water moves us from Scene Seven to Scene Eight.

Scene Eight

Motel room.

Time: September, 1964.

Eva *inadvertently reveals* **Fred's** *guilt to* **Rosy.**

Sound of running water continues.

Perch *sits on the edge of the bed filing his nails. He talks to* **Rosy** *who is brushing her teeth in the bathroom.*

Perch   Brush three minutes. Three full minutes on the clock.

Rosy (*offstage*)   Yes, sir.

Perch   How do you like school so far?

Rosy (*offstage*)   Fine.

Perch   What grade are you in?

Rosy (*offstage*)   Eleventh.

Perch *picks up a flier that is with* **Rosy***'s schoolbooks.*

Perch   You ought to try out for the drill team this year. The Murrah Misses. I'd come watch the game, see you at half-time.

Rosy (*offstage*)   Yes, sir.

Sound of water stops. **Rosy** *enters from the bathroom with a toothbrush. She wears school clothes.*

Rosy   That was four minutes I brushed my teeth.

Perch   Good. How's your mother?

Rosy   She says things are fine.

Perch   Things are fine. Anybody asks you tell them things are fine.

Rosy   I do.

Perch   Did she get the flowers I sent? The roses?

Rosy   Yes, sir.

Perch   I send them every Monday so she'll have them for the week. I hope she likes them.

Rosy   She likes them.

Perch   Your mother likes flowers. But she has difficulties. I know she'll come around. Things are going to be fine. You tell her I help you with your homework?

Rosy   Yes, sir. She's glad because she can't do algebra.

Perch   Do you have any algebra for homework?

Rosy   Yes, sir.

He takes the paper and studies it.

Perch   I can help you. Hand me a pencil.

She hands him a pencil. Throughout the following he writes answers handily.

Perch   I always made good grades. That's why I could become a dentist. A professional. My brother Jim could not cut it. Daddy always let him know he had let him down. Mothers forgive your failures but if you're a man's son, he sees you as a reflection. I've always looked good in my father's eyes. Bright. Impressive. Jim did not make the grade. Daddy tried but could not instill in him the simple principle that privileges must be earned. "Every *right* must be *balanced* by an accompanying *responsibility*."

She has heard this many times before and joins in with him on "an accompanying responsibility."

Perch   Maybe someday Jim would have been able to find his way. But he's gone now. We won't ever know about that. Have they got you in remedial math?

He returns the completed page of algebra to her.

Rosy   No, sir.

Perch   How are your grades?

Rosy   Fine.

Perch   Someday you'll be out of the ugly duckling phase.

Rosy   I know.

Eva *knocks on the door.*

Eva   I got the fan, Dr. Perch.

Perch   Thank you, Miss Eva.

Eva *enters with a fan.*

Rosy *goes and sits on the bed.*

Perch   Always feels like it will cool off in September. But it seems just to get hotter.

Eva   I'll set it up here.

Perch   The heat does still.

Eva   Y'all hear the news?

Perch   What news?

Eva   That old nigger got a stay of execution. Doesn't make sense to spare his life a day longer. They got the nigger that done it.

Perch   What negro?

Eva   The one robbed that Texaco station and shot the lady cashier. I never knew you could stay a nigger's execution.

Perch   Negro.

Eva   Nigra.

Perch   Knee-grow.

Eva   Doesn't matter what you call 'em. Ain't nothing gonna make 'em white.

Perch   Well . . . it is hot. The heat does still.

He heads for the door.

Rosy   Where are you going?

Perch   Get something out of the car.

He exits.

Eva   Your daddy's cute. Always so well groomed. Thing is the nigger's old and blind. Could die in the jail if they don't gas him fast. The law has *got* to stop monkeying around. Murder happened back in April. Now some Yankee's coming down here making appeals to the court. Got the law out hunting new evidence.

She plugs in the fan.

Running out investigating innocent white people out of prejudice, pure prejudice 'cause they sick of having all them coloreds filling up the jail. Want some white suspects for a change. Fred ought to be clear of all suspicion. He has an alibi. An airtight alibi.

Rosy   About what? What, Eva? What alibi?

Eva *goes to* **Rosy**.

Eva   They came here inquiring about his whereabouts concerning the night the cashier woman got robbed and killed. Some passerby saw a car looked like Fred's driving off after shots was heard. Got three numbers off the license plate that matched Fred's. Which was nothing but circumstantial coincident.

Fred let them know he was nowhere near that situation. He was with me, his fiancée and no one else.

I swore to them it was all the truth. They took me in for questioning. Deposited me in front of a whole line of fancy rich men in suits with their secretaries. I had to tell the truth about me and Fred, what we were doing that night the cashier got shot. All of it was none of their business. It involved sexual relations. You might not know about that.

Rosy   I know what it is.

Eva   They didn't spare my modesty in any way. Everything. Every *detail*. Even told them that after the sexual relations I got up and went to the bathroom to douche out the seed. Did it three times for safety. I didn't like revealing that private information. I wanted people to believe I was a virgin. Pure and unsoiled till my wedding day. / But the truth is the truth and God will forgive me. Every Sunday I ask Jesus to forgive me. Forgive me, Jesus, for every breath I take. He has to do it— forgive me. That's all He was born for. Every Sunday I get His forgiveness. Regular, like a bowel movement.

She gives **Rosy** *a superior look.*

Rosy *clutches her skin. A shudder runs through her.*

Eva *turns the electric fan on high. It is loud and blows on her forcefully.*

Eva   In the end they will execute that nigger in a gas chamber. All alone but with spectators. I'd like to see it. I'd look at him with pity. Christian pity. It wouldn't be hate.

Rosy   Oh Lord.

Scene Nine

Bar/restaurant.

Time: November 1964, afternoon.

The day **Bill Perch** *did something bad to his patient Phil Boone.*

Fred *is smoking behind the bar. The red tip of his cigarette burns.*

Susan *enters.*

Susan   Hello, Fred.

Fred   Nice to see you, Mrs. Perch. Scotch with ice.

Susan   Yes.

He gives her a drink.

Thank you. Have you seen Dr. Perch?

Fred   Not this day.

Susan   I called his room. He wasn't there. He's not at the office. Maybe he is somewhere off . . . doing something.

Fred   On a chore.

Susan   He's not coming home. I believe he's not.

Fred   You mean Dr. Perch?

Susan   No, I don't know who I mean.

Fred   Oh. You looking forward to Thanksgiving, Mrs. Perch?

Susan   Yes. Are you?

Fred   Yes, ma'am.

Susan   Thinking about a turkey or a goose?

Fred   Goose.

Susan   I like your tattoo. Strawberries and a black snake. Where did you get it?

Fred   Gulfport.

Susan   Are you from around here?

Fred   Yes, ma'am. Born and raised outside of Meridian. How about yourself?

Susan   I was born at St. Dominic's Hospital right here in Jackson.

Fred   I went away for a time. Went traveling. I was a performer for a time. But I came back here after all.

Susan   I'll end my days here. I don't want to, but I will.

Fred   Have you thought of going somewhere?

Susan   Nowhere to go. Where would I go? There's nowhere to go.

Fred   Some place.

Susan   Really it's nice here. It's familiar.

Fred   Sure.

Susan   I'm happy to live in Mississippi. I hear outside this state, it's very different. People are not genuine.

Fred   This particular region has a lot to offer. Many good things.

Susan   The magnolia. The dogwoods.

Fred   This state invented the portable electric chair.

Susan   Really?

Fred   No other state had one. We were the first. Had it custom-built in Memphis. Folks were loath to give up hanging because it allowed the criminal to be executed right there in the place where he had committed his crime and been convicted. With the portable electric chair the tradition of geographical retribution could be maintained.

Susan   I see.

Fred   'Course now we have the gas chamber. It's not portable. Stays up at the Parchman Penitentiary. There was a good deal of opposition from the people of Sunflower County. They did not want all the evil blood in the state spilled on their land alone.

Susan   I understand their reluctance. I'd feel the same.

Fred   Yes, ma'am.

Susan   But it must be more humane? Less painful? The gas chamber.

Fred   First fellow they put in was low-dosed. Took him forty-five ugly minutes to die. They try to prevent that now by testing the chamber on an animal before they bring in the man. Cats, rabbits. Could be a dog. Anything breathing.

Susan   My you have quite a store of knowledge concerning our system of capital punishment.

Fred   It's a subject that interests me. I'm revealing myself to you. Do you mind?

Susan   No.

Fred   I think about it. I think even if they had the cyanide dose exactly correct, I'd rather be hung from a tree than die choking on poison strapped down in a box.

Susan   I hate living here. There's something in the humidity that makes me perspire drops of blood.

Swirling her finger in the glass of melting ice.

The water has melted. I mean the ice, the ice has melted. Water cannot melt. It evaporates or someone drinks it or bathes in it. Something happened with my husband. I heard it at the garden club. My husband loves his job more than anything else; he takes pride . . . He is a painless dentist. I'm not feeling well. Of all things. I'd better have my check.

Fred   I'll put it on your husband's room.

Susan   Very kind and gracious of you, Fred. The people here, in this state, they're kind. Why would anyone ever want to leave?

Fred   They don't.

As **Susan** *stands to leave,* **Perch** *enters disheveled. He is messed up on liquid morphine but maintaining.*

Perch   Susan, what are you doing here?

Susan   Having a drink.

Perch   Would you like another? We'll have scotch. But he knows that. Fred's peripheral vision is keen. How are you?

Susan   Very well.

Perch   Good. I hope it gets colder by Thanksgiving. I like a frost in the air.

Fred *serves their drinks in silence.*

Susan   Today I was at my garden club . . .

Perch   Green thumb. Thumbs. Both of your thumbs are green.

Susan   I heard something awful.

Perch   People are always running their mouths. It's nice to be a dentist. You don't have to listen to people going on and on. They can't talk with a drill down their throat.

Susan   No, no, no, no drill. Your patient, Phil Boone—nothing happened today, did it? This man, Phil Boone, his teeth? A patient you had today?

Perch   Phil Boone? He's fine. Let me explain. I made an error in judgment. There need to be more precautions in dentistry. Some safeguards.

Susan   What safeguards?

Perch   In the future, devices will be invented and errors will be a thing of the past. There may be accidents but not errors. No deliberate errors.

Susan   Bill, are you . . .?

Perch   What? Yes? Is there a question?

Susan   Could they take your license?

Perch   My dental license? Where did you hear that? Dentistry is the meat and potatoes of my goddamn life.

Susan   I was concerned about our livelihood. How you would provide for us?

Perch   I'll always provide for you. You're my wife.

Susan   I don't have anyone else but you.

Perch   I know you don't.

Susan   You still have your parents. Both of them.

Perch   Don't tell them about this.

Susan   I won't.

Perch   They'd be upset for no reason. They only want me to succeed.

Susan   Well, you do. You always succeed. You always do. I feel whirly, of all things. I need to go home and lie down.

Perch   I'll take you. Let me.

Susan   No. It's better when you are gone. Easier. A fresher smell all around. You need to stay here. At the Jacksonian.

She exits.

Perch   I worry about her nature. She can be cruel. Say things no one could mean.

He takes a brown bottle of morphine from his pocket.

Fred *brings* **Perch** *a second scotch.*

Perch *displays the bottle of morphine to* **Fred**.

Perch   Morpheus. God of oblivion.

He drinks from the bottle.

Susan had an operation. A hysterectomy. She blames me, even though Dr. Carpenter believed it was a necessity. I try to get along but there are times . . . I hit her. It may have been more than once. Most men in their right minds would not be able to stop themselves. They would not.

Rosy *is revealed. She wears her coat unbuttoned.*

Rosy   He's not coming home.

I believe he's not.

Fred *exits.* **Perch** *exits.*

Rosie   The swamp is rising to cover us all.

Another fire bomb in Meridian.

I don't let time go but it goes.

It pulls forward to the night of murder.

And I am released.

I want to get it over. Hurt me now, get it over.

Like Patsy Cline in the song.

Singing:

"If you've got leaving on your mind. Tell me now, get it over. Hurt me now get it over. If you got leaving on your mind."

Scene Ten

Time: The night of the murder, December 17, 1964.

Motel room.

Lights come up on **Eva** *strutting around the room in her undergarments. She is lit on alcohol and cocaine.*

Eva   Don't you just love people who have fun with their bodies? Those are the people you want to be with. People who love showing off because it's a whirlwind of pleasure.

Perch *enters from the bathroom carrying his medicine kit. His shirt is unbuttoned and his pants are falling down. Throbbing cocaine numbness has overtaken him.*

Eva   All these things! You got these things! All these things!

She feels her breasts, ass, mouth, and crotch.

Don't hide! Don't hunch your shoulders! Have fun with your body! Look how it jiggles! Once I was nothing like this. I had to *learn*! I had to *learn* to be natural. They don't teach you that at school.

Perch   No, they don't.

Eva   Hey.

Perch   Yeah?

Eva   Fred is dying. Did you know Fred is dying?

Perch   No.

Eva   I hope I live a *long* time. It's the only time I have not to be in hell. Would you marry me?

Perch   I don't think I would. But could I do something to you?

Eva   What?

Perch   I'd like to look inside your mouth. Put my hands into your mouth.

Eva   Why would you do that?

Perch   I miss it.

Eva   What?

Perch   The mouth.

Eva   Ain't you a dentist?

Perch   Yes, I am. Let me see inside your mouth.

Eva   Only if you'll marry me.

Perch   Alright, that's a deal.

Eva   Yeah! I'm getting married! My fiancé.

Perch   Now stay still just a minute. Let me feel the lips. Upper, lower, vermilion border. Full of nerve endings, blood vessels, erogenous outside organ. Real strong, real flexible muscles.

He moves her mouth with his fingers.

Just a beautiful range of motion.

He lets go and talks to her in a soothing voice as he puts on a latex glove and removes dental tools from the medical kit.

Now please, Miss White, relax, please. There is nothing to be afraid of. This procedure will be completely painless. Now I'm going to need for you to open up your mouth. Wider, please. Wider. Good.

She opens her mouth wide.

He feels inside her mouth.

Fine-looking tongue. Grand whale of the mouth. Powerful muscles—able to emerge and reemerge into this phantasmagorical maw—the mouth. / Wider. That's good. Here they are, the beauties, the teeth. Every one has a mind of its own. A particular design and function. Grind, pierce, cut, chew. Tear.

He moves her jaw with his hand.

You have a slight malocclusion.

Eva   What?

Perch   The teeth in your upper and lower jaw don't meet properly.

Eva   My teeth meet properly.

Perch   I could fix it for you.

Eva   No!

She pours herself a scotch.

Perch   Painlessly. With anesthesia. An-esthesia, an-esthesia. A Greek word. "An" for without. "Esthesia" for sensibility. Without sensibility. Wouldn't you like that? To be without sensibility?

Eva   I don't even have a dentist.

He snorts cocaine.

Perch   I'm a terrific dentist. Painless. I like to make people smile. My own daddy won't smile. Has bad teeth, terrible gums, severe halitosis which leads to social awkwardness. / I've implored him but he won't let me touch his teeth.

Gingivitis has spread to the supporting structures, causing irreparable damage to his mouth. / He's a good man, my father. Tried to instill values in me and my brother. He always told us, "*Every* right must be *balanced* by an accompanying *responsibility.*"

Eva   Oh yeah! Yeah, yeah. "With rare exceptions people of other backgrounds simply cannot comprehend the Anglo-Saxon principle of Equal Justice under the Law and the fact that *every* right must be *balanced* by an accompanying *responsibility.*" "Get out your Bible and pray! You will hear from us!" That's another part of the leaflet.

Perch   What leaflet?

Eva   The one for the KKK.

Perch   What my daddy said—what he said wasn't from any goddamn leaflet. It's an aphorism. An original aphorism.

Eva   No, it's from the KKK leaflet.

Perch   You don't know basically shit, Eva.

She makes a "K" sound and mimes shooting a machine gun.

Eva   K-K-K-K!

He opens a drawer and retrieves a brown bottle of morphine. He drinks from the bottle. She pulls him toward her.

Eva   I got a good memory for things said out loud. I can recite for you whole passages from the Bible. Psalm 63, "Oh God, thou art my God; early will I seek thee: my soul thirsteth for thee, my flesh longeth for thee in a dry and thirsty land, where no water is."

The phone rings. She goes to answer it.

"To see thy power and thy glory."

Picking up the phone.

Hello? . . . Yeah, he's right here . . . Oh, hi, Mrs. Perch . . . I had to deliver towels. Clean sheets . . . She hung up.

Perch   Susan?

Eva   Your wife.

Perch   What did she say?

Eva   "Is this Dr. Perch's room . . . Is that you, Eva? . . . Why are *you* in my husband's room?"

Perch   Oh God, God, God. Things have gotten—they are going down the hill. She's divorcing me. Susan. She is.

He inhales nitrous oxide.

I can see why. I tried to adjust to the professional life—be a good husband and father. I seem like a friendly man. But I stopped going along with the program. Phil Boone— but before that—other things—chloroform—before that . . . Phil Boone had a smell like dead skin and garbage. Came in with an impacted third molar. He was hurting, throbbing. Whole side of his mouth swollen with fever, infection. Didn't like showing his weakness. / Started in claiming to be in on bombing the negro church in Meridian. Bragged he lit the match. / I thought I'd give him some ether to help with the pain of extraction. He kept removing the mask, kept talking, telling me it was time to dynamite the synagogue, go blow up the rabbi's house. / I prepared a shot of Sodium Pentothal because he needed to go under the wire. I take in some of the nitrous oxide to lighten my mood.

He snorts cocaine.

And I pulled out all of his teeth! The molars, the fangs, central and lateral incisors. I'm used to blood on my hands, on my smock. A lot of blood comes from the mouth. It's full of veins. / My secretary, Miss Burwell, helped me clean up. I explained it was an emergency. The teeth were life threatening and had to be extracted or Mr. Boone's chances of survival were some percent that wasn't much. I couldn't stop laughing. / She never came back, Miss Burwell.

Although she did call Mrs. Boone to come pick up her husband.

It took a while for the lawyers and dentist examiners to get their ducks in a row. Now things have gotten bad. I've been hoping for some deus ex machina. Allowing the winds of oblivion to prevail. Oblivion. Has a good smell. Smells like chloroform. Ever tried it? Chloroform?

He opens a bottle of chloroform and pours some on a towel.

Eva   What will it do to me?

Perch   It can be lethal, cause brain impairment, insanity, visions, extreme dizziness. Chloroform comes with risks but it does stop sensibility.

Eva   Alright. Dr. Perch. My fiancé.

Breathing in the chloroform he holds over her mouth and nose.

It's sweet.

Perch   Breathe in deep.

Eva It's strong. It makes me feel . . .

She breathes in more and more chloroform. She staggers and dances around.

La-day, laa-daay—la, la, la, la . . . day.

She keels over. He looks at her. He shakes her.

Perch Eva. You in there?

She shakes her head, confused.

Chloroform is something you should never probably do.

He gets the ice bucket and dumps ice over her.

Eva Shit! That's fucking cold!

He takes the cloth of chloroform and inhales deep and hard.

Perch I got into the chloroform this past summer. Staying at the Jacksonian. Breathing in chloroform made me forget I should worry. I never ought to have let it happen. You know it's wrong but you want to do it more than you know it's wrong. And there is a second—static white noise—and the action has occurred and you did not choose to do or not do it. I feel at home in fog. Life makes sense.

White noise. Zigzag of lights. Time passes . . .

Scene Eleven

Ice machine.

Time: The night of the murder, December 17, 1964.

Wearing a mink coat over her nightgown, **Susan** *stands at the ice machine holding a crystal whiskey glass half-filled with scotch. She opens the lid, claws out pieces of ice, and drops them into her glass. The lid slams down.*

Bar/restaurant.

Fred *is cleaning up around the bar/restaurant.*

Rosy *enters wearing pajamas and wrapped in a blanket.*

Rosy Mama told me to wait in the car. She didn't want to leave me at home where someone might kill me.

Motel room.

Susan *is banging on the door.*

Eva *has passed out.* **Perch** *is in a stupor.*

Susan   Open the door, Bill! Bill, let me in! It's Susan! Your wife! Son of a bitch—bastard!

Perch *tries to dress himself and hide evidence of debauchery.*

Susan   How dare you shut me out! I know you're in there! I hear you in there! Who else is there?! Some whore?! You have a whore!

She kicks and bangs on the door.

I'll kick down this door! Open the door! Fucking please! Let me in!

Perch *drags a practically unconscious* **Eva** *to the bathroom.* **Eva** *struggles a little and says something unintelligible but he dumps her inside and half shuts the door.*

Susan   I'm your wife! I'm your wife! I'm your wife!

Perch *opens the door.*

Susan *enters.*

Perch   Susan.

Susan *looks at him. She sees all of the bizarre paraphernalia.*

Susan   God. What? What is this?

Perch   Things are easier without me.

Susan *opens the bathroom door. She sees* **Eva.** *She steps into the bathroom.*

Susan *(offstage)*   Is she dead?

Perch   No.

Susan *(offstage)*   What's wrong with her?

Perch   I believe she has been over-served.

Susan *(offstage)*   Ohmygod. God!

Susan *sobs from the bathroom.* **Perch** *listens to her. He dresses himself with strange detachment. Sound of water rushing from the sink.*

Bar/restaurant.

Rosy *sits at a table. She is still.*

Fred   I'm wondering, Rosy, if you are dehydrated?

Rosy   I'm thirsty.

Fred   I could see it.

He brings her a glass of water.

Here's some water.

She doesn't drink.

Fred Pinch your skin. If it stays up like a wall, it means you are dehydrated.

She doesn't respond. He pinches her arm.

Fred No. You're not dehydrated.

Rosy Don't pinch my skin.

Fred It was just a test to see if you were dehydrated.

She pinches her skin. It does not stand up like a wall.

Rosy I'm not dehydrated.

Fred No.

He goes behind the bar and pours himself a drink.

Rosy My parents . . .

Fred What?

Rosy My parents are divorcing.

Fred Yeah.

Rosy Fred?

Fred Huh?

Rosy I'll go away with you. Soon if you want.

Fred Go where? I'm not going.

Rosy You're going. To save your own skin. You should take me away and I would never return.

Fred Your folks would be upset. They would miss you.

Rosy Because I was gone, they would miss me in their minds.

Because I was gone. Would you give me the ring?

Fred What ring?

Rosy The one you gave Eva.

Fred I don't have it.

Rosy I know you have it. I know where you got it from.

Fred Where?

Rosy From the Texaco lady. Off her ring finger.

We'll use the money you stole that night. All the money, where you killed the cashier. Where you shot her in the throat.

Fred What did Eva tell you?

Rosy   Nothing. I surmised it. I see through people. Involuntarily. Even when I shut my eyes.

Fred   Maybe we could go somewhere. To greener pastures.

Rosy   My parents are divorcing and then I'll be deserted. I won't be deserted. Take me away and I will not talk and tell anyone—what you have done.

Fred   You really want to go with me?

Rosy   Yeah.

He watches her from behind the bar.

Fred   Come here, Rosy. I want you to come here behind the bar and let me show you something.

Rosy   What?

Fred   Don't ask what. Just come here.

She stands.

Leave the blanket. If you really want me to take you away, you have to trust me.

She removes the blanket and walks up to the bar.

I've got something for you. Right here. But you have to come back here to get it. Come on.

She goes behind the bar.

Rosy   What?

Fred   I've got a ring for you.

*He gives her the same ring he gave **Eva** earlier.*

Rosy   That's nice. I've always wanted something around my finger.

Fred   Good.

She puts the ring on her finger and pulls it off; puts it on, off, on.

Rosy   I like putting my finger in this little gold hole.

Fred   Rosy?

Rosy   Yeah?

Fred   Do you really want to be with me? Go away with me?

Rosy   And never return.

Fred   Prove to me you want to be with me. Show me. Feel this right here.

He exposes himself to her.

Rosy   No.

Fred   Just touch it with your finger. Go on. Do it, Rosy. I want you to.

She lightly touches him.

Rosy   There.

Fred   Hold it. It's different than you think.

Rosy   We'll go away?

Fred   To greener pastures. A place you won't recognize. Now take all of it in your hand.

She holds him for three beats then lets go.

Rosy   There, I did it.

Fred   How did it feel?

Rosy   Like an animal born too soon.

Fred   Rosy—

She moves away from him. She comes from behind the bar and goes to get her blanket.

Rosy   Fred . . .

Fred   What?

Rosy   After you kill me, don't take back the ring.

A moment between them.

Fred   I won't kill you. Of course I won't. You know that. I'm not like that. I'm good.

Sound of water rushing.

Motel room.

Perch *files his nails.* **Susan** *'s crying is subsiding. The sound of running water stops.*

Susan *enters from the bathroom wiping tears off her face with the arm of her fur coat.*

Susan   This is sick. All of it.

Perch   I agree.

Susan   What is she doing here?

Perch   The things people do.

Susan   Were you intimate with her?

Perch   I looked into her mouth.

Susan   You're trash. Why did I marry into trash? Motherfucking trash!

She goes to attack him.

He hits her, almost for the sport of it. She gasps with pain.

All you do—you hurt people! You are a people hurter! That's why they took your dental license away. To stop you from hurting people.

Perch   I'm a good dentist. That's the one thing I can swear is true. I'm a good dentist.

Susan   You're not *allowed* to be a dentist. Everyone knows. They've dismantled you and you're not a dentist. You're not allowed to dispense toothpaste, hand out toothpicks in a box! You have failed in every way a man can fail!

She slings the Christmas tree in his direction.

I'm divorcing you. I'm divorcing you because you have nothing to provide! / You provide nothing.

Perch (*overlapping from /*)   What do you provide? Parasite! Leech. Living off me, all this time—Sucking my blood.

Susan   There's no blood to suck! Grown man can't support his family. Your KKK daddy's sending you checks.

Perch   That's lies.

Susan   You're lies. Full of hate like him.

Grabbing a sheet.

Here's your sheet! Join the lynching! Be like your daddy!

Join the KKK!

She slings a bedsheet over his head.

Throughout the following **Perch** *removes the sheet and douses it with chloroform.*

Susan   Kill, bomb, tie an engine block to the body and throw it in the swamp! Let the terror—the terror.

He grabs her. She struggles to get away. He shakes her violently.

Susan   Purify our blood . . . Rosy . . . Rosy . . .

He covers her face with the sheet soaked in chloroform and strangles her.

He bangs her head against the wall. Three times. The last time very hard.

She stops struggling and goes limp.

He removes the sheet. Her head is bleeding.

He holds her in his arms a moment.

Perch   You're fine. Just fine. Wake up. Susan. Baby. Pretty girl. Tell me something.

He sits her up.

Susan   Hot. Thirsty. Hot.

Perch   Let's get you out of this coat. It's too hot. There.

He partly removes her coat.

Yes. Better?

Susan   Thirsty. Water.

He reaches for the empty ice bucket. He gets up and exits to the ice machine.

Susan   Water. Please. Water.

Lights up on ice machine.

Time: Return to beginning scene of the play.

Perch *stands by the ice machine. He has blood on his hands and shirt. He pulls down the ice handle. Ice crashes out of the machine.*

Lights up on motel room.

Susan *is still. She feels the blood on her head. She says something we cannot understand.*

Rosy *enters the motel wearing the blanket.*

Rosy   Mama? What happened?

Susan   Thirsty.

Thirsty . . . Water.

Rosy   Daddy.

She exits.

Susan   Water . . .

Her movements are discombobulated. Like an insect that has been almost killed but not quite.

She says something we cannot understand.

Scene Twelve

Sound of sirens. Red lights flood across the sky. Chaotic noise of police cars, ambulances arriving.

Rosy *enters wearing the blanket.*

Rosy   The time is . . . It's not Christmas. It's near around before—before Christmas. A murder happened. At the motel. The Jacksonian Motel.

Daddy called the authorities to come.

I gave the police the filling-station lady's ring. But it was too late.

Fred ran off. He disappeared

Eva lost her mind to the chloroform.

Mama died alone in the room. Daddy is in jail waiting on the gas chamber.

For a long time I knew my father was in trouble and my mother was not well, still I wanted to be together in the family.

If tonight did not happen I expect we could work things out. We'd make an effort. A sincere effort. And things would be changed. There still would be time.

Lights up on ice machine.

Time: June 1964, day.

Rosy *and* **Perch** *have a fine day.*

Perch *enters with a 7UP and a Coke. He opens the drinks at the ice machine.*

Perch   Rosy, I've got your 7UP! You need a drink on this hot day. Cool you off, Little Buddy.

Rosy *enters wearing shorts. She seems younger and lighter than we have seen her throughout the play.*

Rosy   Yes, sir, thank you.

He hands her the bottle of soda.

Perch   It's going to be the Fourth of July soon enough. It will be nice to see some fireworks.

Rosy   Will you come home for the Fourth of July?

Perch   Do you want me home?

Rosy   Yes.

Perch   Good

Rosy   Back when I was real little you—

Perch   What?

Rosy   Do you remember at the zoo?

Perch   The Jackson zoo?

Rosy   I was looking down at the rhinoceroses and my hat fell off my head. You jumped over the wall to get it.

Perch   I don't believe I would jump in a wild animal pit.

Rosy   You did. Mama screamed. I thought a rhinoceros would gut you. But you climbed up the wall of dirt and hauled yourself out of the pit. People were cheering you because you had risked your life to save my hat.

Perch   Well, it's possible. It's entirely possible.

Rosy   I remember—back when I was little.

Perch   . . .

Rosy   Are you coming home?

Perch   Yes.

Rosy   When?

Perch   Maybe today.

Rosy   Good.

Perch   Maybe today.

Rosy   Today.

End of Play.

Introduction to Paula Vogel

Aimée K. Michel

Though Paula Vogel finally achieved the recognition that was due her with a 1998 Pulitzer Prize for her 1997 drama *How I Learned to Drive*, she had been pushing the boundaries of the American theater for over two decades with provocative, fiercely honest, witty works of theater.

Born in Washington, DC, in 1951 during the postwar baby boom to a Catholic mother and a Jewish father, Vogel was one of three children, who included her brothers Carl and Mark. Her family life in suburban Baltimore, and particularly her relationship to Carl, were to inform many of her plays.

It was Carl who encouraged her to attend college, and Vogel began her studies at Bryn Mawr College eventually completing her BA at The Catholic University of America in 1974. She then attended Cornell University to study theater arts and earned an MA in 1976. She quickly distinguished herself in playwrighting, winning the Forbes Herman and George McCalmon playwriting competition for both *The Swan Song of Sir Henry* and *A Woman for All Reasons*, consecutively in her first two years. An expanded, full-length version of *Woman* was newly titled *Meg* and won the American College Theater Festival's National Student Playwriting Award in 1977. Years later, in 2003, ACTF established the Paula Vogel Award in Playwrighting.

Vogel also began teaching playwriting and dramatic literature at Cornell while pursuing her doctorate. Her commitment to teaching and mentorship at the same time that she pursued an active career as a working playwright led her to Brown University where she taught generations of young American playwrights from 1984 to 2008 while helping to found the Brown/Trinity Rep Consortium with then artistic director Oscar Eustis. She left Brown in 2008 to join the faculty at Yale School of Drama as the Eugene O'Neill Professor of Playwriting, heading the Playwriting program as well as serving as playwright in residence at the Yale Repertory Theater.

In a 2002 interview on *Women in Theatre*, Vogel describes to host Linda Winer her "cockroach theory" which is that if someone lets her in the door, she will bring ten playwrights in with her. Indeed, the many students from her classes and workshops writing for the American theater today include award winners Bridget Carpenter, Adam Bock, Sarah Ruhl, Nilo Cruz, Lynn Nottage, and Quiara Alegria Hudes.

After two decades of writing plays which boldly expressed female sexuality, giving voice to older, sexually active women such as the prostitutes in *The Oldest Profession* (1981) and to lesbian women in committed relationships wanting to have children of their own in the highly imaginative and theatrical *And Baby Makes Seven* (1984), Vogel finally gained critical recognition and success with her 1992 drama *The Baltimore Waltz* which was written out of her profound grief at the death of her brother Carl from AIDS.

For the next five years, Vogel continued to write plays which exposed taboo areas of women's lives and sexuality. *Desdemona, A Play about a Handkerchief* (1993) turns the tables on the *Othello* story by giving us a fuller accounting of the relationship between Emilia and Desdemona and presenting Desdemona as a sexually adventurous woman rather than the meek woman of Shakespeare's tale. In her dark 1997 play *Hot 'N' Throbbing*, she creates a female character who writes powerful sexually explicit material for a living while she is trapped in a violent domestic relationship with her ex-spouse who kills her at the end of the play. The bold theatricality of this play combined with the incendiary subject matter was challenging for producers, and it has never played in New York City.

In 1996 and 1997 Vogel completed *The Mineola Twins* and *How I Learned to Drive*, which she has said were written in tandem, with *The Mineola Twins* being a burlesque version of *How I Learned to Drive*. *The Mineola Twins* is a wacky satire which blatantly explores sexual stereotypes using the age-old theatrical trick of one actress playing two very different characters, in this case identical twins who hold opposing political views. But it was *How I Learned to Drive*, a play that delved into the taboo topics of sexual abuse and incest in a startlingly honest way, that won Vogel the coveted Pulitzer Prize in Drama in 1998. Clearly speaking to the immediate moment of its time, the play won a slate of awards including the Lortel Prize, the Drama Desk Award, the Outer Critics' Circle Award, the New York Drama Critics' Circle Award for Best Play, a second OBIE, and the Susan Smith Blackburn Prize. Vogel claims it was inspired by Nabokov's *Lolita* in the nuanced way in which he presented that story. "To me emotional issues are grey and not black and white . . . You can't just write Lil bit . . . you have to write Peck," she asserted in the *Women in Theatre* interview with Linda Winer. Indeed, it was her authentic portrayal of both characters that gave the play its depth and touched audiences.

Over the next decade, Vogel continued to explore themes of family and relationships, while creating work that was highly experimental and theatrical. In *The Long Christmas Ride Home* (2003), a play about a family of five heading to grandmother's house for Christmas, she uses bunraku puppetry and Japanese music to summon up a redemptive poetic vision. In *A Civil War Christmas* (2008) she weaves carols and traditional American songs with stories of both historical and fictitious figures to portray the Christmas of 1864 when a weary country struggled through the last months of the Civil War. Vogel has professed a love of musical theater, and with this play and her more recent *Indecent*, she masterfully incorporates this element into her theatrical vision. In her 2014 drama *Don Juan Comes Home from Iraq* Vogel collaborated extensively with her director and a company of actors to breathe life into the stories shared with her by Iraq War veterans in writing workshops and conversations. The resulting work is two intermission-less hours of immersion into the surreal world of war and PTSD.

During this decade, recognition from the American theater also continued including the PEN/Laura Pels International Foundation for Theater Award for a playwright in mid-career in 1999, an Award for Literature from the American Academy of Arts and Letters in 2004, and in 2013 Vogel was inducted into the American Theater Hall of Fame. In 2015 Vogel became the first female playwright to have her literary archive included in the Beinecke Rare Book and Manuscript Library's Collection of American Literature at Yale University.

Yet, with these many accolades and a devoted audience, Vogel had still not made it to the pinnacle of the American theater where playwrights get not only more exposure but more money for their work. Finally, in 2017, Vogel had her breakthrough play

Indecent arrive on Broadway, ironically the same spring that one of her most celebrated students, Lynn Nottage, also premiered on the Broadway stage with *Sweat*.

Though *Indecent* seemed to burst on the scene in a poetic spectacle of music, dance, and a dramatic story, it was, in truth, the effort of an eight-year collaboration with director Rebecca Taichman and a two-year journey through workshop productions with the company of actors and musicians. The play, which honestly and poignantly portrayed a sexual love between two women culminating in an intimate kiss, was nominated for three Tony Awards including Best Play and winning for Best Direction of a Play and Best Lighting Design of a Play. It was also nominated as Best Play by the Drama League Award, the Outer Critics Circle Award, and the Drama Desk Award. It was a finalist for the 2016 Edward M. Kennedy Prize for Drama Inspired by American History.

Vogel's early play and first major success *The Baltimore Waltz*, included in this anthology, embodies many stylistic elements which would be further developed through her later body of work: a metaphoric, non-realistic approach to setting; bold female sexuality and the political made personal. Vogel has expressed that this play is a favorite of hers because it invokes her brother Carl's spirit wherever and whenever it is played on a stage. In an interview for the Dramatists Guild Foundation's Traveling Masters Program Vogel said of this play, "It was the first time I looked at theater as a pure expression of emotion; the first time that I tried anything that was that immediate to me." The idea of the framing of the drama came from an invitation Carl made to her over a year before he died. "He wanted to go to Europe and I couldn't afford it and he offered to pay but I didn't want him to do that," she confessed to Winer in the *Women in Theatre* interview. Carl hadn't revealed that he was HIV positive when he proposed the trip so she hadn't realized the depth of the lost opportunity to spend such intimate time with him. Vogel's solution to approaching such intimate, painful material was to not write a play about Carl dying but to write, instead, a play about the missed trip to Europe. "It's a way of sending messages maybe not to the living but a bottle and a cork and you put the letter in and pray that it washes up on shore where the dead reside."

She has also credited the "flashback" nature of the play to Ambrose Bierce's short story "An Occurrence at Owl Creek Bridge" in which a soldier about to hang suddenly imagines he is alive and escaped in the moment between the noose tightening and his neck breaking. In a similar way, Vogel has Anna imagine the entire trip to Europe at the moment of Carl's death. *The Baltimore Waltz* thus becomes a loving sister's fantasy of all that could have been: what if it had been she who was sick and not he; what if we *had* been able to go on a trip together and spend so much quality time with each other? In the poignant drama, Anna contracts ATD (Acquired Toilet Disease), and she and Carl travel frantically trying to find a doctor who can cure it. From a distance of over thirty years, the AIDS crisis which devastated the American theater population of artists in the late 1980s and 1990s seems historical yet the vilification of the gay population, which was hardest hit, continues in our modern political climate and Vogel's play stands strong, reminding us of this ugly undercurrent in American politics.

Striking a deep chord in a community devastated by the AIDS crisis, the play won an OBIE Award, a Pulitzer Prize nomination, and a Guggenheim fellowship for Vogel, and these recognitions identified her as a force to be reckoned with.

The Baltimore Waltz

Paula Vogel

To the memory of Carl—because I cannot sew.

I always saw myself as a surrogate who, in the absence of anyone else, would stand in for him. And even now, when I'm in front of an audience and I feel good, I hearken back to that feeling, that I'm standing in for them.

—*Ron Vawter*
(From *Breaking the Rules*
by David Savran)

Production History

The Baltimore Waltz was workshopped in October–November 1990 at the Perseverance Theatre in Douglas, Alaska, under Molly D. Smith, Artistic Director, and Deborah B. Baley, Producing Director. The production was directed by Annie Stokes-Hutchinson, with sets by Bill Hudson, costumes by Barbara Casement and Kari Minnick, lights by John E. Miller, and sound by Katie Jensen. The cast was as follows:

Anna	Deborah Holbrook
Carl	Rick Bundy
The Third Man/Doctor	Charles Cardwell

The Baltimore Waltz was produced in February 1992 at the Circle Repertory Company in New York City under Tanya Berezin, Artistic Director, and Terrence Dwyer, Managing Director, with a grant from AT&T OnStage. It was directed by Anne Bogart, with sets by Loy Arcenas, costumes by Walker Hicklin, lights by Dennis Parichy, and sound and score by John Gromada. The dramaturg was Ronn Smith. The cast was as follows:

Anna	Cherry Jones
Carl	Richard Thompson
The Third Man/Doctor	Joe Mantello

Playwright's Note

In 1986, my brother Carl invited me to join him in a joint excursion to Europe. Due to pressures of time and money, I declined, never dreaming that he was HIV positive. This is the letter he wrote me after his first bout with pneumonia at Johns Hopkins Hospital in Baltimore, Maryland. He died on January 9, 1988.

As executor of his estate, I give permission to all future productions to reprint Carl's letter in the accompanying program. I would appreciate letting him speak to us in his own words.

The Baltimore Waltz—a journey with Carl to a Europe that exists only in the imagination—was written during the summer of 1989 at the MacDowell Colony, New Hampshire.

—Paula Vogel

March 1987

Dear Paula:

I thought I would jot down some of my thoughts about the (shall we say) production values of my ceremony. Oh God—I can hear you groaning—everybody wants to direct. Well, I want a good show, even though my role has been reduced involuntarily from player to prop.

First, concerning the choice between a religious ceremony and a memorial service. I know the family considers my Anglican observances as irrelevant as Shinto. However, I wish prayers in some recognizably traditional form to be said, prayers that give thanks to the Creator for the gift of life and the hope of reunion. For reasons, which you appreciate, I prefer a woman cleric, if possible, to lead the prayers. Here are two names: Phebe Coe, Epiphany Church; the Rev. Doris Mote, Holy Evangelists. Be sure to make a generous contribution from the estate for the cleric.

As for the piece of me I leave behind, here are your options:

1. Open casket, full drag.
2. Open casket, bum up. (You'll know where to place the calla lilies, won't you?)
3. Closed casket, interment with the grandparents.
4. Cremation and burial of my ashes.
5. Cremation and dispersion of my ashes in some sylvan spot.

I would really like good music. My tastes in these matters run to the highbrow: Fauré's "Pie Jesu" from his *Requiem*, Gluck's "Dance of the Blessed Spirits" from *Orfeo*, "La Vergine degli Angeli" from Verdi's *Forza*. But my favorite song is "I Dream of Jeannie," and I wouldn't mind a spiritual like "Steal Away." Also, perhaps, "Nearer My God to Thee." Didn't Jeanette MacDonald sing that di-vinely in *San Francisco*?

Finally, would you read or have read A. E. Housman's "Loveliest of Trees"?

Well, my dear, that's that. Should I be lain with Grandma and Papa Ben, do stop by for a visit from year to year. And feel free to chat. You'll find me a good listener.

Love,

Brother

Characters

Anna
Carl, *her brother*
The Third Man/Doctor, *who also plays:*

Airport Security Guard	Radical Student Activist
Public Health Official	Concierge
Harry Lime	Munich Virgin
Garçon	Dr. Todesrocheln
Customs Official	and all other parts
The Little Dutch Boy at Age Fifty	

The Baltimore Waltz takes place in a hospital lounge in Baltimore, Maryland.

Production Notes

The lighting should be highly stylized, lush, dark, and imaginative, in contrast to the hospital white silence of the last scene. Wherever possible, prior to the last scene, the director is encouraged to score the production with music—every cliché of the European experience as imagined by Hollywood.

Anna might be dressed in a full slip/negligee and a trench coat. Carl is dressed in flannel pajamas and a blazer or jacket. The stuffed rabbit should be in every scene with Carl after Scene Six. The Third Man should wear latex gloves throughout the entire play.

Scene One

Three distinct areas on stage: **Anna**, *stage right, in her trench coat, clutching the* Berlitz Pocket Guide to Europe; **Carl**, *stage left, wearing pajamas and blazer;* **The Third Man/Doctor**, *in his lab coat, with stethoscope, is center.*

Anna *reads from her book. Her accents are execrable.*

Anna "Help me please." (*Recites from memory.*) Dutch: "*Kunt U mij helpen, alstublieft?*" "There's nothing I can do." French: (*Searches in vain.*) I have no memory. (*Reads from the* Berlitz) "*Il n'y a rien à faire.*" "Where are the toilets?" "*Wo sind die Toiletten?*"

I've never been abroad. It's not that I don't want to—but the language terrifies me. I was traumatized by a junior high school French teacher, and after that, it was a lost cause. I think that's the reason I went into elementary education. Words like brioche, bidet, bildungsroman raise a sweat.

Oh, I want to go. Carl—he's my brother, you'll meet him shortly—he desperately wants to go. But then, he can speak six languages. He's the head librarian of literature and languages at the San Francisco Public. It's a very important position.

The thought of eight-hundred-year-old houses perched on the sides of mountains and rivers whose names you've only seen in the Sunday *Times* crossword puzzles—all of that is exciting. But I'm not going without him. He's read so much. I couldn't possibly go without him. You see, I've never been abroad—unless you count Baltimore, Maryland.

Carl Good morning, boys and girls. It's Monday morning, and it's time for "Reading Hour with Uncle Carl" once again, here at the North Branch of the San Francisco Public Library. This is going to be a special reading hour. It's my very last reading hour with you. Friday will be my very last day with the San Francisco Public as children's librarian. Why? Do any of you know what a pink slip is? (*Holds up a rectangle of pink.*) It means I'm going on a paid leave of absence for two weeks. Shelley Bizio, the branch supervisor, has given me my very own pink slip. I got a pink slip because I wear this. (*He points to a pink triangle on his lapel.*) A pink triangle. Now, I want you all to take the pink construction paper in front of you, and take your scissors, and cut out pink triangles. There's tape at every table, so you can wear them too! Make some for Mom and Dad, and your brothers and sisters. Very good. Very good, Fabio. Oh, that's a beautiful pink triangle, Tse Heng.

Now before we read our last story together, I thought we might have a sing-along. Your parents can join in, if they'd like to. Oh, don't be shy. Let's do "Here We Go Round the Mulberry Bush." Remember that one? (*He begins to sing. He also demonstrates.*) "Here we go round the mulberry bush, the mulberry bush, the mulberry bush / Here we go round the mulberry bush, so early in the morning.

"This is the way we pick our nose, pick our nose, pick our nose / This is the way we pick our nose, so early in the morning."

Third verse! (*He makes a rude gesture with his middle finger.*) "This is the way we go on strike, go on strike, go on strike / This is the way we go on strike, so early in the—"

What, Mrs. Bizio? I may leave immediately? I do not have to wait until Friday to collect unemployment? Why, thank you, Mrs. Bizio.

Well, boys and girls, Mrs. Bizio will take over now. Bear with her, she's personality-impaired. I want you to be very good and remember me. I'm leaving for an immediate vacation with my sister on the East Coast, and I'll think of you as I travel. Remember to wear those pink triangles.

(*To his supervisor.*) I'm going. I'm going. You don't have to be rude. They enjoyed it. We'll take it up with the union. (*Shouting.*) In a language you might understand: Up-pay ours-yay!

Anna   It's the language that terrifies me.

Carl   Lesson Number One: Subject Position. I. *Je. Ich. Ik.* I'm sorry. *Je regrette. Es tut mir leid.*

Anna   But we decided to go when the doctor gave us his verdict.

Doctor   I'm sorry.

Carl   I'm sorry.

Doctor   There's nothing we can do.

Anna   But what?

Carl   How long?

Anna   Explain it to me. Very slowly. So I can understand. Excuse me, could you tell me again?

Doctor   There are exudative and proliferative inflammatory alterations of the endocardium, consisting of necrotic debris, fibrinoid material, and disintegrating fibroblastic cells.

Carl   Oh, sweet Jesus.

Doctor   It may be acute or subacute, caused by various bacteria: streptococci, staphylococci, enterococci, gonococci, gramnegative bacilli, etc. It may be due to other microorganisms, of course, but there is a high mortality rate with or without treatment. And there is usually rapid destruction and metastases.

Carl   Anna—

Anna   I'm right here, darling. Right here.

Carl   Could you explain it very slowly?

Doctor   Also known as Löffler's Syndrome, i.e., eosinophilia, resulting in fibroblastic thickening, persistent tachycardia, hepatomegaly, splenomegaly, serious effusions into the pleural cavity with edema. It may be *Brugia malayi* or *Wuchereria bancofti*—also known as Weingarten's Syndrome. Often seen with effusions, either exudate or transudate.

Anna   Carl—

Carl   I'm here, darling. Right here.

Anna   It's the language that terrifies me.

Scene Two

Carl   Medical Straight Talk: Part One.

Anna   So you're telling me that you really don't know?

Doctor   I'm afraid that medical science has only a small foothold in this area. But of course, it would be of great benefit to our knowledge if you would consent to observation here at Johns Hopkins—

Carl   Why? Running out of laboratory rats?!

Anna   Oh, no. I'm sorry. I can't do that. Can you tell me at least how it was . . . contracted?

Doctor   Well—we're not sure, yet. It's only a theory at this stage, but one that seems in great favor at the World Health Organization. We think it comes from the old cultus ornatus—

Carl   Toilet seats?

Anna   Toilet seats! My God. Mother was right. She always said—

Carl   And never, ever, in any circumstances, in bus stations . . .

Anna   Toilet seats? Cut down in the prime of youth by a toilet seat?

Doctor   Anna—I may call you Anna? You teach school, I believe?

Anna   Yes, first grade. What does that have—

Doctor   Ah, yes. We're beginning to see a lot of this in elementary schools.

Anna—I may call you Anna? With assurances of complete confidentiality, we need to ask you very specific questions about the body, body fluids, and body functions. As mature adults, as scientists and educators. To speak frankly . . . when you needed to relieve yourself . . . where did you make wa-wa?

Anna   There's a faculty room. But why—how—?

Doctor   You never, ever used the johnny in your classroom?

Anna   Well, maybe once or twice. There's no lock, and Robbie Matthews always tries to barge in. Sometimes I just can't get the time to—surely you're not suggesting that—

Doctor   You did use the facilities in your classroom? (*The **Doctor** makes notes from this.*)

Carl   Is that a crime? When you've got to go, you've got to—

Anna   I can't believe that my students would transmit something like this—

Doctor You have no idea. Five-year-olds can be deadly. It seems to be an affliction, so far, of single schoolteachers. School-teachers with children of their own develop an immunity to ATD—Acquired Toilet Disease.

Anna I see. Why hasn't anybody heard of this disease?

Doctor Well, first of all, the Center for Disease Control doesn't wish to inspire an all-out panic in communities. Secondly, we think education on this topic is the responsibility of the NEA, not the government. And if word of this pestilence gets out inappropriately, the PTA is going to be all over the school system demanding mandatory testing of every toilet seat in every lavatory. It's kindling for a political disaster.

Anna (*taking the* **Doctor** *aside*) I want to ask you something confidentially. Something that my brother doesn't need to hear. What's the danger of transmission?

Doctor There's really no danger to anyone in the immediate family. You must use precautions.

Anna Because what I want to know is . . . can you transmit this thing by . . . by doing—what exactly do you mean by precautions?

Doctor Well, I guess you should do what your mother always told you. You know, wash your hands before and after going to the bathroom. And never lick paper money or coins in any currency.

Anna So there's no danger to anyone by . . . what I mean, Doctor, is that I can't infect anyone by—

Doctor Just use precautions.

Anna Because, in whatever time this schoolteacher has left, I intend to fuck my brains out.

Doctor Which means, in whatever time is left, she can fuck her brains out.

Scene Three: Carl and the Doctor

Carl (*agitated*) I'll tell you what. If Sandra Day O'Connor sat on just one infected potty, the media would be clamoring to do articles on ATD. If just one grandchild of George Bush caught this thing during toilet training, that would be the last we'd hear about the space program. Why isn't someone doing something?!

I'm sorry. I know you're one of the converted. You're doing . . . well, everything you can. I'd like to ask you something in confidence, something my sister doesn't need to hear. Is there any hope at all?

Doctor Well, I suppose there's . . . always hope.

Carl Any experimental drugs? Treatments?

Doctor Well, they're trying all sorts of things abroad. Our hands are tied here by the NIH and the FDA, you understand. There is a long-shot avenue to explore, nothing, you understand, that I personally endorse, but there is an eighty-year-old urologist overseas who's been working in this field for some time—

Carl   We'll try anything.

Doctor   His name is Dr. Todesrocheln. He's somewhat unorthodox, outside the medical community in Vienna. It's gonna cost you. Mind you, this is not an endorsement.

Anna   You hear the doctor through a long-distance corridor. Your ears are functioning, but the mind is numb. You try to listen as you swim toward his sentences in the florescent light in his office. But you don't believe it at first.

This is how I'd like to die: with dignity. No body secretions—like Merle Oberon in *Wuthering Heights*. With a somewhat becoming flush, and a transcendental gaze. Luminous eyes piercing the veil of mortal existence. The windows are open to the fresh breeze blowing off the moors. Oh. And violins in the background would be nice, too.

Music: Violins playing Strauss swell in the background.

Scene Four: The Phone Call

The Third Man   Lesson Number Two: Basic Dialogue. The phone call. Hello. I would like to speak to Mr. Lime, please.

Carl   *Entschuldigen Sie, bitte*—operator? Operator? Hello? *Guten Tag*? *Kann ich bitte mit Herr Lime sprechen*? Harry? Harry? *Wie geht es dir*?! Listen, I . . . can you hear . . . no, I'm in Baltimore . . . yeah, not since Hopkins . . . no, there's—well, there is something up. No, dear boy, that hasn't been up in a long time. No, seriously—it's my sister. ATD.

The Third Man   ATD? Jesus, that's tough, old man. You've got to watch where you sit these days. She's a sweet kid. Yeah. Yeah. Wait a second.

(*Offstage.*) Inge? Inge, baby? *Ein Bier*, *bitte*, baby. *Ja. Ja.* You too, baby.

Pause.

Okay. Dr. Todesrocheln? Yeah, you might say I know him. But don't tell anybody I said that. There's also a new drug they've got over here. Black market. I might be able to help you. I said might. But it's gonna cost you.

(*Cautiously, ominously.*) Do you still have the rabbit?

Carl   I'll bring the rabbit.

The Third Man   Good. A friend of mine will be in touch. And listen, old man . . . if anybody asks you, you don't know me. I'll see you in a month. You know where to find me.

The Third Man and Carl (*simultaneously*)   Click.

Scene Five

The Third Man   Lesson Number Three: Pronouns and the Possessive Case. I, you, he, she and it. They and we. Yours, mine and ours.

Voice of Anna   There's nothing I can do. There's nothing you can do. There's nothing he, she or it can do. There's nothing we can do. There's nothing they can do.

Anna   So what are we going to do?

Carl   Start packing, sister dear.

Anna   Europe? You mean it?

Carl   We'll mosey about France and Germany, and then work our way down to Vienna.

Anna   What about your job?

Carl   It's only a job.

Anna   It's a very important job! Head of the entire San Francisco Public—

Carl   They'll hold my job for me. I'm due for a leave.

Anna   Oh, honey. Can we afford this?

Carl   It's only money.

Anna   It's your money.

Carl   It's our money.

Scene Six

The Third Man   Lesson Four: Present Tense of Faire. What are we going to do? *Qu'est-ce qu'on va faire?*

Anna   So what are we going to do?

Carl   We'll see this doctor in Vienna.

Anna   Dr. Todesrocheln?

Carl   We have to try.

Anna   A urologist?

Carl   He's working on a new drug.

Anna   A European urologist?

Carl   What options do we have?

Anna   Wait a minute. What are his credentials? Who is this guy?

Carl   He was trained at the Allgemeines Krankenhaus during the Empire.

Anna   Yeah? Just what was he doing from, say, 1938 to 1945? Research?

Carl   It's best not to ask too many questions. There are people who swear by his work.

Anna   What's his specialty?

Carl   Well, actually, he's a practitioner of uriposia.

Anna   He writes poems about urine?

Carl   No. He drinks it.

Anna   I'm not going.

Carl   Let's put off judgment until we arrange a consultation—my God, you're so messy. Look at how neat my suitcase is in comparison. You'll never find a thing in there.

Anna   I refuse to drink my own piss for medical science.

Carl *grabs a stuffed rabbit and thrusts it in* **Anna**'*s suitcase.*

Anna   What are you doing?

Carl   We can't leave bunny behind.

Anna   What is a grown man like you doing with a stuffed rabbit?

Carl   I can't sleep without bunny.

Anna   I didn't know you slept with . . . stuffed animals.

Carl   There's a lot you don't know about me.

Scene Seven

The Third Man   Lesson Five: Basic Dialogue. At the airport. We are going to Paris. What time does our flight leave? *Nous allons à Paris. A quelle heure depart notre vol?*

The Third Man *becomes an* **Airport Security Guard**.

Airport Security Guard   Okay. Next. Please remove your keys and all other metallic items. Place all belongings on the belt. Next.

Carl *and* **Anna** *carry heavy luggage.* **Carl** *halts.*

Carl   Wait. I need your suitcase.

He opens **Anna**'*s luggage and begins to rummage around.*

Anna   Hey!

Carl   It was a mess to begin with.

Ah . . . (*He retrieves the stuffed rabbit.*) There.

Anna   Are you having an anxiety attack?

Carl   You hold it.

Carl *and* **Anna** *stamp, sit and stand on the baggage.* **Carl** *manages to relock the bag.*

Anna   What is wrong with you?

Carl   X-rays are bad for bunny.

Airport Security Guard   Next. Please remove all metallic objects. Keys. Eyeglasses. Gold fillings.

Carl   Go on. You first.

Airport Security Guard   Metallic objects?

Anna *passes through, holding the stuffed rabbit.* **Carl** *sighs, relieved. He passes through. The* **Airport Security Guard** *stops him.*

Airport Security Guard   One moment, please.

He almost strip-searches **Carl***. He uses a metallic wand which makes loud, clicking noises. Finally, he nods. He hands* **Anna** *and* **Carl** *their bags, still suspiciously looking at* **Carl***.*

Anna   Okay, bunny—Paris, here we come!

Scene Eight

The Third Man   At the hotel.

(*Simultaneously with* **Carl***'s next lines*) Lesson Six: Direct Pronouns. I am tired. And my sister looks at herself in the mirror.

Carl (*simultaneously with* **The Third Man**)   *Sixieme Leçon: Pronoms— Compléments Directs. Je suis fatigué. Et ma soeur elle se regarde dans la glace.*

Carl *climbs into a double bed with the stuffed rabbit.* **Anna** *stares into a mirror.* **The Third Man**, *apart, stands in their bedroom.*

The Third Man   The first separation—your first sense of loss. You were five; your brother was seven. Your parents would not let you sleep in the same bed anymore. They removed you to your own bedroom. You were too old, they said. But every now and then, when they turned off the lights and went downstairs—when the dark scared you—you would rise and go to him. And he would let you nustle under his arm, under the covers, where you would fall to sleep, breathing in the scent of your own breath and his seven-year-old body.

Carl   Come to bed, sweetie. Bunny and I are waiting. We're going to be jet-lagged for a while.

Anna (*continues to stare in the mirror*)   It doesn't show yet.

Carl   No one can tell. Let's get some sleep, honey.

Anna   I don't want anyone to know.

Carl   It's not a crime. It's an illness.

Anna   I don't want anybody to know.

Carl   It's your decision. Just don't tell anyone . . . what . . . you do for a living.

Anna *joins* **Carl** *in the bed. He holds her hand.*

Anna   Well, there's one good thing about traveling in Europe . . . and about dying.

Carl   What's that?

Anna   I get to sleep with you again.

Scene Nine

Carl   Medical Straight Talk: Part Two.

The Third Man *becomes a* **Public Health Official.**

Public Health Official   Here at the Department of Health and Human Services we are announcing Operation Squat. There is no known cure for ATD right now, and we are acknowledging the urgency of this dread disease by recognizing it as our eighty-second national health priority. Right now ATD is the fourth major cause of death of single schoolteachers, ages twenty-four to forty—behind school buses, lockjaw, and playground accidents.

The best policy, until a cure can be found, is of education and prevention.

Anna *and* **Carl** *hold up posters of a toilet seat in a circle with a red diagonal slash.*

Public Health Official   If you are in the high-risk category—single elementary schoolteachers, classroom aides, custodians, and playground drug pushers—follow these simple guides.

Anna *and* **Carl** *hold up copies of the educational pamphlets.*

Public Health Official   *Do*: Use the facilities in your own home before departing for school.

Do: Use the facilities in your own home as soon as you return from school.

Do: Hold it.

Don't: Eat meals in public restrooms.

Don't: Flush lavatory equipment and then suck your digits.

If absolutely necessary to relieve yourself at work, please remember the Department of Health and Human Services' ATD slogan: Don't sit, do squat!

Scene Ten

Music: Accordion playing a song like "La Vie en rose."

Anna *and* **Carl** *stroll.*

Carl   Of course, the Left Bank has always been a haven for outcasts, foreigners, and students, since the time that Abelard fled the Île de La Cité to found the university here.

Anna   Oh, look. Is that the Eiffel Tower? It looks so . . . phallic.

Carl   And it continued to serve as a haven for the avant-garde of the twenties, the American expatriate community that could no longer afford Montparnasse.

Anna   My God, they really do smoke Gauloise here.

Carl   And, of course, the Dada and Surrealists who set up camp here after World War I and their return from Switzerland—

The Third Man, *in a trench coat and red beret, crosses the stage.*

Anna   Are we being followed?

Carl   Is your medication making you paranoid?

Pause.

Now, over here is the famous spot where Gertrude supposedly said to her brother Leo—

The Third Man *follows them.*

Anna   I know. "God is the answer. What is the question?"—I'm not imagining it. That man has been trailing us from the Boulevard St. Michel.

Carl   Are you getting hungry?

Anna   I'm getting tired.

Carl   Wait. Let's just whip around the corner to the Café St. Michel where Hemingway, after an all-night bout, threw up his shrimp heads all over Scott's new suede shoes—which really was a movable feast.

The Third Man *is holding an identical stuffed rabbit and looks at them.*

Anna   Carl! Carl! Look! That man over there!

Carl   So? They have stuffed rabbits over here, too. Let's go.

Anna   Why is he following us? He's got the same—

Carl   It's your imagination. How about a little déjeuner?

Anna *and* **Carl** *walk to a small table and chairs.*

Scene Eleven

Garçon (*with a thick Peter Sellers French accent*)   It was a simple bistro affair by French standards. He had le veau Prince Orloff, she le boeuf à la mode—a simple dish of haricots verts, and a médoc to accompany it all. He barely touched his meal. She mopped the sauces with the bread. As their meal progressed, Anna thought of the lunches she packed back home. For the past ten years, hunched over in the faculty room at McCormick Elementary, this is what Anna ate: on Mondays, pressed chipped chicken sandwiches with mayonnaise on white; on Tuesdays, soggy tuna sandwiches; on Wednesdays, Velveeta cheese and baloney; on Thursdays, drier pressed chicken on the now stale white bread; on Fridays, Velveeta and tuna. She always had a small wax envelope of carrot sticks or celery, and a can of Diet Pepsi. Anna, as she ate in the bistro, wept. What could she know of love?

Carl   Why are you weeping?

Anna   It's just so wonderful.

Carl   You're a goose.

Anna   I've wasted over thirty years on convenience foods.

The **Garçon** *approaches the table.*

Garçon   Is everything all right?

Anna   Oh God. Yes . . . yes—it's wonderful.

Carl   My sister would like to see the dessert tray.

Anna *breaks out in tears again. The* **Garçon** *shrugs and exits. He reappears a few minutes later as* **The Third Man**, *this time with a trench coat and blue beret. He sits at an adjacent table and stares in their direction.*

Anna   Who is that man? Do you know him?

Carl (*hastily looks at* **The Third Man**)   No, I've never seen him before.

The Third Man *brings the stuffed rabbit out of his trench coat.*

Anna   He's flashing his rabbit at you.

Carl (*rises*)   Excuse me. I think I'll go to les toilettes.

Anna   Carl! Be careful! Don't sit!

Carl *exits.* **The Third Man** *waits a few seconds, looks at* **Anna**, *then follows* **Carl** *without expression.*

Anna   What is it they do with those rabbits?

A split second later, the **Garçon** *reenters with the dessert tray.* **Anna** *ogles him.*

Garçon   Okay. We have *la crème plombière pralinée, un bavarois à l'orange, et ici* we have *une Charlotte Malakoff aux framboises.* Our *specialité* is *le gâteau de crêpes à la Normande.* What would mademoiselle like?

Anna *has obviously not been looking at the dessert tray.*

Anna (*sighing*)   Ah, yes.

Garçon (*smiles*)   *Vous êtes américaîne*? This is your first trip to Paris?

Anna   Yes.

Garçon   And you do not speak at all French?

Anna   No.

The **Garçon** *smiles.*

Garçon (*suggestively*)   Bon. Would you like *la specialité de la maison*?

Scene Twelve

Carl   Exercise: *La carte. La specialité de la maison.*

Back at the hotel, Anna sampled the Garçon's *specialité de la maison* while her brother browsed the Louvre.

Anna *and the* **Garçon** *are shapes beneath the covers of the bed;* **Carl** *clutches his stuffed rabbit.*

Carl   Jean Baptiste Camille Corot lived from 1796 to 1875. Although he began his career by studying in the classical tradition, his later paintings reveal the influence of the Italian style.

Anna (*muffled*)   Ah! Yes!

Garçon (*also muffled*)   Ah! Oui!

Carl   He traveled extensively around the world, and in the salon of 1827 his privately lauded techniques were displayed in public.

Anna   Yes—oh, yes, yes!

Garçon   *Mais oui!*

Carl   Before the Academy had accepted realism, Corot's progressive paintings, his clear-sighted observations of nature, revealed a fresh, almost spritely, quality of light, tone and composition.

Anna   Yes—that's right—faster—

Garçon   *Plus vite?*

Anna   Faster—

Garçon   *Encore! Plus vite!*

Anna   Wait!

Garçon   *Attends?*

Carl   It was his simplicity, and his awareness of color that brought a fresh wind into the staid Academy—

Garçon   *Maintenant?*

Anna   Lower—faster—lower—

Garçon   *Plus bas—plus vite—plus bas—*

Carl   He was particularly remembered and beloved for his championing the cause of younger artists with more experimental techniques, bringing the generosity of his advancing reputation to their careers.

Anna   Yes—I—I—I—I—!

Garçon   *Je—je! Je! Je!*

Pause.

Carl   In art, as in life, some things need no translation.

Garçon   Gauloise?

Carl   For those of you who are interested, in the next room are some stunning works by Delacroix.

Scene Thirteen: Back at the Hotel

Carl   Lesson Seven: Basic Vocabulary. Parts of the Body.

Carl, *slightly out of the next scene, watches them.*

Anna *sits up in bed. The* **Garçon** *is asleep beneath the sheet.*

Anna   I did read one book once in French. *Le Petit Prince.* Lying here, watching him sleep, I look at his breast and remember the rose with its single, pathetic thorn for protection. And here—his puckered red nipple, lying poor and vulnerable on top of his blustering breast plate. It's really so sweet about men.

She kisses the **Garçon**'s *breast. The* **Garçon** *stirs.*

Garçon   *Encore?*

Anna   What is the word—in French—for this? (*She fingers his breast.*)

Garçon   For *un homme: le sein.* For *une femme: la mamelle.*

Anna   *Le sein?*

Garçon   *Oui. Le sein.*

Anna (*she kisses his neck*)   And this?

Garçon   *Le cou.*

Anna   *Et ici?*

Garçon   *Bon. Décolleté.*

Anna *begins to touch him under the sheet.*

Anna   And this?

The **Garçon** *laughs.*

Garçon   *S'il vous plâit* . . . I am tickling there. Ah. *Couille.*

Anna   *Culle?*

Garçon   *Non. Couille. Le cul* is something much different. *Ici c'est le cul.*

Anna   Oh, yes. That's very different.

Garçon (*taking her hand under the sheet*)   We sometimes call these also *Le Quatrième État.* The Fourth Estate.

Anna   Really? Because you press them?

Garçon   *Bien sûr.*

Anna   And this?

Garçon (*with pride*)   Ah. *Ma Tour Eiffel.* I call it *aussi* my *Charles de Gaulle.*

Anna   Wow.

Garçon   My grandfather called his *Napoléon.*

Anna   I see. I guess it runs in your family.

Garçon (*modestly*)   *Oui. Grand-mère—qu'est-ce que c'est le mot en anglais?* Her *con—*here—*ici—*do you know what I am meaning?

Anna   You're making yourself completely clear.

Garçon   We called hers the *Waterloo de mon grand-père—*

Anna (*digs under the sheet more*)   And this?

Garçon (*scandalized*)   *Non.* There is no word *en français. Pas du tout.*

Anna   For this? There must be—

Garçon   *Non!* Only the Germans have a word for that.

Carl *enters and casually converses with* **Anna***. Startled, the* **Garçon** *covers himself with the sheet.*

Carl   Hello, darling. Are you feeling better?

He walks to the chair beside the bed and removes the **Garçon***'s clothing.*

Anna   Yes, much. I needed to lie down. How was the Louvre?

The **Garçon** *carefully rises from the bed and takes his clothing from* **Carl***, who is holding them out. He creeps cautiously stage left and begins to pull on his clothes.*

Carl   Oh, Anna. I'm so sorry you missed it. The paintings of David were amazing. The way his paintbrush embraced the body—it was just incredible to stand there and see them in the flesh.

Anna   Ah yes—in the flesh. (*She smiles at the confused* **Garçon**.)

Carl   Well, sweetie. It's been a thoroughly rewarding day for both of us. I'm for turning in. How about you?

The **Garçon** *is now fully dressed.*

Anna   Yes, I'm tired. Here—I've warmed the bed for you. (*She throws back the sheet.*)

Carl   Garçon—*l'addition*!

Anna (*to the* **Garçon**)   *Merci beaucoup.*

Anna *blows him a kiss. The* **Garçon** *takes a few steps out of the scene as* **Carl** *climbs into bed.*

Scene Fourteen

The Third Man   Anna has a difficult time sleeping. She is afflicted with night thoughts. According to Elizabeth Kübler-Ross, there are six stages the terminal patient travels in the course of her illness.

The First Stage: Denial and Isolation.

The Third Man *stays in the hotel room and watches* **Carl** *and* **Anna** *in the bed. They are sleeping, when* **Anna** *sits upright.*

Anna   I feel so alone. The ceiling is pressing down on me. I can't believe I am dying. Only at night. Only at night. In the morning, when I open my eyes, I feel absolutely well—without a body. And then the thought comes crashing in my mind. This is the last spring I may see. This is the last summer. It can't be. There must be a mistake. They mixed the specimens up in the hospital. Some poor person is walking around, dying, with the false confidence of my prognosis, thinking themselves well. It's a clerical error.

Carl! I can't sleep. Do you think they made a mistake?

Carl   Come back to sleep.

He pulls **Anna** *down on the bed to him, and strokes her brow.*

They change positions on the bed.

The Third Man   The Second Stage: Anger.

Anna (*sits bolt upright in bed, angry*)   How could this happen to me! I did my lesson plans faithfully for the past ten years! I've taught in classrooms without walls—kept up on new audio-visual aids—I read Summerhill! And I believed it!

When the principal assigned me the job of the talent show—and nobody wants to do the talent show—I pleaded for cafeteria duty, bus duty—but no, I got stuck with the talent show. And those kids put on the best darnn show that school has ever seen! Which one of them did this to me? Emily Baker? For slugging Johnnie MacIntosh? Johnnie MacIntosh? Because I sent him home for exposing himself to Susy Higgins? Susy Higgins? Because I called her out on her nose-picking? Or those Nader twins? I've spent the best years of my life giving to those kids—it's not—

Carl   Calm down, sweetie. You're angry. It's only natural to be angry. Elizabeth Kübler-Ross says that—

Anna   What does she know about what it feels like to die?!

Elizabeth Kübler-Ross can sit on my face!

Carl *and* **Anna** *change positions on the bed.*

The Third Man   The Third Stage: Bargaining.

Anna   Do you think if I let Elizabeth Kübler-Ross sit on my face I'll get well?

Carl *and* **Anna** *change positions on the bed.*

The Third Man   The Fourth Stage: Depression.

Carl (*sits on the side of the bed beside* **Anna**)   Anna . . . honey—come on, wake up.

Anna   Leave me alone.

Carl   Come on, sweetie . . . you've been sleeping all day now, and you slept all yesterday. Do you want to sleep away our last day in France?

Anna   Why bother?

Carl   You've got to eat something. You've got to fight this. For me.

Anna   Leave me alone.

Carl *lies down beside* **Anna**. *They change positions.*

The Third Man   The Fifth Stage: Acceptance.

Anna *and* **Carl** *are lying in bed, awake. They hold hands.*

Anna   When I'm gone, I want you to find someone.

Carl   Let's not talk about me.

Anna   No, I want to. It's important to me to know that you'll be happy and taken care of after . . . when I'm gone.

Carl   Please.

Anna   I've got to talk about it. We've shared everything else. I want you to know how it feels . . . what I'm thinking . . . when I hold your hand, and I kiss it . . . I try to memorize what it looks like, your hand . . . I wonder if there's any memory in the grave?

The Third Man   And then there's the Sixth Stage: Hope.

Anna *and* **Carl** *rise from the bed.*

Carl   How are you feeling?

Anna   I feel good today.

Carl   Do you feel like traveling?

Anna   Yes. It would be nice to see Amsterdam. Together. We might as well see as much as we can while I'm well—

Carl   That's right, sweetie. And maybe you can eat something—

Anna   I'm hungry. That's a good sign, don't you think?

Carl   That's a wonderful sign. You'll see. You'll feel better when you eat.

Anna   Maybe the doctor in Vienna can help.

Carl   That's right.

Anna   What's drinking a little piss? It can't hurt you.

Carl   Right. Who knows? We've got to try.

Anna   I'll think of it as . . . European lager.

Carl   Golden Heidelberg.

Carl *and* **Anna** *hum/sing the drinking song from* The Student Prince.

Scene Fifteen

The Third Man   And as Anna and Carl took the train into Holland, the seductive swaying of the TEE-train aroused another sensation. Unbeknownst to Elizabeth Kübler-Ross, there is a Seventh Stage for the dying. There is a growing urge to fight the sickness of the body with the health of the body.

The Seventh Stage: Lust.

Anna *and* **Carl** *are seated in a train compartment.* **Carl** *holds the stuffed rabbit out to* **Anna.**

Anna   Why?

Carl   Just take it. Hold it for me. Just through customs.

Anna   Only if you tell me why.

Carl   Don't play games right now. Or we'll be in deep, deep do-do.

Anna *reluctantly takes the stuffed rabbit and holds it.*

Anna   You're scaring me.

Carl   I'm sorry, sweetie. You're the only one I can trust to hold my rabbit. Trust me. It's important.

Anna   Then why won't you tell me—?

Carl   There are some things you're better off not knowing.

Anna   Are you smuggling drugs? Jewels?

Carl (*whispers*)   It's beyond measure. It's invaluable to me.

That's all I'll say.

(*In a louder tone.*) Just act normal now.

Customs Official   *Uw paspoort, aistublieft.*

Anna *and* **Carl** *give him their passports.* **Carl** *is nervous.* **Anna** *smiles at the* **Customs Official** *a bit lasciviously.*

Customs Official   Have you anything to declare?

Anna (*whispering*)   Yes, Captain, I'm smuggling contraband.

I demand to be searched. In private.

Customs Official (*blushes*)   Excuse me?

Anna   Yes. I said—*waar is het damestoilet?*

Customs Official   Oh . . . I thought . . .

The **Customs Official** *giggles.*

Anna   Yes?

Customs Official   First left.

He returns their passports.

Have a very pleasant stay.

Anna *waves bunny's arm goodbye. The* **Customs Official** *looks at her, blushes again, and retreats.* **Carl** *relaxes.*

Carl   You're good at this. Very good.

Anna   When in Holland, do like the Dutch . . . Mata Hari was Dutch, you know.

Scene Sixteen

Carl   *Questions sur le dialogue. Est-ce que les hommes hollandais sont comme les français?* Are Dutch men like the French?

Anna *and* **The Little Dutch Boy at Age Fifty.** *He wears traditional wooden shoes, trousers and vest. His Buster Brown haircut and hat make him look dissipated.*

The Little Dutch boy at Age Fifty   It was *kermis* time, the festival in my village. And I had too much *bier* with my school friends, Piet and Jan. *Ja.* Soo, Piet thought we should go to the outer dyke with cans of spray paint, after the kermis. So we went.

Here in Noord Brabant there are three walls of defenses against the cruelty of the North Sea. The first dyke is called the *Waker*—the Watcher; the second dyke is *de Slaper*—the Sleeper; and the last dyke, which had never before been tested, is known as the *Dromer*—the Dreamer.

And when we got to the Dreamer, Piet said to me: "Willem, you do it." Meaning I was to write on the walls of the Dreamer. This is why I was always in trouble in school—Piet and Jan would say, "Willem, you do it." And whatever it was, I would do it.

Soo, I took up a can of the paint and in very big letters, I wrote in Dutch that our schoolmaster, Mijnheer Van Doorn, was a gas-passer. Everyone could read the letters from far away. And just as I was finishing this, and Piet and Jan were laughing behind me, I looked—I was on my knees, pressed up against the dyke—and I could see that the wall of the Dreamer was cracking its surface, very fine little lines, like a goose egg when it breaks from within.

And I yelled to my friends: Look! And they came a bit closer, and as we looked, right above my head, a little hole began to peck its way through the clay. And there was just a small trickle of water. And Jan said: "Willem, put your thumb in that hole." And by that time, the hole in the dyke was just big enough to put my thumb in. "Why?" I asked of Jan. "Just do it," he said. And so I did.

And once I put my thumb in, I could not get it out. Suddenly we could hear the waves crashing as the Sleeper began to collapse. Only the Dreamer remained to hold off the savage water. "Help me!" I yelled to Jan and Piet—but they ran away. "Vlug!" I cried—but no one could hear me. And I stayed there, crouching, with my thumb stuck into the clay. And I thought what if the Dreamer should give in, too. How the waves would bear my body like a messenger to the village. How no one would survive the flood. Only the church steeple to mark the spot where we had lived. How young we were to die.

Pause.

Have you ever imagined what it would be like to be face to face with death?

Anna   Yes . . . yes I have.

The Little Dutch Boy at Age Fifty   And have you ever prayed for deliverance against all hope?

Anna   I—no. I haven't been able to get to that stage. Yet.

The Little Dutch Boy at Age Fifty   But the Dreamer held. And finally there came wagons with men from the village, holding lanterns and sand and straw. And they found me there, strung up by my thumb, beside the big black letters: *Mijnheer Van Doorn is een gas-passer*. And they freed me and said I was a hero, and I became the boy who held back the sea with his thumb.

Anna   Golly. You were very brave.

The Little Dutch Boy at Age Fifty   I was stupid. Wrong place, wrong time.

Anna   How long ago did this happen?

The Little Dutch Boy at Age Fifty (*sadly*)   Let us just say it happened a long time ago.

Anna   You've faced death. I wish my brother were here to meet you.

The Little Dutch Boy at Age Fifty   Where is he? *Wo ist dein bruder?*

Anna   Oh, he stayed in Amsterdam to see the Rijksmuseum and the Van Gogh Museum.

The Little Dutch Boy at Age Fifty   And you did not go? You should see them, they are really fantastic.

Anna   Why? What's the use? I won't remember them, I'll have no memory.

The Little Dutch Boy at Age Fifty   So you are an American?

Anna   Yes.

The Little Dutch Boy at Age Fifty   So do you want to sleep with me? All the women toeristen want to sleep with the little Dutch boy who put his thumb in the dyke.

Anna   Do you mind so much?

The Little Dutch Boy at Age Fifty (*shrugs*)   *Nee.* It's a way to make a living, is it *niet?*

Anna (*quietly*)   Let's go then.

Scene Seventeen

Carl   *Répétez. En français.* Where is my brother going? *Où va mon frère? Bien.*

Anna   I had just returned from my day trip and left the Centraal Station. The sun sparkled on the waters of the canal, and I decided to walk back to the hotel. Just then I saw my brother.

Carl *enters in a trench coat, sunglasses, holding the stuffed rabbit.*

Anna   I tried to catch up with Carl, dodging bicycles and pedestrians. And then, crossing the Amstel on the Magere Brug, he appeared.

The Third Man *enters, in a trench coat, sunglasses, and with black gloves, holding a stuffed rabbit.*

Anna   I trailed them from a discreet distance.

The Third Man *and* **Carl** *walk rapidly, not glancing at each other.* **Carl** *stops;* **The Third Man** *stops a few paces behind.* **Carl** *walks;* **The Third Man** *walks.* **Carl** *stops;* **The Third Man** *stops. Finally, they face each other and meet. Quickly, looking* *surreptitiously around,* **Carl** *and* **The Third Man** *stroke each other's stuffed rabbits. They quickly part and walk off in opposite directions.*

Anna *rushes to center stage, looking in both directions.*

Anna   I tried to follow the man in the trench coat, and crossed behind him over the Amstel, but I lost sight of him in the crowd of men wearing trench coats and sunglasses.

I want some answers from my brother. Whatever trouble he's in, he has to share it with me. I want some answers back at the hotel. He's going to talk.

Scene Eighteen

Carl   *Questions sur le dialogue.* You must learn. *Sie müssen lernen.*

Anna *enters the empty hotel room. On the bed, propped up on pillows, lies a stuffed rabbit.*

Anna   Carl? Carl? Are you back? Carl?

She stops and looks at the stuffed rabbit.

Carl (*from the side*)   You were not permitted to play with dolls; dolls are for girls. You played with your sister's dolls until your parents found out. They gave you a stuffed animal—a thin line was drawn. Rabbits were an acceptable surrogate for little boys. You named him Jo-Jo.

You could not sleep without him. Jo-Jo traveled with you to the seashore, to the hotel in New York City when you were seven, to your first summer camp.

He did not have the flaxen plastic hair of your sister's Betsey-Wetsy, but he had long, furry ears, soft white on one side, pink satin inside. He let you stroke them. He never betrayed you. He taught you to trust in contact. You will love him always.

Anna (*moves toward the stuffed rabbit*)   My brother left you behind, did he? Alone at last. Okay, bunny, now you're going to talk. I want some answers. What have you got that's so important?

Just as she reaches for the stuffed rabbit, **The Third Man** (*in trench coat, sunglasses, and black gloves*) *steps out into the room.*

The Third Man (*threateningly*)   I wouldn't do that, if I were you.

Anna *screams in surprise.*

The Third Man   Now listen. Where is your brother? I have a message for him. Tell him he's running out of time. Do you understand?

Anna, *scared, nods.*

The Third Man   Good. He'd better not try to dupe us. We're willing to arrange a swap—his sister for the rabbit. Tell him we're waiting for him in Vienna. And tell him he'd better bring the rabbit to the other side.

He disappears. **Anna***, shaken, sits on the bed and holds the stuffed rabbit. She strokes it for comfort.* **Carl** *enters, in a frenzy. He carries his stuffed rabbit.* **Anna** *stares as* **Carl** *tosses the decoy rabbit away.*

Carl   Don't ask me any questions. I can't tell you what's happening. Are you able to travel? Good. We have to leave Amsterdam tonight. There's a train in an hour. We'll go to Germany. Are you packed?

Scene Nineteen

Anna and The Third Man (*simultaneously*)   *Wann fahrt der nächste Zug nach Hamburg?*

German band music swells as **Anna** *and* **Carl** *sit in their railroad compartment, side by side.* **Anna***, pale, holds the stuffed rabbit in her lap.*

Carl   Ah, Saxony, Bavaria, the Black Forest, the Rhineland . . . I love them all. I think perhaps now would be a good time to show the slides.

Anna   I'm so sorry. I hate it when people do this to me.

Carl   Nonsense. People like to see slides of other people's trips. These are in no particular order. We'll only show a few, just to give a taste of the German countryside.

Anna   Carl took over two hour's worth of slides.

Carl   If you'll just dim the lights, please.

The Third Man *wheels in the projector and operates it throughout the travelogue.*

Carl   Well. Bonn's as good a place to start as anywhere. This is the view from our snug little hotel we stayed in. The gateway to the Rhine, the birthplace of Beethoven and the resting place of Schumann.

Slide: The view of downtown Baltimore from the Ramada Inn near Johns Hopkins Hospital, overlooking the industrial harbor.

Anna   Looks a lot like Baltimore to me.

Carl   My sister jests. As you can see in the slide, one night we splurged and stayed in a rather dear inn near the Drachenfels Mountains, where Lord Byron had sported.

Slide: A close-up of the balcony railing looking into the Ramada Inn hotel room.

Anna (*deadpan*)   This is the room I slept in while I stayed with my brother Carl.

Slide: Gutted ruins of inner-city Baltimore near the Jones-Fall Expressway; rubble and obvious urban blight.

Carl   Alas, poor Köln. Practically wiped out by airplane raids during World War II, and yet, out of this destruction, the cathedral of Köln managed to survive—one of the most beautiful Gothic churches in the world, with a superb altar painted by the master artist of Köln, Stefan Lochner.

Slide: An impoverished storefront church, a black Evangelical sect in Baltimore.

Carl   Let's see—what do we have next?

Slide: A Sabrett hotdog cart with its blue and orange umbrella in front of Johns Hopkins Hospital.

Carl   Oh, yes. Let's talk about the food. Whereas I snapped mementos of the regal pines of the Black Forest, Anna insisted on taking photos of everything she ate.

Anna   I can remember things I feel.

Carl   Well, then, let's talk about the food. Germany has a more robust gustatory outlook than the delicate palate of France. The Germans positively celebrate the pig from snout to tail. I could not convince Anna to sample the Sulperknochen, which is a Rheingau concoction of ears, snout, tail, and feet.

Anna   Ugh.

Slide: A close-up of a vendor placing a hotdog on a bun and lathering it with mustard; there are canned sodas in a wide variety.

Carl   And of course, everything is washed down with beer.

*Slide: **Anna** sipping a Bud Light.*

Anna   It was delicious.

Carl   Enough of food. May we talk about culture, sister, dear?

Next slide, please.

Slide: The Maryland National Armory; the state penitentiary.

Carl   Ah, Heidelberg. Dueling scars and castles. Spectacular ruin which serves as the locale for open-air concerts and fireworks . . .

Slide: The Baltimore smokestack.

Carl   And by a quaint cable car, you can reach the peak at Königstuhl, 2,000 feet high, with its breathtaking view of the Neckar Valley.

Slide: The Bromo Seltzer tower in Baltimore.

Slide: The interstate highways viewed from the tower.

Carl   Every cobblestoned street, every alleyway, was so pristine and clean.

Slide: The rowhouses on Monument Street.

Slide: A corridor of Johns Hopkins Hospital, outside the basement laboratories.

Carl   Wasn't it, Anna?

Anna (*deadpan*)   Yes. Sterile.

Slide: A hospital aide washing the floor.

Carl   Even the Black Forest looked swept. We splurged once again and stayed at the Waldhorn Post here, outside of Wildbad.

Slide: Exterior of Johns Hopkins Hospital.

Carl   The hotel dates back to 1145—the chef there is renowned for his game dishes.

Slide: **Anna** *in front of a vending machine dispensing wrapped sandwiches in the Johns Hopkins Hospital cafeteria.*

Anna   I wasn't too hungry.

Carl   I was ravenous.

Slide: Route 95 outside the harbor tunnel; the large toll signs are visible.

Carl   Let's see—the Romantic Road . . . *Die Romantishe Strasse* . . . a trek through picture-book Bavaria and the Allgau Alpen . . . Füssen to Wurzburg.

Anna   Honey, perhaps they've seen enough. It's hard to sit through this many—

Carl   Wait. Just one more. They've got to see Neuschwanstein, built by mad King Ludwig II. It's so rococo it's Las Vegas.

Slide: The castle at Disneyland.

Carl   I believe that Ludwig was reincarnated in the twentieth century as Liberace.

Wait a moment, that's not the castle.

Anna   Yes, it is.

Carl (*upset*)   It looks like—how did that get in here?

Anna   I don't know which castle you're referring to, but it's definitely a castle.

Slide: A close-up of the castle, with a large Mickey Mouse in the picture.

Carl   That's not funny, Anna! Are you making fun of me?

Anna   Don't get upset.

Slide: Donald Duck has joined Mickey Mouse with tourists.

Carl   I went to Europe. I walked through Bavaria and the Black Forest. I combed through Neuschwanstein! I did these things, and I will remember the beauty of it all my life! I don't appreciate your mockery!

Anna   It's just a little—

Carl   You went through Germany on your back. All you'll remember are hotel ceilings. You can show them your Germany!

He rushes off, angry.

Anna   Sometimes my brother gets upset for no apparent reason. Some wires cross in his brain and he—I'm sorry. Lights, please.

The Third Man *wheels the projector offstage.*

Anna   I would like to show you my impressions of Germany. They were something like this . . .

Scene Twenty: In Munich

Anna *is under the sheet beside the* **Munich Virgin**, *who is very young.*

Anna   Are you comfortable?

Munich Virgin   *Ja, ja . . . danke.*

Anna   Good. Have you been the bellhop here for a long time?

Munich Virgin   Not so very long a time. My *vater* owns the hotel, and says I must learn and work very hard. Soon I will be given the responsibility of the front desk.

Anna   My. That's exciting.

Pause.

Are you cold?

Munich Virgin   *Nein.* Just a . . . *klein nervös.* My English is not so very good.

Anna   Is this your first time? You always remember your first time.

Pause.

I'm very honored.

Pause.

Listen. I'm a schoolteacher. May I tell you something? A little lesson? When you're a much older man, and you've loved many women, you'll be a wonderful lover if you're just a little bit nervous . . . like you are right now. Because it will always be the first time.

Munich Virgin   You are a very nice woman.

Anna   The human body is a wonderful thing. Like yours. Like mine. The beauty of the body heals all the sickness, all the bad things that happen to it. And I really want you to feel this. Because if you feel it, you'll remember it. And then maybe you'll remember me.

Scene Twenty-One

Anna *and the* **Munich Virgin** *rise.* **Carl** *gets into the bed with his stuffed rabbit.* **Anna** *gets ready to leave.*

The Third Man   Conjugations of the verb *verlassen.* To leave, to abandon, to forsake. The present tense.

Carl   Are you leaving me alone?

Anna   Yes. Just for a little while. I need to take a walk. I'm restless. It's perfectly safe.

Carl   Okay, sweetie. Don't be too long. Bunny and I are ready for bed.

Anna   I won't stay out long. I'll be right back.

The Third Man   The future tense of the verb *verlassen*.

Carl   Will you be leaving me alone again tonight? I'm ready for bed.

Anna   I will be leaving you alone. Just for a little while.

Carl   Who will it be tonight? The bellhop? The desk clerk? Or the maître d'?

Anna   Don't be mean. You said you didn't make judgments.

Carl   I don't. I just want to spend time with you.

Anna   I'll be back in time for a bedtime story.

The Third Man   The past tense of the verb *verlassen*.

Carl   Again? Again? You went out last night. And the night before.

Anna   I can't help it. I've been a good girl for the past thirty years. Now I want to make up for lost time.

Carl   And what am I supposed to do while you're out traipsing around with every Thomas, Deiter, *und* Heinrich?

Anna   Hug bunny.

The Third Man   There are three moods of the verb *verlassen*: the indicative, the imperative, and the subjunctive. Anna and Carl are never in the same mood.

Carl   Leave me alone.

Anna   Carl, don't be like that.

Carl   Why? It doesn't matter what I want. You are going to leave.

Anna   I never stay out very long.

Carl   All I can say is if this establishment charges us for room service, they've got some nerve—

Anna   I've got to take what opportunities come along—

Carl   I wish you wouldn't go—

Anna   Please understand. I don't have much time. I spend as much time with you as I can, but while I still have my health . . . please?

Scene Twenty-Two

The Third Man   As children they fought.

Carl   We never fought, really.

Anna   Not in a physical way. He was a sickly child.

Carl   She was very willful.

Anna   No roughhousing. But he knew all of my weak points. My secret openings. He could be ruthless.

Carl   She'd cry at the slightest thing.

Anna   He has a very sharp tongue.

Carl   But when one of you is very, very sick, you can't fight. It's not fair. You've got to hold it in. We never fight.

Anna   But we had a doozy in the hotel room in Berlin.

Carl   Well, my God, Anna, even though you're sick, I have the right to get angry.

Anna   We'd been traveling too long. We were cranky. The rooms were closing in.

Carl   I'm just saying that we should spend a little more time together. I don't get to see you alone enough. You're always restless.

Anna   Fine. You go out without me for a change.

Carl   I'm going out for a walk.

Anna (*starting to weep*)   I don't care.

Carl   When she was little, this would be the time I'd bribe her. With a comic book or an ice cream. I always had pennies saved up for these little contingencies.

Anna   But sometimes, for the sake of my pride, I would be inconsolable. I would rush off and then feel just awful alone. Why didn't I take the bribe?

(*To* **Carl**.) I'm going out.

Carl   To fuck?

Anna   No, dear. The passive voice is used to emphasize the subject, to indicate the truth of the generalization. I'm going out. To get fucked.

Scene Twenty-Three

Music: Kurt Weill.

Anna *goes over to a small cabaret table. There is a telephone on the table. The* **Radical Student Activist** *sits at another identical table, smoking, watching her.*

Anna   I'm going to enjoy Berlin without him. I'll show him. I'm going to be carefree, totally without scruples. I'll pretend I've never taught first-graders.

Beat.

I'm going to have a perfectly miserable time.

The **Radical Student Activist** *picks up the telephone. The telephone at* **Anna***'s table rings.*

Anna   Oh my goodness. My miserable time is calling me.

(*Picks up the phone.*) Yes?

Radical Student Activist   Are you alone, Fraülein?

Anna   Well, uh, actually . . . yes, I am.

Radical Student Activist   *Gut. Du willst mal richtig durchgefickt werden, ja?*

Anna   I'm sorry. I don't speak a word of German.

The **Radical Student Activist** *laughs.*

Radical Student Activist   *Ja.* Even better. I said, would you like to get fucked?

Anna   Do you always come on to single women like that?

Radical Student Activist   Would you like it better if I bought you tall drinks with umbrellas? Told to you the stories of how hard a time my parents had during the war? Tell you how exciting I find foreign women, how they are the real women, not like the pale northern *mädchen* here at home? How absolutely bourgeois.

Anna   I see. Why do you come here?

Radical Student Activist   I don't come here for the overpriced drinks. I come here because of the bored Western women who come here, who leave their tired businessmen husbands in the hotel rooms behind.

Anna   You're cute. In a hostile way.

Radical Student Activist   Fucking is a revolutionary act.

Anna   Your hovel or my hotel?

Scene Twenty-Four

In the hotel room. **Anna**, *awake, lies in the middle of the bed. To her left,* **Carl** *sleeps, curled up. To her right, the* **Radical Student Activist**, *curled on her breast, slumbers.*

Anna *is awake with an insomniacal desperation.*

Anna (*singing softly*)   Two and two are four; four and four are eight; eight and eight are sixteen; sixteen and sixteen are thirty-two . . .

Radical Student Activist (*groggy*)   *Wo ist die Toilette?*

He rises and stumbles stage left.

Anna   In lovemaking, he's all fury and heat. His North Sea pounding against your Dreamer. And when you look up and see his face, red and huffing, it's hard to imagine him ever having been a newborn, tiny, wrinkled, and seven pounds. That is, until afterwards. When he rises from sleep and he walks into the bathroom. And there he exposes his soft little derrière, and you can still see the soft baby flesh.

(*As the* **Radical Student Activist** *comes back into the room.*) I've got to put a name to that behind. What's your name? *Wie heissen Sie?*

Radical Student Activist (*starts dressing in a hurry*)   *Auf Wiedersehn.* Next thing you'll ask for my telephone number.

Anna   No, I won't. I was just curious—

Radical Student Activist   *Ja, ja . . . und* then my sign of the zodiac. I'll get cards from Hallmark und little scribblings like "I'll never forget the night we shared."

Anna   Forget it.

Radical Student Activist   There is something radical in two complete strangers committing biological necessity without having to give into bourgeois conventions of love, without breeding to produce workers for a capitalist system, without the benediction of the church, the family, the bosses—

Anna   I have something to confess to you. I lied to you.

Radical Student Activist   About what?

Anna   I'm not here on business. I don't specialize in corporate takeovers. I don't work on Wall Street. I only told you that because I thought that was what you wanted to hear.

Radical Student Activist   Okay. So you do estate planning?

Income tax?

Anna   No. You just committed a revolutionary act with a first-grade schoolteacher who lives in low-income housing. And I'm tired. I think you should go.

Radical Student Activist   And your husband?

Anna   Not too loud. And he's not my husband. He's my brother.

A maiden librarian for the San Francisco Public.

(*As the* **Radical Student Activist** *starts to leave.*) And by the way—the missionary position does not a revolution make.

The **Radical Student Activist** *leaves.* **Anna**, *depressed, lies down.* **Carl** *rises from the bed.*

Scene Twenty-Five

Carl   And as she lay in the bed, sleepless, it swept over her—the way her classroom smelled early in the morning, before the children came. It smelled of chalk dust—

The Third Man   It smelled of Crayola wax, crushed purple and green—

Carl   The cedar of hamster cage shavings—

The Third Man   The sweet wintergreen of LePage's paste—

Carl   The wooden smell of the thick construction paper—

The Third Man   The spillings of sticky orange drink and sour milk—

The Third Man and Carl (*simultaneously*)   And the insidious smell of first-grader pee.

Carl   It smelled like heaven.

Anna   And the first thing I did each morning was put up the weather map for today on the board under the flag. A bright, smiling sun or Miss Cloud or Mr. Umbrella. On special days I put up Suzy Snowflake. And when I opened my desk drawer, scattered like diamonds on the bottom were red, silver and gold stars.

Beat.

I want to go home. Carl, I want to go home.

Carl   Soon, sweetie. Very soon.

Anna   I've had enough. I've seen all of the world I want to see. I want to wake up in my own bed. I want to sit with you at home and we'll watch the weather. And we'll wait.

Carl   We've come so far. We have to at least go to Vienna. Do you think you can hold out long enough to meet Dr. Todesrocheln?

Anna, *miserable and homesick, nods.*

Carl   That a girl. I promise you don't have to undertake his . . . hydrotherapy unless you decide to. I have a friend in Vienna, a college chum, who might be able to get us some black-market stuff. It's worth a shot.

Anna   Then you'll take me home?

Carl   Then I'll take you home.

Scene Twenty-Six

Music: A song such as the zither theme from The Third Man.

Carl *and* **Anna** *stand, with their luggage, in front of a door buzzer.*

Carl   First we'll just look up Harry. Then we'll cab over to Dr. Todesrocheln.

He rings the buzzer. They wait. He rings the buzzer again. They wait. An aging **Concierge** *comes out.*

Carl   *Entschuldigung. Wir suchen* Harry Lime? Do you speak English?

Concierge   *Nein. Ich spreche kein Englisch.*

Carl *and the* **Concierge** *start to shout as if the other one was deaf.*

Carl   Herr Lime? Do you know him? Herr Harry Lime?

Concierge   *Ach. Ach. Ja*, Herr Harry Lime. You come . . . too *spät*.

Carl   He's gone? Too *spät*?

Concierge   *Fünf minuten too spät. Er ist tot—*

Carl   What?

Concierge   *Ja. Ein auto mit Harry splatz-machen auf der Strasse. Splatz!*

Anna   *Splatz*!?

Carl   *Splatz*?!

It dawns on **Carl** *and* **Anna** *what the* **Concierge** *is saying.*

Concierge   *Ja, ja. Er geht über die Strasse, und ein auto . . . spppllllaattz!*

Anna   Oh, my God.

Concierge (*gesturing with hands*)   *Ja. Er hat auch eine rabbit. Herr rabbit auch—spplllaattz!* They are . . . *diggen ein grab in den Boden. Jetz.*

Carl   Now? You saw this happen?

Concierge   *Ja.* I . . . saw it *mit meinen* own *Augen. Splatz.*

(*As he exits.*) *Splatzen, splatzen, über alles . . .*

Carl   Listen, darling. I want you to take a cab to the doctor's office.

Anna   Where are you going?

Carl   *Ich verlasse.* I'll find out what happened to Harry.

Anna   I wish you wouldn't leave . . .

Carl   I'll come back. Okay?

Scene Twenty-Seven

Anna *climbs onto a table and gathers a white paper sheet around her. She huddles.*

Anna   Some things are the same in every country. You're scared when you see the doctor, here in Vienna just like in Baltimore. And they hand you the same paper cup to fill, just like in America. Then you climb up onto the same cold metal table, and they throw a sheet around you and you feel very small. And just like at home, they tell you to wait. And you wait.

As she waits, dwarfed on the table, the scene with **Harry Lime** *and* **Carl** *unfolds. Music, such as* The Third Man *theme, comes up.*

Scene Twenty-Eight: On the Ferris Wheel in the Prater

Carl *holds the stuffed rabbit closely.*

Carl   Why are we meeting here?

Harry Lime   Have you looked at the view from up here? It's quite inspiring. No matter how old I get, I always love the Ferris wheel.

Carl   I just came from your funeral.

Harry Lime   I'm touched, old man. Was it a nice funeral?

Carl   What are you doing?

Harry Lime   It's best not to ask too many questions. The police were beginning to do that. It's extremely convenient, now and then in a man's career, to die. I've gone underground. So if you want to meet me, you have to come here. No one asks questions here.

Carl   Can you help us?

Harry Lime *at first does not answer. He looks at the view.*

Harry Lime   Where is your sister? She left you alone?

Carl   She's—she needs her rest. You were my closest friend in college.

Harry Lime   I'll be straight with you. I can give you the drugs—but it won't help. It won't help at all. Your sister's better off with that quack Todesrocheln—we call him the Yellow Queen of Vienna—she might end up drinking her own piss, but it won't kill her.

Carl   But I thought you had the drugs—

Harry Lime   Oh, I do. And they cost a pretty penny. For a price, I can give them to you. At a discount for old times. But you have to know, we make them up in my kitchen.

Carl   Jesus.

Harry Lime   Why not? People will pay for these things. When they're desperate people will eat peach pits or aloe or egg protein—they'll even drink their own piss. It gives them hope.

Carl   How can you do this?

Harry Lime   Listen, old man, if you want to be a millionaire, you go into real estate. If you want to be a billionaire, you sell hope. Nowadays the only place a fellow can make a decent career of it is in Mexico and Europe.

Carl   That's . . . disgusting.

Harry Lime   Look. I thought you weren't going to be . . . sentimental about this. It's a business. You have to have the right perspective. Like from up here . . . the people down on the street are just tiny little dots. And if you could charge a thousand dollars, wouldn't you push the drugs?

I could use a friend I can trust to help me.

Carl   When we were at Hopkins together, I thought you were God. You could hypnotize us into doing anything, and it would seem . . . charming. "Carl, old man," you'd say, "just do it." Cutting classes, cribbing exams, shoplifting, stupid undergraduate things—and I would do it. Without knowing the consequences. I would do it.

The Third Man   Oh, you knew the consequences, old man. You knew. You chose not to think about them.

Carl   I've grown old before my time from the consequences, I'm turning you in.

Harry Lime   I wouldn't do that, old man.

(*Pats a bulge on the inside of his trench coat.*) By the time you hit the ground, you'll be just a tiny little dot. (**Carl** and **Harry Lime** *look at each other, waiting.*)

Harry Lime   And I think you have something I want. The rabbit, *bitte.*

Carl   No. You're not getting it. I'm taking it with me.

Harry Lime *puts his arms in position for a waltz and begins to sway, seductively.*

Harry Lime   Come on, give it up. Come to my arms, my only one. Dance with me, my beloved, my sweet—

Carl *takes the stuffed rabbit and threatens to throw it out the window of the Ferris wheel. A Strauss waltz plays very loudly, and* **Harry Lime** *and* **Carl** *waltz-struggle for the rabbit.* **Carl** *is pushed and* **Harry Lime** *waltzes off with the rabbit.*

Scene Twenty-Nine: Meanwhile, Back at Dr. Todesrocheln

Anna   You begin to hope that the wait is proportionate to the medical expertise.

My God. My feet are turning blue. Where am I? An HMO?

Waits.

The problem with being an adult is that you never forget why you're waiting. When I was a child, I could wait blissfully unaware for hours. I used to read signs and transpose letters, or count tiles in the floor. And in the days before I could read, I would make up stories about my hands—Mr. Left and Mr. Right.

Beat.

(*Demonstrates.*) Mr. Left would provoke Mr. Right. Mr. Right would ignore it. The trouble would escalate, until my hands were battling each other to the death.

Beat.

Then one of them would weep. Finally, they became friends again, and they'd dance.

Her two hands dance together. She is unaware that **Dr. Todesrocheln** *has entered and is watching her. He clears his throat. He wears a very dirty lab coat with pockets* *filled with paper and a stale doughnut. He wears a white fright wig and glasses. He also wears one sinister black glove. With relish, he carries a flask of a golden liquid.*

Anna   Oh, thank goodness.

Dr. Todesrocheln   *Ja.* So happy to meet you. Such an interesting specimen. I congratulate you. Very, very interesting.

Anna   Thank you.

Dr. Todesrocheln   We must have many more such specimens from you—for the urinocryoscopy, the urinometer, the urinoglucosometer, the uroacidimeter, uroazotometer, *und mein* new acquirement in *der laboratorium—ein* urophosphometer.

Anna   My goodness.

Dr. Todesrocheln *has put the flask down on a table. Quietly, his left hand reaches for it; the right hand stops the left.*

Dr. Todesrocheln   *Ja.* Nowadays, we have learned to discover the uncharted mysteries of the fluids discharged through the urethra. We have been so primitive in the past. Doctors once could only analyze by taste and smell—but thanks to the advancement of medical science, there are no limits to our thirst for knowledge.

Anna   Uh-huh.

Dr. Todesrocheln's *left hand seizes the flask. Trembling, with authority, his right hand replaces the flask on the table, and soothes the left hand into quietude.*

Dr. Todesrocheln   So much data has been needlessly, carelessly destroyed in the past—the medical collections of Ravensbruck senselessly annihilated—and that is why as a scientist, I must be exacting in our measurements and recordings.

Anna   What can I hope to find out from these . . . specimens?

Dr. Todesrocheln   Ah, yes—the layman must have his due! Too much pure research und no application makes Jack . . . *macht* Jack . . . (*Loses his train of thought.*)

Fraülein Anna—I may call you Fraülein Anna? Let us look at the body as an alchemist, taking in straw and mud *und schweinefleisch* and processing it into liquid gold which purifies the body. You might say that the sickness of the body can only be cured by the health of the body. To your health!

His left hand seizes the flask in a salute, and raises the flask to his lips. In time, the right hand brings the flask down. A brief struggle. It appears the flask might spill, but at last the right hand triumphs.

Anna   You know, even though I really grew up in the suburbs of Baltimore, I like to think of myself as an open-minded person—

Dr. Todesrocheln   The ancient Greeks knew that the aromatic properties of the fluid could reveal the imbalances of the soul itself . . .

The left hand sneaks toward the flask.

Anna   I'm always very eager to try new foods, or see the latest John Waters film—

Dr. Todesrocheln   Its use in the purification rites of the Aztecs is, of course, so well known that it need not be mentioned . . .

The hand has grasped the flask and begins to inch it off the table.

Anna   And whenever I meet someone who cross-dresses, I always compliment him on his shoes or her earrings—

Dr. Todesrocheln   It is the first golden drop that marks the infant's identity separate from the womb.

The hand has slipped the flask beneath the table; his right hand is puzzled.

Anna   But still, it's important to know where your threshold is . . . and I think we're coming dangerously close to mine . . .

Dr. Todesrocheln   Until the last precious amber releases the soul from the body— ashes to ashes, drop to drop—excuse me—

His left hand, with the flask, swings in an arc behind his body. He swivels his body to the flask, his back turned to us. We can hear him drink in secrecy.

(*With his back turned.*) Ahhh . . .

*He orders himself. Composed, he turns around to face **Anna** again, and demurely sets down the flask. Its level is noticeably lower.*

Anna *is aghast.*

Dr. Todesrocheln   I can sense your concern. I have been prattling on without regard to questions you must surely have—

Anna   Is that your real hair?

Dr. Todesrocheln   Of course. I can not promise results, but first we must proceed by securing samples—

Anna   I don't believe that's your real hair.

Dr. Todesrocheln   I will need first of all twenty-four hours of your time for a urononcometry—

Anna (*increasingly scared*)   You look familiar to me—

Dr. Todesrocheln   Although I can tell you from a first taste— er, test—that your uroammonica level is high, not unpleasantly so, but full-bodied—

Anna   Oh, my God . . . I think I know who you are . . . you're . . . you're . . .

She rises to snatch his toupee. **Dr. Todesrocheln** *suddenly stands, menacing.*

The light changes.

Dr. Todesrocheln   *WO IST DEIN BRUDER?*

He takes off his wig and glasses and appears as the **Doctor** *in the first scene, peeling off the black gloves to reveal latex gloves underneath.*

Dr. Todesrocheln   You fool! You left your brother in the room alone! *WO IST DEIN BRUDER?*

Music: The Emperor Waltz *plays at a very loud volume.*

Anna, *frightened, races from* **Dr. Todesrocheln**'s *office to the hotel room. We see* **Carl**, *lying stiff beneath a white sheet. To the tempo of the Strauss,* **Anna** *tries to wake him. He does not respond.* **Anna** *takes off the sheet and forces him into a sitting position, the stuffed rabbit clenched beneath his arm.* **Carl** *remains sitting, stiff, eyes open, wooden. He is still in his pajamas. Then he slumps.* **Anna** *raises him again. He remains upright for a beat, and begins to fall.* **Anna** *stops him, presses his body against hers, pulls his legs over the bed, tries to stand him up. Frozen, his body tilts against hers. She tries to make him cross the floor, his arms around her neck. She positions him in a chair, but his legs are locked in a perpendicular angle and will not touch the floor. She presses his legs to the floor. He mechanically springs forward. Then suddenly, like the doll in E. T. A. Hoffmann, the body of* **Carl** *becomes animated, but with a strange, automatic life of its own.* **Carl** *begins to waltz with* **Anna**. *Gradually, he winds down, and faltering, falls back to the bed. There is the sound of a loud alarm clock; the* **Doctor** *enters, and covers* **Carl** *with a sheet. Then he pulls a white curtain in front of the scene, as the stage lights become, for the first time, harsh, stark and white.*

Scene Thirty: In the Hospital Lounge

The **Doctor** *holds the stuffed rabbit and travel brochures in his hands. He awkwardly peels off his latex gloves.*

Doctor   I'm sorry. There was nothing we could do.

Anna   Yes. I know.

Doctor   I thought you might want to take this along with you.

He hands **Anna** *the stuffed rabbit.*

Anna (*to the stuffed rabbit*)   There you are!

(*Hugs the stuffed rabbit and sees the* **Doctor** *watching her.*) It's Jo-Jo. My brother's childhood rabbit. I brought it to the hospital as a little surprise. I thought it might make him feel better.

Doctor   Sometimes little things become important, when nothing else will help . . .

Anna   Yes.

They pause and stand together awkwardly.

At least Carl went in his sleep. I guess that's a blessing.

Doctor   If one has to die from this particular disease, there are worse ways to go than pneumonia.

Anna   I never would have believed what sickness can do to the body.

Pause.

Well, Doctor, I want to thank you for all you've done for my brother.

Doctor   I wish I could do more. By the way, housekeeping found these brochures in your brother's bedside table. I didn't know if they were important.

Anna (*takes the brochures*)   Ah, yes. The brochures for Europe. I've never been abroad. We're going to go when he gets—

Stops herself.

(*With control.*) I must learn to use the past tense. We would have gone had he gotten better.

Doctor   Anna—I may call you Anna? I, uh, if there's anything I can do . . .

Anna   Thank you, but there's nothing you can do—

Doctor   I mean, I really would like it if you'd call me for coffee, or if you just want to talk about all this . . .

He trails off. **Anna** *looks at him. She smiles. He squirms.*

Anna   You're very sweet. But no, I don't think so. Not now. I feel it's simply not safe for me right now to see anyone. Thanks again and goodbye.

She starts to exit. The **Doctor***, wistful, watches her go. The lighting begins to change back to the dreamy atmosphere of the first scene. Softly, a Strauss waltz begins.* **Carl,** *perfectly well, waits for* **Anna***. He is dressed in Austrian military regalia. They waltz off as the lights dim.*

End of Play.

Introduction to Suzan-Lori Parks

Wesley Brown

Suzan-Lori Parks was born in Fort Knox, Kentucky, in 1963. She was one of three siblings whose father was a career officer in the US Army. The family lived in many states, including several years in West Germany where she spent her middle and some high school years before returning to the United States. Parks has said that living in so many varied social and cultural environments greatly influenced her writing. It was while a student at Mount Holyoke College in the early 1980s that Parks studied with James Baldwin who encouraged her to write plays. She was also inspired by another former Mount Holyoke graduate, Wendy Wasserstein, who went on to receive the Pulitzer Prize in Drama for her 1989 play *The Heidi Chronicles*.

Ironically, Parks' first play to garner critical attention, *Imperceptible Mutabilities of the Third Kingdom*, was produced the same year Wasserstein received the Pulitzer Prize. Showing a lack of interest with conventional plots, Parks offered a series of related scenes addressing the stereotypes that have stalked African Americans from slavery to the late twentieth century, using comedic situations and, playfully, teasing together formal English and black vernacular speech. In one scene, "Snails," three contemporary black women are besieged by a weird scientist who violates their space with a camera hidden in a huge mechanical contraption resembling a cockroach; in "Open House," open heart surgery on a dying black woman becomes a symbolic exploration of her life during slavery; and in "Greeks,"a black marine sergeant and his family keep up the appearance of dutiful Americans while awaiting recognition from a grateful nation that is not forthcoming.

These unsettling parodies of how the complexities of black lives are often reduced to grotesque and unyielding stereotypes are continued in Parks' next play, *The Death of the Last Black Man in the Whole Entire World AKA the Negro Book of the Dead* (1990), where the watermelon, like Shange's minstrel mask in *Spell #7*, is a burden that cannot be easily cast aside. What gives these early plays a bearable lightness of being that never becomes ponderous is Parks' exuberant use of language. In her 1994 essay "Elements of Style" she writes: "Repetition and Revision is a concept integral to the Jazz aesthetic in which the composer or performer will write or play a musical phrase once and again and again; etc. – with each revisit the phrase is slightly revised. 'Rep & Rev' as I call it is a central element in my work; through its use I'm working to create a dramatic text that departs from the traditional linear narrative style to look and sound more like a musical score . . . With each play I'm finding the only way that that particular dramatic story can be told."

Parks' repetition and revision narrative style continued to evolve in plays that altered and satirized the representations of historical figures such as *The America Play* (1994) about an Abraham Lincoln impersonator who allowed paying customers to reenact the president's assassination; *Venus* (1996 Obie Award) reimagining the life of the carnival attraction Sarah "Saartjie" Baartman, aka the Venus Hottentot; *In the Blood* (1999) and *Fucking A* (2000), two different variations on Hawthorne's *The Scarlet Letter*; and *Topdog/Underdog*, the 2001 Pulitzer Prize-winning play about two black orphaned brothers named Lincoln and Booth who survive by the former earning a living getting shot in a perverse tourist attraction, while the latter tries to master the con game three-card monte.

With the 1999 production of *In the Blood*, the consensus of critical opinion seemed to be in agreement that Suzan-Lori Parks had come into her own as a major American playwright. This recognition was borne out, subsequently, by the Guggenheim Fellowship (2000); the MacArthur Foundation "Genius" Grant (2001); the NAACP Theatre Award (2008); the Edward M. Kennedy Prize for Drama Inspired by American History (2015); and the PEN/Laura Pels International Foundation for Theatre Awards for *Master American Dramatist* (2017).

In Parks' adaptation of *The Scarlet Letter*, she riffs on Hawthorne's protagonist, Hester Prynne, transforming her into a black American woman, Hester, La Negrita, whose lived experience has gone, in Parks' words, "unrecorded, dismembered, washed out . . ." And Parks has set herself the task in all of her plays "to locate the ancestral burial ground, dig for bones, find bones, hear the bones sing, write it down." However, we are not in Salem but New York City where Hester lives on public assistance under a bridge with her five children, each one by a different father. And like Hester in Hawthorne's novel, La Negrita has internalized the judgments imposed on her by the word "slut" scrawled on a wall that she cannot read, having only learned the letter "A." The oldest son is teaching her to read, but refuses to utter the word on the wall in her presence.

La Negrita struggles mightily to keep her family together but is undone by the symbolic representatives of the state and others (alternating in the roles played by her children) she expects will assist her: a community doctor, Amiga Gringa, a white friend, the Welfare Lady, a minister, and her oldest son's father who was her first love. Each one addresses the audience with rationalizations to explain away how they have used La Negrita. Parks is unflinching in her refusal to offer the audience any falsely uplifting triumph over adversity. But what is exhilarating is the integrity Suzan-Lori Parks brings to writing a play that earns every moment no matter how terrifying.

In the Blood

Suzan-Lori Parks

Production History

In the Blood premiered at The Joseph Papp Public Theater/New York Shakespeare Festival (George C. Wolfe, Producer; Rosemarie Tichler, Artistic Producer; Mark Litvin, Managing Director) in New York City in November 1999. It was directed by David Esbjornson; the set design was by Narelle Sissons; the lighting design was by Jane Cox; the sound design was by Don DiNicola; the costume design was by Elizabeth Hope Clancy; the production dramaturg was John Dias; and the production stage manager was Kristen Harris. The cast was as follows:

Hester, La Negrita	Charlayne Woodard
Chilli/Jabber	Rob Campbell
Reverend D./Baby	Reggie Montgomery
Welfare Lady/Bully	Gail Grate
Doctor/Trouble	Bruce MacVittie
Amiga Gringa/Beauty	Deirdre O'Connell

Author's Elements of Style

I'm continuing the use of my slightly unconventional theatrical elements. Here's a road map:

- (*Rest*)
  Take a little time, a pause, a breather; make a transition.

- A Spell
  An elongated and heightened (*Rest*). Denoted by repetition of figures' names with no dialogue. Has sort of an architectural look:

  Reverend D.
  Hester
  Reverend D.
  Hester

  This is a place where the figures experience their pure true simple state. While no action or stage business is necessary, directors should fill this moment as they best see fit.

- [Brackets in the text indicate optional cuts for production.]

- (Parentheses around dialogue indicate softly spoken passages (asides; sotto voce)).

Characters

Hester, La Negrita
Chilli/Jabber, *her oldest son*
Reverend D./Baby, *her youngest son*
Welfare Lady/Bully, *her oldest daughter*
Doctor/Trouble, *her middle son*
Amiga Gringa/Beauty, *her youngest daughter*

Place

Here

Time

Now

Author's Note

This play requires a cast of six adult actors, five of whom double as adults and children. The setting should be spare, to reflect the poverty of the world of the play.

Prologue

All clustered together.

All   THERE SHE IS!

WHO DOES SHE THINK

SHE IS

THE NERVE SOME PEOPLE HAVE

SHOULDNT HAVE IT IF YOU CANT AFFORD IT

AND YOU KNOW SHE CANT

SHE DONT GOT NO SKILLS

CEPT ONE

CANT READ CANT WRITE

SHE MARRIED?

WHAT DO YOU THINK?

SHE OUGHTA BE MARRIED

THATS WHY THINGS ARE BAD LIKE THEY ARE

CAUSE OF

GIRLS LIKE THAT

THAT EVER HAPPEN TO ME YOU WOULDNT SEE ME HAVING IT

YOU WOULDNT SEE THAT HAPPENING TO ME

WHO THE HELL SHE THINK SHE IS

AND NOW WE GOT TO PAY FOR IT

THE NERVE

SOME PEOPLE HAVE

BAD LUCK

SHE OUGHTA GET MARRIED

TO WHO?

THIS AINT THE FIRST TIME THIS HAS HAPPENED TO HER

NO?

THIS IS HER FIFTH

FIFTH?

SHE GOT FIVE OF THEM

FIVE BRATS

AND NOT ONE OF THEM GOT A DADDY

PAH!

They spit.

WHOS THE DADDY?

SHE WONT TELL

SHE WONT TELL CAUSE SHE DONT KNOW

SHE KNOWS

NO SHE DONT

HOW COULD A GIRL NOT KNOW

WHEN YOU HAD SO MUCH ACTION YOU LOSE A FRACTION

OF YR GOOD SENSE

THE PART OF MEN SHE SEES ALL LOOK THE SAME ANYWAY

WATCH YR MOUTH

I DIDNT SAY NOTHING

YOU TALKING ALL NASTY AND THAT AINT RIGHT

THERES CHILDREN HERE

WHERES THE CHILDREN I DONT SEE NO CHILDREN

SHE MARRIED?

SHE AINT MARRIED

SHE DONT GOT NO SKILLS

CEPT ONE

CANT READ CANT WRITE

SHE MARRIED?

WHAT DO YOU THINK?

All
All
All

SHE KNOWS SHES A NO COUNT

SHIFTLESS

HOPELESS

BAD NEWS

BURDEN TO SOCIETY

HUSSY

SLUT

PAH!

They spit.

JUST PLAIN STUPID IF YOU ASK ME AINT NO SMART WOMAN GOT 5 BASTARDS

AND NOT A PENNY TO HER NAME

SOMETHINGS GOTTA BE DONE TO STOP THIS SORT OF THING

CAUSE I'LL BE DAMNED IF SHE GONNA LIVE OFF ME

HERE SHE COMES

MOVE ASIDE

WHAT SHE GOTS CATCHY

LET HER PASS

DONT GET CLOSE

YOU DONT WANNA LOOK LIKE YOU KNOW HER

STEP OFF!

They part like the Red Sea would.

Hester, La Negrita *passes through them.*

She holds a newborn baby in her arms.

All   IT WONT END WELL FOR HER

HOW YOU KNOW?

I GOT EYES DON'T I

BAD NEWS IN HER BLOOD

PLAIN AS DAY.

All
Hester
All

Hester *lifts the child up, raising it toward the sky.*

Hester   My treasure. My joy.

All   PAH!

They spit.

Scene One: Under the Bridge

Home under the bridge. The word "SLUT" scrawled on a wall. **Hester**'s *oldest child* **Jabber**, *thirteen, studies that scrawl.* **Hester** *lines up soda cans as her youngest child* **Baby**, *two years old, watches.*

Hester   Zit uh good word or a bad word?

Jabber
Jabber

Hester   Aint like you to have yr mouth shut, Jabber. Say it to me and we can figure out the meaning together.

Jabber   Naaaa—

Hester   What I tell you bout saying "Naa" when you mean "no"? You talk like that people wont think you got no brains and Jabbers got brains. All my kids got brains, now.

(Rest)

Lookie here, Baby. Mamma set the cans for you. Mamma gonna show you how to make some money. Watch.

Jabber   Im slow.

Hester   Slow aint never stopped nothing, Jabber. You bring yr foot down on it and smash it flat. Howabout that, Baby? Put it in the pile and thats that. Now you try.

Baby *jumps on the can smashing it flat, hollering as he smashes.*

Baby   Ha!

Hester   Yr a natural! Jabber, yr little baby brothers a natural. We gonna come out on top this month, I can feel it. Try another one, Baby.

Jabber   They wrote it in yr practice place.

Hester   Yes they did.

Jabber   They wrote in yr practice place so you didnt practice today.

Hester   I practiced. In my head. In the air. In the dirt underfoot.

Jabber   Lets see.

With great difficulty **Hester** *makes an "A" in the dirt.*

Hester   The letter A.

Jabber   Almost.

Hester   You gonna disparage me I aint gonna practice.

Baby   Mommmmieee!

Hester   Gimmieuhminute, Baby-child.

Jabber   Legs apart hands crost the chest like I showd you. Try again.

Baby   Mommieee!

Hester   See the pretty can, Baby?

Baby   Ha!

Jabber   Try again.

Baby   Mommmieee!

Hester   Later. Read that word out to me, huh? I like it when you read to me.

Jabber   Dont wanna read it.

Hester   Cant or wont?

Jabber   —Cant.

Hester
Jabber

He knows what the word says, but he wont' say it.

Hester   I was sick when I was carrying you. Damn you, slow fool. Aaah, my treasure, cmmeer. My oldest treasure.

She gives him a quick hug.

She looks at the word, its letters mysterious to her.

Baby *smashes can after can.*

Hester   Go scrub it off, then. I like my place clean.

Jabber *dutifully scrubs the wall.*

Hester   We know who writ it up there. It was them bad boys writing on my home. And in my practice place. Do they write on they own homes? I dont think so. They come under the bridge and write things they dont write nowhere else. A mean ugly word, I'll bet. A word to hurt our feelings. And because we aint lucky we gotta live with it. 5 children I got. 5 treasures. 5 joys. But we aint got our leg up, just yet. So we gotta live with mean words and hurt feelings.

Jabber   Words dont hurt my feelings, Mamma.

Hester   Dont disagree with me.

Jabber   Sticks and stones, Mamma.

Hester   Yeah. I guess.

(Rest)

Too late for yr sisters and brother to still be out. Yr little brother Babys gonna make us rich. He learns quick. Look at him go.

She lines up more cans and **Baby** *jumps on them, smashing them all.* **Bully**, *her twelve-year-old girl, runs in.*

Bully   Mommieeeeeeeee! Mommie, Trouble he has really done it this time. I told him he was gonna be doing life and he laughed and then I said he was gonna get the electric chair and you know what he said?

Hester   Help me sack the cans.

Bully   He said a bad word!

Hester   Sack the cans.

They sack the crushed cans.

Bully   Trouble he said something really bad but Im not saying it cause if I do yll wash my mouth. What he said was bad but what he did, what he did was worse.

Hester   Whatd he do?

Bully   Stole something.

Hester   Food?

Bully   No.

Hester   Toys?

Bully   No.

Hester   I dont like youall stealing toys and I dont like youall stealing food but it happens. I wont punish you for it. Yr just kids. Trouble thinks with his stomach. He hungry he takes, sees a toy, gotta have it.

Bully   A policeman saw him steal and ran after him but Trouble ran faster cause the policeman was fat.

Hester   Policeman chased him?

Bully   He had a big stomach. Like he was pregnant. He was jiggling and running and yelling and red in the face.

Hester   What he steal?

Bully   —Nothing.

Hester   You talk that much and you better keep talking, Miss.

Bully *buttons her lips.*

Hester *pops her upside the head.*

Bully   Owwww!

Hester   Get outa my sight. Worse than a thief is a snitch that dont snitch.

Trouble, *age ten, and* **Beauty**, *age seven, run in, breathless.*

They see **Hester** *eyeing them and stop running; they walk nonchalantly.*

Hester   What you got behind you?

Trouble   Nothing. Jabber, what you doing?

Jabber   Cleaning the wall.

Beauty   My hair needs a ribbon.

Hester   Not right now it dont. You steal something?

Trouble   Me? Whats cookin?

Hester   Soup of the day.

Trouble   We had soup the day yesterday.

Hester   Todays a new day.

Beauty   Is it a new soup?

Hester   Wait and see. You gonna end up in the penitentiary and embarass your mother?

Trouble   No.

Hester   If you do I'll kill you. Set the table.

Jabber   Thats girls work.

Trouble   Mommiee—

Bully   Troubles doing girls work Troubles doing girls work.

Hester   Set the damn table or Ima make a girl outa you!

Trouble   You cant make a girl outa me.

Hester   Dont push me!

(*Rest*)

Look, Baby. See the soup? Mommies stirring it. Dont come close, its hot.

Beauty   I want a ribbon.

Hester   Get one I'll tie it in.

Beauty *gets a ribbon.*

Trouble *gets bowls, wipes them clean, hands them out.*

Hester *follows behind him and, out of the back of his pants, yanks a policemans club.*

Hester   Whered you get this?

Trouble
Hester
Trouble

Hester   I said—

Trouble   I found it. On the street. It was just lying there.

Bully   You stole it.

Trouble   Did not!

Hester   Dont lie to me.

Trouble   I found it. I did. It was just lying on the street. I was minding my own business.

Hester   That why the cops was chasing you?

Trouble   Snitch!

Bully   Jailbait!

He hits **Trouble** *hard.*

They fight. Pandemonium.

Hester   Suppertime!

Order is restored.

Hester *slips the club into the belt of her dress; it hangs there like a sword.*

She wears it like this for most of the play.

Her children sit in a row holding their bowls.

She ladles out the soup.

Hester   Todays soup the day, ladies and gents, is a very special blend of herbs and spices. The broth is chef Mommies worldwide famous "whathaveyou" stock. Theres carrots in there. Theres meat. Theres oranges. Theres pie.

Trouble   What kinda pie?

Hester   What kind you like?

Trouble   Apple.

Hester   Theres apple pie.

Jabber   Pumpkin.

Bully   And cherry!

Hester   Theres pumpkin and cherry too. And steak. And mash potatoes for Beauty. And milk for Baby.

Beauty   And diamonds.

Jabber   You cant eat diamonds.

Hester   So when you find one in yr soup whatll you do?

Beauty   Put it on my finger.

They slurp down their soup quickly.

As soon as she fills their bowls, they're empty again.

The kids eat. **Hester** *doesn't.*

Jabber   You aint hungry?

Hester   I'll eat later.

Jabber   You always eating later.

Hester   You did a good job with the wall, Jabber. Whatd that word say anyway?

Jabber   —Nothing.

The soup pot is empty.

Hester

Jabber/Bully/Trouble/Beauty/Baby

(*Rest*)

Hester   Bedtime.

Bully   Can we have a story?

(*Rest*)

Hester   All right.

(*Rest*)

There were once these five brothers and they were all big and strong and handsome and didnt have a care in the world. One was known for his brains so they called him Smarts and one was known for his muscles, so they called him Toughguy, the third one was a rascal so they called him Wild, the fourth one was as goodlooking as all get out and they called him Looker and the fifth was the youngest and they called him Honeychild cause he was as young as he was sweet. And they was always together these five brothers. Everywhere they went they always went together. No matter what they was always together cause they was best friends and wasnt nothing could divide them. And there was this Princess. And she lived in a castle and she was lonesome. She was lonesome and looking for love but she couldnt leave her castle so she couldnt look very far so every day she would stick her head out her window and sing to the sun and every night she would stick her head out and sing to the moon and the stars: "Where are you?" And one day the five brothers heard her and came calling and she looked upon them and she said: "There are five of you, and each one is wonderful and special in his own way. But the law of my country doesnt allow a princess to have more than one husband." And that was such bad news and they were all so in love that they all cried. Until the Princess had an idea. She was after all the Princess, so she changed the law of the land and married them all.

(*Rest*)

And with Bro Smarts she had a baby named Jabber. And with Bro Toughguy she had Bully. With Bro Wild came Trouble. With Bro Looker she had Beauty. With Bro

Honeychild came Baby. And they was all happy.

Jabber   Until the bad news came.

Hester   No bad news came.

Jabber   Theres always bad news.

Hester   Bedtime.

Beauty   Where did the daddys go?

Hester   They went to bed.

Trouble   They ran off.

Jabber   The war came and the brothers went off to fight and they all died.

Beauty   They all died?

Jabber   And they fell into the ground and the dirt covered up they heads.

Hester   Its bedtime. Now!

Beauty   Im scared.

Trouble   I aint scared. Jabber, you a spook.

Bully   Yr the spook.

Trouble   Yr a bastard.

Bully   Yr a bastard.

Hester   Yr all bastards!

The children burst into tears.

Hester   Cmmeer. Cmmeer. Mama loves you. Shes just tired is all. Lemmie hug you.

They nestle around her and she hugs them.

Hester   My five treasures. My five joys.

Hester
Jabber/Bully/Trouble/Beauty/Baby
Hester

Hester   Lets hit the sack! And leave yr shoes for polish and yr shirts and blouses for press. You dont wanna look like you dont got nobody.

They take off their shoes and tops and go inside leaving **Hester** *outside alone.*

Hester
Hester
Hester

(*Rest*)

Hester *examines the empty soup pot, shines the kids shoes, "presses" their clothes.*

A wave of pain shoots through her.

Hester   You didnt eat, Hester. And the pain in yr gut comes from having nothing in it.

(*Rest*)

Kids ate good though. Ate their soup all up. They wont starve.

(*Rest*)

None of these shoes shine. Never did no matter how hard you spit on em, Hester. You get a leg up the first thing you do is get shoes. New shoes for yr five treasures. You got yrself a good pair of shoes already.

From underneath a pile of junk she takes a shoebox.

Inside is a pair of white pumps.

She looks them over then puts them away.

Hester   Dont know where yr going but yll look good when you get there.

[**Hester** *takes out a small tape player.*

Pops in a tape.

She takes a piece of chalk from her pocket and, on the freshly scrubbed wall, practices her letters: she writes the letter "A" over and over and over.

The cassette tape plays as she writes.

On tape:

Reverend D.   If you cant always do right then you got to admit that some times, some times my friends you are going to do wrong and you are going to have to *live* with that. Somehow work that into the fabric of your life. Because there aint a soul out there that is spot free. There aint a soul out there that has walked but hasnt stumbled. Aint a single solitary soul out there that has said "hello" and not "goodbye," has said "yes" to the lord and "yes" to the devil too, has drunk water and drunk wine, loved and hated, experienced the good side of the tracks and the bad. That is what they call "Livin," friends. L-I-V-I-N, friends. Life on earth is full of confusion. Life on earth is full of misunderstandings, reprimandings, and we focus on the trouble, friends, when it is the solution to those troubles we oughta be looking at. "I have fallen and I cant get up!" How many times have you heard that, friends? The fellow on the street with his whisky breath and his outstretched hand, the banker scraping the money off the top, the runaway child turned criminal all cry out "I have fallen, and I cant get up!" "I have fallen, and I cant get up!" "I have fallen—"

Hester *hears someone coming and turns the tape off.*]

She goes back to polishing the shoes.

Amiga Gringa *comes in.*

Amiga Gringa   Look at old Mother Hubbard or whatever.

Hester   Keep quiet. Theyre sleeping.

Amiga Gringa   The old woman and the shoe. Thats who you are.

Hester   I get my leg up thats what Im getting. New shoes for my treasures.

Amiga Gringa   Thatll be some leg up.

Hester   You got my money?

Amiga Gringa   Is that a way to greet a friend? "You got my money?" What world is this?

Hester   You got my money, Amiga?

Amiga Gringa   I got *news* for you, Hester. News thats better than gold. But first— heads up.

The **Doctor** *comes in.*

He wears a sandwich board and carries all his office paraphernalia on his back.

Doctor   Hester! Yr due for a checkup.

Hester   My guts been hurting me.

Doctor   Im on my way home just now. Catch up with me tomorrow. We'll have a look at it then.

He goes on his way.

Amiga Gringa   Doc! I am in pain like you would not believe. My hips, Doc. When I move them—blinding flashes of light and then—down I go, flat on my back, like Im dead, Doc.

Doctor   I gave you something for that yesterday.

Doctor

Amiga Gringa

He slips her a few pills.

He goes on his way.

Amiga Gringa   Hes a saint.

Hester   Sometimes.

Amiga Gringa   Want some?

Hester   I want my money.

Amiga Gringa   Patience, girl. All good things are on their way. Do you know what the word is?

Hester   What word?

Amiga Gringa   Word is that yr first love is back in town, doing well and looking for you.

Hester   Chilli? Jabbers daddy? Looking for me?

Amiga Gringa   Thats the word.

Hester

Hester

Hester   Bullshit. Gimmie my money, Miga. I promised the kids cake and ice cream. How much you get?

Amiga Gringa   First, an explanation of the economic environment.

Hester   Just gimmie my money—

Amiga Gringa   The Stock Market, The Bond Market, Wall Street, Grain Futures, Bulls and Bears and Pork Bellies. They all impact the price a woman such as myself can get for a piece of "found" jewelry.

Hester   That werent jewelry I gived you that was a watch. A mans watch. Name brand. And it was working.

Amiga Gringa   Do you know what the Dow did today, Hester? The Dow was up twelve points. And that prize fighter, the one everyone is talking about, the one with the pretty wife and the heavyweight crown, he rang the opening bell. She wore a dress cut down to here. And the Dow shot up forty-three points in the first minutes of trading, Hester. Up like a rocket. And men glanced up at the faces of clocks on the walls of their offices and women around the country glanced into the faces of their children and time passed. [And someone looks at their watch because its lunchtime, Hester. And theyre having— lunch. And they wish it would last forever. Cause when they get back to their office where they—work, when they get back the Dow has plummeted. And theres a lot of racing around and time is brief and something must be done before the closing bell. Phone calls are made, marriages dissolve, promises lost in the shuffle, Hester, and all this time your Amiga Gringa is going from fence to fence trying to get the best price on this piece of "found" jewelry. Numbers racing on lightboards, Hester, telling those that are in the know, the value of who knows what. One man, broken down in tears in the middle of the avenue, "Oh my mutual funds" he was saying.] The market was hot, and me, a suspicious looking mother, very much like yrself, with no real address and no valid forms of identification, walking the streets with a hot watch.

(*Rest*)

Here.

She gives **Hester** *dollars.*

Hester   Wheres the rest?

Amiga Gringa   Thats it.

Hester   Five bucks?

Amiga Gringa   It wasnt a good day. Some days are good some days are bad. I kept a buck for myself.

Hester   You stole from me.

Amiga Gringa   Dont be silly. We're friends, Hester.

Hester   I shoulda sold it myself.

Amiga Gringa   But you had the baby to watch.

Hester   And no ones gonna give money to me with me carrying Baby around. Still I coulda got more than 5.

Amiga Gringa   Go nextime yrself then. The dangers I incur, working with you. You oughta send yr kids away. Like me. I got three kids. All under the age of three. And do you see me looking all baggy eyed, up all night shining little shoes and flattening little shirts and going without food? Theres plenty of places that you can send them. Homes. Theres plenty of peoples, rich ones especially, that cant have kids. The rich spend days looking through the newspaper for ads where they can buy one. Or they go to the bastard homes and pick one out. Youd have some freedom. Youd have a chance at life. Like me.

Hester   My kids is mine. I get rid of em what do I got? Nothing. I got nothing now, but if I lose them I got less than nothing.

Amiga Gringa   Suit yrself. You wouldnt have to send them all away, just one or two or three.

Hester   All I need is a leg up. I get my leg up I'll be ok.

Bully *comes outside and stands there watching them.*

She wears pink, one-piece, flame-retardant pajamas.

Hester   What.

Bully   My hands stuck.

Hester   Why you sleep with yr hands in fists?

Amiga Gringa   Yr an angry girl, arentcha, Bully.

Bully   Idunno. This ones stuck too.

Hester   Maybe yll grow up to be a boxer, huh? We can watch you ringside, huh? *Wide World of Sports.*

Amiga Gringa   Presenting in this corner weighing 82 pounds the challenger: Bully!

Bully   Ima good girl.

Hester   Course you are. There. You shouldnt sleep with yr hands balled up. The good fairies come by in the night with treats for little girls and they put them in yr hands. How you gonna get any treats if yr hands are all balled up?

Bully   Jabber is bad and Trouble is bad and Beauty is bad and Baby is bad but I'm good. Bullys a good girl.

Hester   Go on back to bed now.

Bully   Miga. Smell.

Amiga Gringa   You got bad breath.

Bully   I forgot to brush my teeth.

Hester   Go head.

Bully *squats off in the "bathroom" and rubs her teeth with her finger.*

Amiga Gringa   Babys daddy, that Reverend, he ever give you money?

Hester   No.

Amiga Gringa   Hes a gold mine. I seen the collection plate going around. Its a full plate.

Hester   I aint seen him since before Baby was born.

Amiga Gringa   Thats two years.

Hester   He didnt want nothing to do with me. His heart went hard.

Amiga Gringa   My second kids daddy had a hard heart at first. But time mushed him up. Remember when he comed around crying about his lineage and asking whered the baby go? And I'd already gived it up.

Hester   Reverend D., his heart is real hard. Like a rock.

Amiga Gringa   Worth a try all the same.

Hester   Yeah.

(Rest)

Who told you Chilli was looking for me?

Amiga Gringa   Word on the street, thats all.

Trouble, *dressed in superhero pajamas, comes in.*

He holds a box of matches. He lights one.

Hester   What the hell you doing?

Trouble   Sleepwalking.

Hester   You sleepwalk yrself back over here and gimmie them matches or Ima kill you.

Trouble *gives her the matches.*

Bully *has finished with her teeth.*

Bully   You wanna smell?

Hester   Thats ok.

Bully   Dont you wanna smell?

Hester *leans in and* **Bully** *opens her mouth.*

Bully   I only did one side cause I only ate with one side today.

Hester   Go on to bed.

Bully *passes* **Trouble** *and hits him hard.*

Trouble   Aaaaah!

Bully   Yr a bad person!

He hits him again.

Trouble   Aaaaaaaaah!

Hester   Who made you policewoman?

Trouble   Ima blow you sky high one day you bully bitch!

Bully *goes to hit him again.*

Hester   Trouble I thought you said you was sleep. Go inside and lie down and shut up or you wont see tomorrow.

Trouble *goes back to sleepwalking and goes inside.*

Hester   Bully. Go over there. Close yr eyes and yr mouth and not a word, hear?

Bully *goes a distance off curling up to sleep without a word.*

Hester   I used to wash Troubles mouth out with soap when he used bad words. Found out he likes the taste of soap. Sometimes you cant win. No matter what you do.

(Rest)

Im gonna talk to Welfare and get an upgrade. The worldll take care of the women and children.

Amiga Gringa   Theyre gonna give you the test. See what skills you got. Make you write stuff.

Hester   Like what?

Amiga Gringa   Like yr name.

Hester   I can write my damn name. Im not such a fool that I cant write my own goddamn name. I can write my goddamn name.

Inside, **Baby** *starts crying.*

Hester   HUSH!

Baby *hushes.*

Amiga Gringa   You should pay yrself a visit to Babys daddy. Dont take along the kid in the flesh thatll be too much. For a buck I'll get someone to take a snapshot.

Jabber *comes in. He wears mismatched pajamas.*

He doesnt come too close, keeps his distance.

Jabber   I was in a rowboat and the sea was flat like a blue plate and you was rowing me and it was fun.

Hester   Go back to bed.

Jabber   It was a good day but then Bad News and the sea started rolling and the boat tipped and I fell out and—

Hester   You wet the bed.

Jabber   I fell out the boat.

Hester   You wet the bed.

Jabber   I wet the bed.

Hester   Thirteen years old still peeing in the bed.

Jabber   It was uh accident.

Hester   Whats wrong with you?

Jabber   Accidents happen.

Hester   Yeah you should know cause yr uh damn accident. Shit. Take that off.

Jabber *strips.*

Amiga Gringa   He aint bad looking, Hester. A little slow, but some women like that.

Hester   Wear my coat. Gimmie a kiss.

Jabber *puts on* **Hester**'*s coat and kisses her on the cheek.*

Jabber   Mommie?

Hester   Bed.

Jabber   All our daddys died, right? All our daddys died in the war, right?

Hester   Yeah, Jabber.

Jabber   They went to war and they died and you cried. They went to war and died but whered they go when they died?

Hester   They into other things now.

Jabber   Like what?

Hester   —. Worms. They all turned into worms, honey. They crawling around in the dirt happy as larks, eating the world up, never hungry. Go to bed.

Jabber *goes in.*

(*Rest*)

Amiga Gringa   Worms?

Hester   Whatever.

Amiga Gringa   Hes yr favorite. You like him the best.

Hester   Hes my first.

Amiga Gringa   Hes yr favorite.

Hester   I dont got no *favorite*.

(*Rest*)

Five bucks. Three for their treats. And one for that photo. Reverend D. aint the man I knew. Hes got money now. A salvation business and all. Maybe his stone-heart is mush, though. Maybe.

Amiga Gringa   Cant hurt to try.

Scene Two: Street Practice

Hester *walks alone down the street.*

She has a framed picture of **Baby**.

Hester   Picture, it comed out pretty good. Got him sitting on a chair, and dont he look like he got everything one could want in life? Hes two years old. Andll be growd up with a life of his own before I blink.

(*Rest*)

Picture comed out good. Thought Amiga was cheating me but it comed out good.

Hester *meets the* **Doctor**, *coming the other way.*

As before he carries all of his office paraphernalia on his back. He wears a sandwich board; the words written on it are hidden.

Doctor   Hester. Dont move a muscle, I'll be set up in a jiffy.

Hester   I dont got more than a minute.

Doctor   Hows yr gut?

Hester   Not great.

Doctor   Say "Aaaah!"

Hester   Aaaah!

As she stands there with her mouth open, he sets up his roadside office: a thin curtain, his doctor's shingle, his instruments, his black bag.

Doctor   Good good good good good. Lets take yr temperature. Do you know what it takes to keep my road-side practice running? Do you know how much The Higher

Ups would like to shut me down? Every blemish on your record is a blemish on mine. Take yr guts for instance. Yr pain could be nothing or it could be the end of the road—a cyst or a tumor, a lump or a virus or an infected sore. Or cancer, Hester. Undetected. There youd be, lying in yr coffin with all yr little ones gathered around motherlessly weeping and The Higher Ups pointing their fingers at me, saying I should of saved the day, but instead stood idly by. You and yr children live as you please and Im the one The Higher Ups hold responsible. Would you like a pill?

Hester   No thanks.

She doubles over in pain.

My gut hurts.

The **Doctor** *takes a pill.*

Doctor   In a minute. We'll get to that in a minute. How are yr children?

Hester   Theyre all right.

Doctor   All five?

Hester   All five.

Doctor   Havent had any more have you?

Hester   No.

Doctor   But you could. But you might.

Hester   —Maybe.

Doctor   Word from The Higher Ups is that one more kid outa the likes of you and theyre on the likes of me like white on rice. I'd like to propose something—. Yr running a temperature. Bit of a fever. Whats this?

Hester   Its a club. For protection.

Doctor   Good thinking.

He examines her quickly and thoroughly.

Doctor   The Higher Ups are breathing down my back, Hester. They want answers! They want results! Solutions! Solutions! Solutions! Thats what they want.

He goes to take another pill, but doesnt.

I only take one a day. I only allow myself one a day.

(*Rest*)

He goes back to examining her.

Breathe in deep. Lungs are clear. Yr heart sounds good. Strong as an ox.

Hester   This falls been cold. The wind under the bridge is colder than the wind on the streets.

Doctor   Exercise. Thats what I suggest. When the temperature drops, I run in place. Hold yr hands out. Shaky. Experiencing any stress and tension?

Hester   Not really.

Doctor   Howre yr meals?

Hester   The kids come first.

Doctor   Course they do. Howre yr bowels. Regular?

Hester   I dunno.

Doctor   Once a day?

Hester   Sometimes. My gut—

Doctor   In a minute. Gimmie the Spread & Squat right quick. Lets have a look under the hood.

Standing, **Hester** *spreads her legs and squats.*

Like an otter, he slides between her legs on a dolly and looks up into her privates with a flashlight.

Doctor   Last sexual encounter?

Hester   Thats been a while, now.

Doctor   Yve healed up well from yr last birth.

Hester   Its been two years. His names Baby.

Doctor   Any pain, swelling, off-color discharge, strange smells?

Hester   No.

Doctor   L.M.P.?

Hester   About a week ago.

(Rest)

How *you* been feeling, Doc?

Doctor   Sometimes Im up, sometimes Im down.

Hester   You said you was lonesome once. I came for a checkup and you said you was lonesome. You lonesome today, Doc?

Doctor   No.

Hester   Oh.

Far away, **Chilli** *walks by with his picnic basket on his arm.*

He pauses, checks his pocket watch, then continues on.

Doctor   Yr intelligent. Attractive enough. You could of made something of yrself.

Hester   Im doing all right.

Doctor   The Higher Ups say yr in a skid. I agree.

Hester   Oh, I coulda been the Queen of Sheba, it just werent in the cards, Doc.

Doctor   Yr kids are five strikes against you.

Hester   I dont need no lecture. Gimmie something for my gut so I can go.

Doctor   The Higher Ups, they say Im not making an impact. But what do you care.

Hester   My gut—

Doctor   Stand right here.

He draws a line in the dirt, positions her behind it, and walks a few steps away. He reveals the writing on his sandwich board. It is an eye exam chart.

The letters on the first line spell "SPAY."

Read.

Hester   —. A.

Doctor   Good.

He takes a step closer decreasing the distance between them.

Read.

Hester   __.__.__.

(Rest)

I need glasses for that.

Doctor   Uh huhn.

He steps closer.

How about now?

Hester   I need glasses I guess.

Doctor   I guess you do.

He steps even closer.

Hester   ((somethin-somethin-A-somethin.))

(Rest)

I need glasses.

Doctor   You cant read this?

Hester   I gotta go.

She turns to go and he grabs her hand, holding her fast.

Doctor   When I say removal of your "womanly parts" do you know what parts Im talking about?

Hester   Yr gonna take my womans parts?

Doctor   My hands are tied. The Higher Ups are calling the shots now.

(*Rest*)

You have five healthy children, itll be for the best, considering.

Hester   My womans parts.

Doctor   Ive fowarded my recommendation to yr caseworker. Its out of my hands. Im sorry.

Hester   I gotta go.

But she doesn't move.

She stands there numbly.

Doctor   Yr gut. Lets have a listen.

He puts his ear to her stomach and listens.

Growling hungry stomach. Heres a dollar. Go get yrself a sandwich.

Hester *takes the money and goes.*

Doctor

Doctor

Doctor

FIRST CONFESSION: THE DOCTOR
"Times Are Tough: What Can We Do?"

Doctor   Times are tough:

What can we do?

When I see a woman begging on the streets I guess I could

bring her in my house

sit her at my table

make her a member of my family, sure.

But there are hundreds and thousands of them

and my house cant hold them all.

Maybe we should all take in just one.

Except they wouldnt really fit.

They wouldnt really fit in with us.

Theres such a gulf between us. What can we do?

I am a man of the people, from way back my streetside practice

is a testement to that

so dont get me wrong

do not for a moment think that I am one of those people haters who does not
understand who does not experience—compassion.

(*Rest*)

Shes been one of my neediest cases for several years now.

What can I do?

Each time she comes to me

looking more and more forlorn

and more and more in need

of affection.

At first I wouldnt touch her without gloves on, but then—

(*Rest*)

we did it once

in that alley there,

she was

phenomenal.

(*Rest*)

I was

lonesome and

she gave herself to me in a way that I had never experienced

even with women Ive paid

she was, like she was giving me something that was not hers to give me but
something that was mine

that I'd lent her

and she was returning it to me.

Sucked me off for what seemed like hours

but I was very insistent. And held back

and she understood that I wanted her in the traditional way.

And she was very giving very motherly very obliging very understanding very phenomenal.

Let me cumm inside her. Like I needed to.

What could I do?

I couldnt help it.

Scene Three: The Reverend on His Soapbox

Late at night. The **Reverend D.** *on his soapbox preaching to no one in particular.*

There are audio recordings of his sermons for sale.

Reverend D.   You all know me. You all know this face. These arms. These legs. This body of mine is known to you. To all of you. There isnt a person on the street tonight that hasnt passed me by at some point. Maybe when I was low, many years ago, with a bottle in my hand and the cold hard unforgiving pavement for my dwelling place. Perhaps you know me from that. Or perhaps you know me from my more recent incarnation. The man on the soapbox, telling you of a better life thats available to you, not after the demise of your physical being, not in some heaven where we all gonna be robed in satin sheets and wearing gossamer wings, but right here on earth, my friends. Right here right now. Let the man on the soapbox tell you how to pick yourself up. Let the man on the soapbox tell you how all yr dreams can come true. Let the man on the soapbox tell you that you dont have to be down and dirty, you dont have to be ripped off and renounced, you dont have to be black and blue, your neck dont have to be red, your clothes dont have to be torn, your head dont have to be hanging, you dont have to *hate* yourself, you dont have to hate yr neighbor. You can pull yrself up.

Hester *comes in with a framed picture of* **Baby**.

She stands a ways off. **Reverend D.** *keeps on talking.*

Reverend D.   And I am an example of that. I am a man who has crawled out of the quicksand of despair. I am a man who has pulled himself out of that never ending gutter—and you notice friends that every city and every towns got a gutter. Aint no place in the world that dont have some little trench for its waste. And the gutter, is endless, and deep and wide and if you think you gonna crawl out of the gutter by crawling along the gutter you gonna be in the gutter for the rest of your life. You gotta step out of it, friends and I am here to tell you that you can.

(*Rest*)

He sees **Hester** *but doesnt recognize her.*

Reverend D.   What can I do for you tonight, my sister.

Hester   I been good.

Reverend D.   But yr life is weighing heavy on you tonight.

Hester   I havent bothered you.

Reverend D.   Reverend D. likes to be bothered. Reverend D. enjoys having the tired, the deprived and the depraved come knocking on his door. Come gathering around his soapbox. Come closer. Come on.

Hester *holds the picture of* **Baby** *in front of her face, hiding her face from view.*

Hester   This child here dont know his daddy.

Reverend D.   The ultimate disaster of modern times. Sweet child. Yours?

Hester   Yes.

Reverend D.   Do you know the father?

Hester   Yes.

Reverend D.   You must go to him and say, "Mister, here is your child!"

Hester   Mister here is your child!

Reverend D.   "You are wrong to deny what God has made!"

Hester   You are wrong to deny what God has made!

Reverend D.   "He has nothing but love for you and reaches out his hands every day crying wheres daddy?"

Hester   Wheres daddy?

Reverend D.   "Wont you answer those cries?"

Hester   Wont you answer those cries?

Reverend D.   If he dont respond to that then hes a good-for-nothing dead-beat, and you report him to the authorities. Theyll garnish his wages so at least you all wont starve. I have a motivational cassette which speaks to that very subject. I'll give it to you free of charge.

Hester   I got all yr tapes. I send my eldest up here to get them.

Reverend D.   Wonderful. Thats wonderful. You should go to yr childs father and demand to be recognized.

Hester   Its been years since I seen him. He didnt want me bothering him so I been good.

Reverend D.   Go to him. Plead with him. Show him this sweet face and yours. He cannot deny you.

Hester *lowers the picture, revealing her face.*

Hester
Reverend D.
Hester
Reverend D.

(*Rest*)

Hester   You know me?

Reverend D.   No. God.

Hester   I aint bothered you for two years.

Reverend D.   You should go. Home. Let me call you a taxi. *Taxi!* You shouldnt be out this time of night. Young mother like you. In a neighborhood like this. We'll get you home in a jiff. Where ya live? East? West? North I bet, am I right? *TAXI!* God.

Hester   Hes talking now. Not much but some. hes a good boy.

Reverend D.   I am going to send one of my people over to your home tomorrow. Theyre marvelous, the people who work with me. Theyll put you in touch with all sorts of agencies that can help you. Get some food in that stomach of yours. Get you some sleep.

Hester   Doctor says I got a fever. We aint doing so good. We been slipping. I been good. I dont complain. They breaking my back is all. Five kids. My treasures, breaking my back.

Reverend D.   We'll take up a collection for you.

Hester   You know me.

Reverend D.   You are under the impression that—. Your mind, having nothing better to fix itself on, has fixed on me. Me, someone youve never even met.

Hester   There aint no one here but you and me. Say it. You know me. You know my name. You know my—. You know me and I know you.

Hester

Reverend D.

(*Rest*)

Reverend D.   Here is a card. My lawyer. He'll call you.

Hester   We dont got no phone.

Reverend D.   He'll visit. Write yr address on—. Tell me yr address. I'll write it down. I'll give it to him in the morning and he'll visit you.

(*Rest*)

Do the authorities know the name of the father?

Hester   I dont tell them nothing.

Reverend D.   They would garnish his wages if you did. That would provide you with a small income. If you agree not to ever notify the authorities, we could, through my instutition, arrange for you to get a much larger amount of money.

Hester   How much more?

Reverend D.   Twice as much.

Hester   Three times.

Reverend D.   Fine.

Hester   Theres so many things we need. Food. New shoes. A regular dinner with meat and salad and bread.

Reverend D.   I should give you some money right now. As a promise to you that I'll keep my word. But Im short of cash.

Hester   Oh.

Reverend D.   Come back in two days. Late. I'll have some then.

Hester   You dont got no food or nothing do ya?

Reverend D.   Come back in two days. Not early. Late. And not a word to no one. Okay?

Hester   —. K.

Reverend D.
Hester
Reverend D.
Hester

(*Rest*)

Reverend D.   You better go.

Hester *goes.*

Scene Four: With the Welfare

Outside, **Jabber,** **Trouble,** *and* **Beauty** *sit in the dirt playing with toy cars.*

Trouble   Red light. Greet light. Red light. Green light.

Jabber   Look, a worm.

They all study the worm as it writhes in the dirt. **Welfare** *enters.*

Welfare   Wheres your mommie?

Beauty   Inside.

Jabber   Mommie! Welfares here.

Welfare   Thank you.

Hester *enters.*

Hester   You all go inside.

The kids go inside

Welfare   Hands clean?

Hester   Yes, Maam.

Welfare   Wash them again.

Hester *washes her hands again.*
Dries them.

Welfare   The welfare of the world.

Hester   Maam?

Welfare   Come on over, come on.

Hester *stands behind* **Welfare***, giving her a shoulder rub.*

Welfare   The welfare of the world weighs on these shoulders, Hester.

(*Rest*)

We at Welfare are at the end of our rope with you. We put you in a job and you quit. We put you in a shelter and you walk. We put you in school and you drop out. Yr children are also truant. Word is they steal. Stealing is a gateway crime, Hester. Perhaps your young daughter is pregnant. Who knows. We build bridges you burn them. We sew safety nets, rub harder, good strong safety nets and you slip through the weave.

Hester   We was getting by all right, then I dunno, I been tired lately. Like something in me broke.

Welfare   You and yr children live, who knows where.

Hester   Here, Maam, under the Main Bridge.

Welfare   This is not the country, Hester. You cannot simply—live off the land. If yr hungry you go to the shelter and get a hot meal.

Hester   The shelter hassles me. Always prying in my business. Stealing my shit. Touching my kids. We was making ends meet all right then—ends got further apart.

Welfare   "Ends got further apart." God!

(*Rest*)

I care because it is my job to care. I am paid to stretch out these hands, Hester. Stretch out these hands. To you.

Hester   I gived you the names of four daddys: Jabbers and Bullys and Troubles and Beautys. You was gonna find them. Garnish they wages.

Welfare   No luck as yet but we're looking. Sometimes these searches take years.

Hester   Its been years.

Welfare Lifetimes then. Sometimes they take that long. These men of yours, theyre deadbeats. They dont want to be found. Theyre probably all in Mexico wearing false mustaches. Ha ha ha.

(*Rest*)

What about the newest child?

Hester Baby.

Welfare What about "Babys" father?

Hester —. I dunno.

Welfare Dont know or dont remember?

Hester You think Im doing it with mens I dont know?

Welfare No need to raise your voice no need of that at all. You have to help me help you, Hester.

(*Rest*)

Run yr fingers through my hair. Go on. Feel it. Silky isnt it?

Hester Yes, Maam.

Welfare Comes from a balanced diet. Three meals a day. Strict adherence to the food pyramid. Money in my pocket, clothes on my back, teeth in my mouth, womanly parts where they should be, hair on my head, husband in my bed.

Hester *combs* **Welfare***'s hair.*

Welfare Yr doctor recommends that you get a hysterectomy. Take out yr womans parts. A spay.

Hester Spay.

Welfare I hope things wont come to that. I will do what I can. But you have to help me, Hester.

Hester ((Dont *make* me hurt you.))

Welfare What?

Hester I didnt mean it. Just slipped out.

Welfare Remember yr manners. We worked good and hard on yr manners. Remember? Remember that afternoon over at my house? That afternoon with the teacups?

Hester *Manners*, Maam?

Welfare Yes. Manners.

Hester
Welfare

Welfare   Babys daddy. Whats his name?

Hester   You wont find him no how.

Welfare   We could get lucky. He could be right around the corner and I could walk out and there he would be and then we at Welfare would wrestle him to the ground and turn him upside down and let you and yr Baby grab all the money that falls from Deadbeat Daddys pockets. I speak metaphorically. We would garnish his wages.

Hester   How much would that put in my pocket?

Welfare   Depends how much he earns. Maybe 100. Maybe. We take our finders fee. Whats his name?

Hester   I dunno.

Welfare   You dont have to say it out loud. Write it down.

She gives **Hester** *pencil and paper.*

Hester *writes.* **Welfare** *looks at the paper.*

Welfare   "A."

(*Rest*)

Adam, Andrew, Archie, Arthur, Aloysius, "A" what?

Hester   Looks good dont it?

Welfare   You havent learned yr letters yet, have you?

Hester   I want my leg up is all.

Welfare   You wont get something for nothing.

Hester   I been good.

Welfare   Five bastards is not good. Five bastards is bad.

Hester   Dont make me hurt you!

She raises her club to strike **Welfare**.

Welfare   You hurt me and, kids or no kids, I'll have you locked up. We'll take yr kids away and yll never see them again.

Hester   My lifes my own fault. I know that. But the world dont help, Maam.

Welfare   The world is not here to help us, Hester. The world is simply here. We must help ourselves.

(*Rest*)

I know just the job for you. It doesnt pay well, but the work is very rewarding. Hard honest work. Unless yr afraid of hard honest work.

Hester   I aint afraid of hard work.

Welfare   Its sewing. You can do it at home. No work no pay but thats yr decision.

(*Rest*)

Heres the fabric. Make sure you dont get it dirty.

Hester   Can I express myself?

Welfare   Needles, thread and the pattern, in this bag. Take the cloth. Sew it. If you do a good job therell be more work. Have it sewn by tomorrow morning, yll get a bonus.

Hester *takes the cloth and notions.*

Hester   I dont think the world likes women much.

Welfare   Dont be silly.

Hester   I was just thinking.

Welfare   Im a woman too! And a black woman too just like you. Don't be silly.

Hester
Welfare

(*Rest*)

Hester *puts her hand out, waiting.*

Hester   Yr shoulders. Plus I did yr hair.

Welfare   Is a buck all right?

Hester
Welfare

Welfare   Unless yll change a fifty.

Hester   I could go get change—

Welfare   Take the buck, K? And the cloth. And go.

She owes **Hester** *more dollars, but after a beat,* **Hester** *just leaves.*

SECOND CONFESSION: THE WELFARE
"I Walk the Line"

Welfare   I walk the line

between us and them

between our kind and their kind.

The balance of the system depends on a well-drawn boundary line

and all parties respecting that boundary.

I am

I am a married woman.

I dont—that is have never

never in the past or even in the recent present or even when I look

look out into the future of my life I do not see any interest

any *sexual* interest

in anyone

other than my husband.

(*Rest*)

My dear husband.

The hours he keeps.

The money he brings home.

Our wonderful children.

The vacations we go on.

My dear husband he needed

a little spice.

And I agreed. We both needed spice.

We both hold very demanding jobs.

We put an ad in the paper: "Husband and Bi-Curious Wife, seeking—"

But the women we got:

Hookers. Neurotics. Gold diggers!

"Bring one of those gals home from work," Hubby said. And

Hester,

she came to tea.

(*Rest*)

She came over and we had tea.

From my mothers china.

And marzipan on matching china plates.

Hubby sat opposite in the recliner

hard as Gibraltar. He told us what he wanted and we did it.

We were his little puppets.

She was surprised, but consented.

Her body is better than mine.

Not a single stretchmark on her.

Im a looker too dont get me wrong just in a different way and

Hubby liked the contrast.

Just light petting at first.

Running our hands on each other

then Hubby joined in

and while she and I kissed

Hubby did her and me alternately.

The thrill of it—.

(*Rest*)

I was so afraid I'd catch something

but I was swept away and couldnt stop.

She stuck her tongue down my throat

and Hubby doing his thing on top

my skin shivered.

She let me slap her across the face

and I crossed the line.

(*Rest*)

It was my first threesome

and it wont happen again.

And I should emphasize that

she is a low-class person.

What I mean by that is that we have absolutely nothing in common.

As her caseworker I realize that maintenance of the system depends on a well-drawn boundary line

and all parties respecting that boundary.

And I am, after all,

I am a married woman.

She exits.

Hester *reenters, watches* **Welfare** *exit.*

Hester   Bitch.

Hester, *alone on stage, examines the cloth* **Welfare** *gave her.*

Hester   Sure is pretty cloth. Sewing cant be that hard. Thread the needle stick it in and pull it through. Pretty cloth. Lets see what we making. Oooooh. Uh evening dress. Go to a party in. Drink champagne and shit. Uh huh, "Dont mind if I do," and shit and la de *dah* and come up in a limo and everybody wants a picture. So many lights Im blinded. Wear dark glasses. Strut my stuff.

She has another painful stomach attack which knocks the wind out of her and doubles her over.

Far away, **Chilli** *walks by with his picnic basket on his arm.*

He pauses, checks his pocket watch, then continues on.

Hester, *recovering from her attack, sees him just before he disappears.*

Hester   Chilli!

Intermission.

Scene Five: Small Change and Sandwiches

Late at night. The children inside, all sleeping.

Lots of "A's" written in **Hester**'s *practice place.*

Hester, *working on her sewing, tries to thread the needle.*

Hester   Damn needle eyes too damn small. Howmy supposed to get the thread through. Theres a catch to everything, Hester. No easy money nowheres. Wet the thread good. Damn.

She squeezes her eyes shut and opens them, trying to focus. Having difficulty threading the needle, she takes out an object wrapped in brown paper.

Looks cautiously around. Begins to unwrap it.

A sandwich.

Hester   Put something in my stomach maybe my eyesll work.

Amiga Gringa *comes in.*

Hester *stashes the package, picks up her sewing.*

Amiga Gringa   Mother Hubbard sewing by street lamp. Very moving.

Hester   I got me uh job. This here is work.

Amiga Gringa   From Welfare?

Hester   Shes getting me back in the workforce. I do good on this she'll give me more.

Amiga Gringa   Whats the pay?

Hester   Its by the piece.

Amiga Gringa   How much?

Hester   Ten bucks maybe.

Amiga Gringa   Maybe?

Hester   I get a bonus for working fast.

Amiga Gringa   Very nice fabric. Very pretty. Very expensive. And oooh, look at what yr making.

Hester   You good with needles? Thread this. My eyes aint good.

Amiga *tries halfheartedly to thread the needle. Quits.*

Amiga Gringa   Sorry.

Hester *continues trying to thread the needle.*

Hester   Today we had uh E-clipse. You seen it?

Amiga Gringa   Cant say I did. Good yr working. Getting some money in yr pocket. Making a good example for the kids. Pulling yrself up by yr bootstraps. Getting with the program. Taking responsibility for yr life. I envy you.

Hester   Me?

Amiga Gringa   Yr working, Im—looking for work.

Hester   I bet I could get you some sewing.

Amiga Gringa   Oh no. Thats not for me. If I work, Hester, I would want to be paid a living wage. You have agreed to work for less than a living wage. May as well be a slave. Or an animal.

Hester   Its a start. She said if I do well—

Amiga Gringa   If you do well shes gonna let you be her slave *for life.* Wouldnt catch me doing that. Chump work. No no no. But its a good thing you are. Example to the kids.

Hester   I aint no chump.

Amiga Gringa   Course you arent. Yr just doing chump work is all.

Hester   Its a leg up. Cant start from the top.

Amiga Gringa   Why not? Plenty of people start from the top. Why not you? Sure is pretty fabric.

Hester   All I gotta do is sew along the lines.

Amiga Gringa   Bet the fabric cost a lot. I wonder how much we could get for it— on the open market.

Hester   Aint mine to sell. Its gonna make a nice dress. Im gonna sew it up and try it on before I give it to her. Just for fun.

But she still hasn't been able to thread the needle.

Amiga Gringa   Bet we could get 100 bucks. For the fabric. A lot more than youd get for sewing it. And you wouldnt have to lift a finger. I'd sell it tonight. Have the money for you in the morning.

Hester   No thanks.

Amiga Gringa   Suit yrself.

Hester *continues trying to thread that damn needle.*

Amiga Gringa   Chump work.

Hester   They make the eyes too small, thats the problem.

(*Rest*)

I seen Chilli right after I was with the Welfare. You said he was looking for me and there he was! Jabbers daddy walking right by with a big gold pocket watch. But did I tell? Did I run after Welfare and say, "Theres Jabbers daddy?" I did not. Can you imagine?

Amiga Gringa   I told ya he was looking for ya. Hes gonna find you too.

Hester   Jabbers daddy, after all these years!

Amiga Gringa   Maybe yr lucks turning.

Hester   You think?

Amiga Gringa   Maybe.

Amiga Gringa

Hester

(*Rest*)

Amiga Gringa   I missed my period.

Hester   Dont look at *me.*

(*Rest*)

Whatcha gonna do.

Amiga Gringa   Have it, I guess.

Hester   You may not be knocked up.

Amiga Gringa   Theres something in here all right. I can feel it growing inside. Just my luck.

Hester   You shoulda been careful.

Amiga Gringa   —Whatever.

Hester   So get rid of it if you dont want it.

Amiga Gringa   Or birth it then sell it.

Hester   You as crazy as they come.

Amiga Gringa

Hester

Amiga Gringa

Amiga *leans toward* **Hester** *to kiss her.*

Hester *pulls back a bit.*

Amiga Gringa   Whassamatter?

Hester   I dont got no love for nobody cept the kids.

Amiga *pulls back, takes up the fabric.*

Amiga Gringa   I'll get you a lot of money for this.

Hester   No.

Amiga Gringa   Whassis?

Amiga Gringa *discovers the brown paper package.*

Hester   Nothing.

Amiga Gringa   Smells like something. Smells like food. Smells like egg salad.

Hester   I was saving it.

Amiga Gringa   Lets celebrate! Come on itll be fun. Kids!

Hester   They *sleep*. Let em sleep.

Amiga Gringa   Lets toast my new kid. Just you and me. A new life has begun. Am I showing? Not yet, right? Will be soon enough. Little bastards in there living high on the hog, taking up space. Little bastard, we toast you with: egg salad.

Amiga *takes a big bite out of the sandwich.*

Hester *grabs at it but* **Amiga** *keeps it from her reach.*

Bully *comes outside.*

Bully   Mommie?

Hester   Yes, Bully.

Bully   My hands.

Hester   Lemmie unlock em.

Bully *comes over.* **Hester** *opens her hands.*

Bully   Egg salad?

Amiga Gringa   Yeah. Its yr mommies sandwich.

Amiga *gives the sandwich to* **Hester** *who almost takes a bite but sees* **Bully** *looking on hungrily.*

Hester *gives the sandwich to* **Bully**. **Bully** *eats.*

Hester *gives* **Amiga** *the fabric.*

Hester   Cheat me and I'll kill you.

Amiga Gringa   Have a little faith, Hester. Amiga will sell this fabric for you. You will not be a chump. In the morning when the sun comes up yll be 100 bucks richer. Sleep tight.

She takes the fabric and leaves.

Bully *sits with her mother, licking her fingers.*

THIRD CONFESSION: AMIGA GRINGA
"In My Head I Got It Going On"

Amiga Gringa   In my head I got it going on.

The triple X-rated movie:

Hester and Amiga get down and get dirty.

Chocolate and Vanilla get into the ugly.

We coulda done a sex show behind a curtain

then make a movie and sell it

for three bucks a peek.

I had me some delicious schemes

to get her out of that hole she calls home.

Im doing well for myself

working my money maker.

Do you have any idea how much cash I'll get for the fruit of my white womb?!

Grow it.

Birth it.

Sell it.

And why shouldnt I?

(*Rest*)

Funny how a woman like Hester

driving her life all over the road

most often chooses to walk the straight and narrow.

Girl on girl action is a very lucrative business.

And someones gotta do something for her.

Im just trying to help her out.

And myself too, ok. They dont call it Capitalizm for nothing.

(Rest)

She liked the idea of the sex

at least she acted like it.

Her looking at me with those eyes of hers.

You looking like you want it, Hester.

Shoot, Miga, she says thats just the way I look she says.

It took a little cajoling to get her to do it with me

for an invited audience.

For a dime a look.

Over at my place.

Every cent was profit and no overhead to speak of.

The guys in the neighborhood got their pleasure

and we was our own boss so we didnt have to pay no joker off the top.

We slipped right into a very profitable situation

like sliding into warm water.

Her breasts her bottom

she let me touch her however I wanted

I let her ride my knees.

She made sounds like an animal.

She put her hand between my legs.

One day some of the guys took advantage.

Ah, what do you expect in a society based on Capitalizm.

I tell you the plight of the worker these days—.

Still one day Im gonna get her to make the movie

cause her and me we had the moves down

very sensual, very provocative, very scientific, very lucrative.

In my head I got it going on.

Scene Six: The Reverend on the Rock

Late at night. Down the road, **Reverend D.** *cleaning his cornerstone, a white block of granite bearing the date in Roman numerals, and practicing his preaching.*

[**Reverend D.**   "It is easier for a camel to go through the eye of a needle than for a rich man to enter the kingdom of God." And you hear that and you say, let me get a tax shelter and hide some of my riches so that when I stand up there in judgment God wont be none the wiser! And that is the problem with the way we see God. For most of us, God is like the IRS. God garnishes yr wages if you dont pay up. God withholds. The wages of sin, they lead to death, so you say, let me give to the poor. But not any poor, just those respectable charities. I want my poor looking good. I want my poor to know that it was me who bought the such and such. I want my poor on tv. I want famous poor, not miscellaneous poor. And I dont want local poor. Local poor dont look good. Gimmie foreign poor. Poverty exotica. Gimmie brown and yellow skins against a non-Western landscape, some savanna, some rain forest some rice paddy. Gimmie big sad eyes with the berri-berri belly and the outstretched hands struggling to say "Thank You" the only english they know, right into the camera. And put me up there with them, holding them, comforting them, telling them everythings gonna be alright, we gonna raise you up, we gonna get you on the bandwagon of our ways, put a smile in yr heart and a hamburger in yr belly, baby.

(Rest)

And that is how we like our poor. At arms length. Like a distant relation with no complication. But folks, we gotta—]

Hester *comes in and watches him.*

After a while, he notices her and stops talking.

Hester   Nice rock.

Reverend D.   Thank you.

Hester   Theres writing on it.

Reverend D.   Dont come close. Its the date its just the date. The date.

Well, the year.

Hester   Like a calendar.

Reverend D.   Its a cornerstone. The first stone of my new church. My backers are building me a church and this is the first stone.

Hester   Oh.

(Rest)

You told me to come back. Im back.

Reverend D.   Theyll start building my church tomorrow. My church will be a beautiful place. Its not much of a neighborhood now but when my church gets built, oh therell be a turnaround. Lots of opportunity for everyone. I feel like one of the pilgrims. You know, they step out of their boats and on to that Plymouth rock. I step off my soapbox and on to my cornerstone.

Hester   You said come back to get my money. Im back.

Reverend D.   Do you know what a "backer" is?

Hester   Uh-uhn.

Reverend D.   Its a person who backs you. A person who believes in you. A person who looks you over and figures you just might make something of yrself. And they get behind you. With kind words, connections to high places, money. But they want to make sure they havent been suckered, so they watch you real close, to make sure yr as good as they think you are. To make sure you wont screw up and shame them and waste their money.

(*Rest*)

My backers are building me a church. It will be beautiful. And to make sure theyre not wasting their money on a man who was only recently a neerdowell, they watch me.

Hester   They watching now?

Reverend D.   Not now. Now theyre in their nice beds. Between the cool sheets. Fast asleep. I dont sleep. I have this feeling that if I sleep I will miss someone. Someone in desperate need of what I have to say.

Hester   Someone like me.

Reverend D.   I dont have your money yet but I will. I'll take up a collection for you on Sunday. I'll tell them yr story, that yr someone in need, and all the money will go to you. Every cent of it. We get good crowds on Sunday.

(*Rest*)

Ive got work to do.

He waits for her to go but she stays.

He goes back to cleaning his cornerstone.

Hester   Today we had uh *E*-clipse. You seen it?

Reverend D.   You should go.

Hester   A shadow passed over the sky. Everything was dark. For a minute.

Reverend D.   It was a cloud. Or an airplane. Happens all the time.

Hester   No clouds out today. It was uh *E*-clipse.

Reverend D.   I am taking a collection for you on Sunday. Youll have to wait until then. Good night.

Hester   Uh *E*-clipse.

Reverend D.   There was no eclipse today! No eclipse!

(*Rest*)

Good night.

Hester   I was crossing the street with the kids. We had a walk sign. White is walk and red is dont walk. I know white from red. Aint colorblind, right? And we was crossing. And a shadow fell over, everything started going dark and, shoot I had to look up. They say when theres uh *E*-clipse you shouldnt look up cause then you go blind and alls I need is to go blind, thank you. But I couldnt help myself. And so I stopped right there in the street and looked up. Never seen nothing like it.

(*Rest*)

I dont know what I expected to see but.

(*Rest*)

It was a big dark thing. Blocking the sun out. Like the hand of fate. The hand of fate with its five fingers coming down on me.

(*Rest*)

(*Rest*)

And then the trumpets started blaring.

(*Rest*)

And then there was Jabber saying "Come on Mommie, Come on!" The trumpets was the taxi cabs. Wanting to run me over. Get out the road.

Reverend D.
Hester
Reverend D.
Hester

Reverend D. *sits on his rock, his back hiding his behavior which has become unseemly.*

Reverend D.   Comeer.

Hester *slowly goes to him.*

Reverend D.   Suck me off.

Hester   No.

Reverend D.   Itll only take a minute. Im halfway there. Please.

She goes down on him. Briefly. He cumms.

Mildly. Into his handkerchief.

She stands there. Ashamed. Expectant.

Reverend D.   Go home. Put yr children to bed.

Hester   Maybe we could get something regular going again—

Reverend D.   Go home. Go home.

Hester
Reverend D.

(Rest)

Reverend D.   Heres something. Its all I have.

He offers her a crumpled bill which she takes.

Reverend D.   Next time you come by—. It would be better if you could come around to the *back*. My churchll be going up and—. If you want your money, it would be better if you come around to the back.

Hester   Yeah.

She goes. **Reverend D.** *sits there, watching her leave.*

FOURTH CONFESSION: REVEREND D.
"Suffering Is an Enormous Turn-on"

Reverend D.   Suffering is an enormous turn-on.

(Rest)

She had four kids and she came to me asking me what to do.

She had a look in her eye that invites liaisons

eyes that say red spandex.

She had four children four fatherless children four fatherless mouths to feed

fatherless mouths fatherless mouths.

Add insult to injury was what I was thinking.

There was a certain animal magnetism between us.

And she threw herself at me

like a baseball in the Minors

fast but not deadly

I coulda stepped aside but.

God made her

and her fatherless mouths.

(Rest)

I was lying in the never ending gutter of the street of the world.

You can crawl along it forever and never crawl out

praying for God to take my life

you can take it God

you can take my life back

you can have it

before I hurt myself somebody

before I do a damage that I cannot undo

before I do a crime that I can never pay for

in the never ending blistering heat

of the never ending gutter of the world

my skin hot against the pavement

but lying there I knew

that I had never hurt anybody in my life.

(*Rest*)

(*Rest*)

She was one of the multitude. She did not stand out.

(*Rest*)

The intercourse was not memorable.

And when she told me of her *predicament*

I gave her enough money to take care of it.

(*Rest*)

In all my days in the gutter I never hurt anyone.

I never held hate for anyone.

And now the hate I have for her

and her hunger

and the *hate* I have for her hunger.

God made me.

God pulled me up.

Now God, through her, wants to drag me down

and sit me at the table

at the head of the table of her fatherless house.

Scene Seven: My Song in the Street

Hester *with the kids. They are all playing freeze tag.*

After a bit, **Hester** *is "it." She runs then stops, standing stock-still, looking up into the sky.*

Bully *gets tagged.*

Bully   1 Mississippi, 2 Mississippi, 3 Mississippi, 4 Mississippi, 5 Mississippi.

Jabber *gets tagged.*

Jabber   1 Mississippi, 2 Mississippi, 3 Mississippi, 4 Mississippi, 5 Mississippi. Yr it.

Hester *gets tagged.*

Hester
Hester

Jabber   Mommie?

Hester   What.

Bully   Whasswrong?

Hester   You think I like you bothering me all day?

Hester

Jabber/Bully/Trouble/Beauty

(Rest)

Hester   All yall. Leave Mommie be. She cant play right now. Shes tired.

She stands there looking up into the sky.

The kids play apart.

Bully   Lemmie see it.

Trouble   What?

Bully   Yr pee.

Trouble
Bully

Bully   Dont got no hair or nothing on it yet. I got hair on mines. Look.

Trouble
Bully

Trouble   Jabber. Lets see yrs.

Trouble
Jabber
Bully

Bully   Its got hair. Not as much as mines though.

Beauty   I had hairs but they fell out.

Trouble   Like a bald man or something?

Beauty   Yeah.

Trouble
Trouble

Bully   Dont be touching yrself like that, Trouble, dont be nasty.

Trouble
Trouble

Jabber   You keep playing with it ssgonna fall off. Yr pee be laying in the street like a dead worm.

Trouble   Mommieeee!

Hester   Dont talk to Mommie just now.

Bully   Shes having a nervous breakdown.

Hester   Shut the fuck up, please.

(*Rest*)

(*Rest*)

Jabber   When I grow up I aint never gonna use mines.

Trouble   Not me. I be *using* mines.

Jabber   Im gonna keep mines in my pants.

Bully   How you ever gonna get married?

Jabber   Im gonna get married but Im gonna keep it in my pants.

Bully   When you get married you gonna have to get on top uh yr wife.

Jabber   I'll get on top of her all right but I'll keep it in my pants.

Trouble   Jabber, you uh tragedy.

Bully   When I get married my husbands gonna get on top of me and—

Hester   No ones getting on top of you, Bully.

Bully   He'll put the ring on my finger and I'll have me uh white dress and he'll get on top of me—

Hester   No ones getting on top of you, Bully, no ones getting on top of you, so shut yr mouth about it.

Trouble   How she gonna have babies if no one gets on top of her?

Hester   Dont *make* me hurt you!

She *raises her hand to* **Trouble** *who runs off.*

Bully *starts crying.*

Hester   Shut the fuck up or I'll give you something to cry about!

The kids huddle together in a knot.

Hester
Jabber/Bully/Beauty Hester
Jabber/Bully/Beauty
Hester

(Rest)

Hester   Bedtime.

Beauty   Its too early for bed—

Hester   BEDTIME!

They hurry off.

Hester *goes back to contemplating the sky.*

Hester
Hester
Hester

Hester   Big dark thing. Gods hand. Coming down on me. Blocking the light out.
Five-fingered hand of fate. Coming down on me.

The **Doctor** *comes on wearing his "SPAY" sandwich board.*

He watches her looking up. After a bit he looks up too.

Doctor   We've scheduled you in for the day after tomorrow. First thing in the
morning. You can send yr kids off to school then come on in. We'll have childcare for
the baby. We'll give you good meals during yr recovery. Yll go to sleep. Yll go to
sleep and when you wake up, whisk! Yll be all clean. No worries no troubles no trials
no tribulations no more mistakes. Clean as a whistle. You wont feel a thing. Day after
tomorrow. First thing in the morning. Free of charge. Itll be our pleasure. And yours.
All for the best. In the long run, Hester. Congratulations.

He walks off. **Hester** *is still looking up.*

Chilli *walks in with his picnic basket on his arm.*

He pauses to check his pocket watch.

Hester *lowers her head.*

The sight of him knocks the wind out of her.

Hester   Oh.

Chilli   Ive been looking for you.

Hester   Oh.

Chilli   Ssbeen a long time.

Hester   I—I—.

Chilli   No need to speak.

Hester   I—

Chilli   Yr glad to see me.

Hester   Yeah.

Chilli   I been looking for you. Like I said. Lifes been good to me. Hows life been to you?

Hester   Ok.—. Hard.

Chilli
Hester

Hester   I was with the Welfare and I seed you. I called out yr name.

Chilli   I didnt hear you. Darn.

Hester   Yeah.

(*Rest*)

I woulda run after you but—

Chilli   But you were weak in the knees. And you couldnt move a muscle.

Hester   Running after you woulda gived you away. And Welfares been after me to know the names of my mens.

Chilli   Mens? More than one?

Hester   I seed you and I called out yr name but I didnt run after you.

(*Rest*)

You look good. I mean you always looked good but now you look better.

(*Rest*)

I didnt run after you. I didnt give you away.

Chilli   Thats my girl.

(*Rest*)

Welfare has my name on file, though, doesnt she?

Hester   From years ago. I—

Chilli   Not to worry couldnt be helped. I changed my name. They'll never find me. Theres no trace of the old me left anywhere.

Hester   Cept Jabber.

Chilli   Who?

Hester   Yr son.

Hester
Chilli

Chilli   Guess what time it is?

Hester   He takes after you.

Chilli   Go on guess. Betcha cant guess. Go on.

Hester   Noon?

Chilli   Lets see. I love doing this. I love guessing the time and then pulling out my watch and seeing how close I am or how far off. I love it. I spend all day doing it. Doctor says its a tick. A sure sign of some disorder. But I cant help it. And it doesnt hurt anyone. You guessed?

Hester   Noon.

Chilli   Lets see. Ah! 3.

Hester   Oh.

Hester *goes back to contemplating the sky.*

Chilli   Sorry.

(*Rest*)

Whats up there?

Hester   Nothing.

Chilli   I want you to look at me. I want you to take me in. Ive been searching for you for weeks now and now Ive found you. I wasnt much when you knew me. When we knew each other I was—I was a shit.

(*Rest*)

I was a shit, wasnt I?

Hester
Chilli

Chilli   I was a shit, agree with me.

Hester   We was young.

Chilli   We was young. We had a romance. We had a love affair. We was young. We was in love. I was infatuated with narcotics. I got you knocked up then I split.

Hester   Jabber, hes yr spitting image. Only hes a little slow, but—

Chilli   Who?

Hester   Jabber. Yr son.

Chilli   Dont bring him into it just yet. I need time. Time to get to know you again. We need time alone together. Guess.

Hester   3:02.

Chilli   Ah! 3:05. But better, yr getting better. Things move so fast these days. Ive seen the world Ive made some money Ive made a new name for myself and I have a loveless life. I dont have love in my life. Do you know what thats like? To be alone? Without love?

Hester   I got my childr—I got Jabber. hes my treasure.

Hester
Chilli

(*Rest*)

Chilli   Im looking for a wife.

Hester   Oh.

Chilli   I want you to try this on.

He takes a wedding dress out of his basket.

He puts it on her, right over her old clothes.

Hester *rearranges the club, still held in her belt, to get the dress on more securely.*

Hester   I seed you and I called out your name, but you didnt hear me, and I wanted to run after you but I was like, Hester, if Welfare finds out Chillis in town they gonna give him hell so I didnt run. I didnt move a muscle. I was mad at you. Years ago. Then I seed you and I was afraid I'd never see you again and now here you are.

Chilli   What do you think?

Hester   Its so clean.

Chilli   It suits you.

Hester *gets her shoes.*

Hester   I got some special shoes. Theyd go good with this. Jabber, come meet yr daddy!

Chilli   Not yet, kid!

(*Rest*)

Lets not bring him into this just yet, K?

He fiddles with his watch.

Chilli   Fourteen years ago. Back in the old neighborhood. You and me and the moon and the stars. What was our song?

Hester
Chilli

Hester   Huh?

Chilli   What was our song?

(*Rest*)

Da dee dah, dah dah dee dee?

Hester   Its been a long time.

Chilli   Listen.

He plays their song, "The Looking Song," on a tinny tape recorder. He sings along as she stands there. After a bit he dances and gets her to dance with him. They sing as they dance and do a few moves from the old days.

Chilli   Im looking for someone

to lose my looks with

looking for someone

to lose my shape with

looking for someone

to-get-my-hip-replaced with

looking for someone

Could it be you?

Im looking for someone

to lose my teeth with

looking for someone

to go stone deef with

looking for someone

to-lie–6-feet-underneath with

looking for someone

Could it be you?

They say, "Seek and ye shall find"

so I will look until Im blind

through this big old universe

for rich or poor better or worse

Singing:

yuck up my tragedy

oh darling, marry me

let's walk on down the aisle, walk on

Down Down Down.

Cause Im looking for someone

to lose my looks with

looking for someone

to lose my teeth with

looking for someone

I'll-lie–six-feet-underneath with

looking for someone

Could it be you?

Theyre breathless from dancing.

This is real. The feelings I have for you, the feelings you are feeling for me, these are all real. Ive been fighting my feelings for years. With every dollar I made. Every hour I spent. I spent it fighting. Fighting my feelings. Maybe you did the same thing. Maybe you remembered me against yr will, maybe you carried a torch for me against yr better judgment.

Hester   You were my first.

Chilli   Likewise.

(*Rest*)

He silently guesses the time and checks his guess against his watch. Is he right or wrong?

"Yuck up my tragedy."

Hester   Huh?

Chilli   "Marry me."

Hester

Chilli

Hester   K.

Chilli   There are some conditions some things we have to agree on. They dont have anything to do with money. I understand your situation.

Hester   And my—

Chilli   And your child—ok. *Our* child—ok. These things have to do with you and me. You would be mine and I would be yrs and all that. But I would still retain my rights to my manhood. You understand.

Hester   Sure. My—

Chilli   Yr kid. We'll get to him. I would rule the roost. I would call the shots. The whole roost and every single shot. Ive proven myself as a success. Youve not done that. It only makes sense that I would be in charge.

Hester   —K.

(*Rest*)

I love you.

Chilli   Would you like me to get down on my knees?

He gets down on his knees, offering her a ring.

Heres an engagement ring. Its rather expensive. With an adjustable band. If I didnt find you I would have had to, well—. Try it on, try it on.

*He checks his watch. As **Hester** fiddles with the ring, **Bully** and **Trouble** rush in. **Beauty** and **Baby** follow them.*

Bully   Mommie!

Hester   No.

Trouble   You look fine!

Hester   No.

Beauty   Is that a diamond?

Hester   No!

Baby   Mommie!

Hester *recoils from her kids.*

Hester
Bully/Trouble/Beauty/Baby

Bully   Mommie?

Chilli   Who do we have here, honey?

Hester

Bully/Trouble/Beauty/Baby

Chilli   Who do we have here?

Hester   The neighbors kids.

Chilli *goes to look at his watch, doesnt.*

Chilli   Honey?

Hester   Bully, wheres Jabber at?

Chilli   Honey?

Hester   Bully, Im asking you a question.

Chilli   Honey?

Trouble   Hes out with Miga.

Chilli   So you all are the neighbors kids, huh?

Trouble   Who the fuck are you?

Hester   Trouble—

Chilli   Who the fuck are you?

Bully   We the neighbors kids.

Chilli
Hester

(*Rest*)

Chilli   Honey?

Hester   Huh?

Chilli   Im—. I'm thinking this through. I'm thinking this all the way through. And I think—I think—.

(*Rest*)

(*Rest*)

I carried around this picture of you. Sad and lonely with our child on yr hip. Stuggling to make do. Stuggling against all odds. And triumphant. Triumphant against everything. Like—hell, like Jesus and Mary. And if they could do it so could my Hester. My dear Hester. Or so I thought.

(*Rest*)

But I dont think so.

He takes her ring and her veil.

He takes her dress. He packs up his basket.

(*Rest*)

Hester   Please.

Chilli   Im sorry.

He looks at his watch, flipping it open and then snapping it shut. He leaves.

FIFTH CONFESSION: CHILLI
"We Was Young"

Chilli   We was young

and we didnt think

we didnt think that nothing we could do would hurt us

nothing we did would come back to haunt us

we was young and we knew all about gravity but gravity was a law that did not apply
to those persons under the age of eighteen

gravity was something that came later

and we was young and we could

float

weightless

I was her first

and zoom to the moon if we wanted and couldnt nothing stop us

we would go

fast

and we were gonna live forever

and any mistakes we would shake off

we were Death Defying

we were Hot Lunatics

careless as all get out

and she needed to keep it and I needed to leave town.

People get old that way.

(*Rest*)

We didnt have a car and everything was pitched toward love in a car

and there was this car lot down from where we worked and we were fearless

late nights go sneak in those rusted Buicks that hadnt moved in years

I would sit at the wheel and pretend to drive

and she would say she felt the wind in her face

surfing her hand out the window

then we'd park

without even moving

in the full light of the lot

making love—

She was my first.

We was young.

Times change.

Scene Eight: The Hand of Fate

*Night. The back entrance to the **Reverend D.**'s new church.*

Hester *comes in with the kids in tow.*

Hester   Sunday night. He had people in there listening to him this morning. He passed the plate in my name. Not in my name directly. Keeps me secret, cause, well, he has his image. I understand that. Dont want to step on everything hes made for himself. And he still wants me. I can tell. A woman can tell when a man eyes her and he eyed me all right.

(Rest)

Yr building this just from talking. Must be saying the right things. Nobodyd ever give me nothing like this for running my mouth. Gonna get me something now. Get something or do something. Fuck you up fuck you up! Hold on, girl, it wont come to that.

(Rest)

[I'll only ask for five dollars. Five dollars a week. That way he cant say no. And hes got a church, so he got five dollars. I'll say I need to buy something for the kids. No. I'll say I need to—get my hair done. There is this style, curls piled up on the head, I'll say. Takes hours to do. I need to fix myself up, I'll say. Need to get my looks back. Need to get my teeth done. Caps, bridges, what they called, fillers, whatever. New teeth, dentures. Dentures. He dont cough up I'll go straight to Welfare. Maybe.]

(Rest)

Jabber *comes running around the building.*

*He sees **Hester** and sneaks up on her, touching her arm.*

Jabber   Yr it.

Hester   I aint playing.

Jabber   K.

Hester   Where you been.

Jabber   Out with Miga.

Hester   Oh.

(Rest)

Jabber   Mommie?

Hester   What.

Jabber
Hester

(*Rest*)

Jabber   I dont like the moon.

Hester   I'll cover it up for you.

She holds her hand up to the sky, hiding the moon from view.

Jabber   Whered it go?

Hester   Its gone to bed. You too.

She nudges him away from her.

He curls up with the others.

Hester
Hester

Reverend D. *comes outside.*

He carries a large neon cross.

Hester   Its Sunday.

He sees the children.

Reverend D.   Oh God.

Hester   Its Sunday.—. Yesterday was—Saturday.

Reverend D.   Excuse me a minute?

He props the cross against a wall.

Hester   Its Sunday.

Reverend D.   I passed the plate and it came back empty.

Hester   Oh.

Reverend D.   But not to worry: I'll have some. Tomorrow morning—

Hester   I was gonna—get myself fixed up.

Reverend D.   —When the bank opens. A hundred bucks. Tomorrow morning. All for you. You have my word.

Hester   I was thinking, you know, in my head, that there was something I can do to stop that hand coming down. Must be something—

Reverend D.   I'll have my lawyer deliver the money. Its better if you dont come back. Its too dangerous. My following are an angry bunch. They dont like the likes of you.

Hester   But you do. You like me.

Reverend D.   Youd better go.

Hester   Why you dont like me? Why you dont like me no more?

He tries to go back inside. She grabs ahold of him.

Dont go.

Reverend D.   Take yr hands off me.

Hester   Why you dont like me?

They struggle as he tries to shake her loose.

Then, in a swift motion, she raises her club to strike him.

He is much stronger than she. He brutally twists her hand.

She recoils in pain and falls to the ground.

Jabber, *wide awake, watches.*

Reverend D.   Slut.

(*Rest*)

Dont ever come back here again! Ever! Yll never get nothing from me! Common slut. Tell on me! Go on! Tell the world! I'll crush you underfoot.

He goes inside.

Hester
Hester
Hester

Jabber   Mommie.

Hester
Hester

Jabber   The moon came out again.

Jabber
Hester
Jabber

(*Rest*)

Jabber   Them bad boys had writing. On our house. Remember the writing they had on our house and you told me to read it and I didnt wanna I said I couldnt but that wasnt really true I could I can read but I didnt wanna.

Hester   Hush up now.

Jabber   I was reading it but I was only reading it in my head I wasn't reading it with my mouth I was reading it with my mouth but not with my tongue I was reading it only with my lips and I could hear the word outloud but only outloud in my head.

Hester Shhhh.

Jabber I didnt wanna say the word outloud in your head.

Hester
Hester

Jabber I didnt wanna say you the word. You wanna know why I didnt wanna say you the word? You wanna know why? Mommie?

Hester
Hester

(*Rest*)

Hester What.

Jabber It was a bad word.

Hester
Hester

Jabber Wanna know what it said? Wanna know what the word said?

Hester What.

Jabber
Jabber

Hester What?

Jabber "Slut."

Hester Go to sleep, Jabber.

Jabber It read "Slut." "Slut."

Hester Hush up.

Jabber Whassa "Slut"?

Hester Go sleep.

Jabber You said if I read it youd say what it means. Slut. Whassit mean?

Hester I said I dont wanna hear that word. How slow are you? Slomo.

Jabber Slut.

Hester You need to close yr mouth, Jabber.

Jabber I know what it means. Slut.

Hester (Shut up.)

Jabber Slut.

Hester (I said shut up, now.)

Jabber I know what it means.

Hester   (And I said shut up! Shut up.)

(*Rest*)

(*Rest*)

Jabber   Slut. Sorry.

The word just popped out, a child's joke.

He covers his mouth, sheepishly. They look at each other.

Hester
Jabber
Hester
Jabber

Hester *quickly raises her club and hits him once.*

Brutally. He cries out and falls down dead. His cry wakes **Bully**, **Trouble**, *and* **Beauty**. *They look on.* **Hester** *beats* **Jabber**'s *body again and again and again.* **Trouble** *and* **Bully** *back away.*

Beauty *stands there watching.*

Jabber *is dead and bloody.*

Hester *looks up from her deed to see* **Beauty** *who runs off.*

Hester *stands there alone—wet with her son's blood.*

Grief-stricken, she cradles his body. Her hands wet with blood, she writes an "A" on the ground.

Hester   Looks good, Jabber, dont it? Dont it, huh?

SIXTH CONFESSION: HESTER, LA NEGRITA
"I Shoulda Had a Hundred-Thousand"

Hester, La Negrita   Never shoulda had him.

Never shoulda had none of em.

Never was nothing but a pain to me:

Five mistakes!

No, dont say that.

—nnnnnnnn—

Kids? Where you gone?

Never shoulda haddem.

Me walking around big as a house

Knocked up and Showing

and always by myself.

Men come near me oh yeah but then

love never sticks longer than a quick minute

wanna see something last forever watch water boil, you know.

I never shoulda haddem!

(*Rest*)

She places her hand in the pool of **Jabber**'s *blood.*

No:

I shoulda had a hundred

a hundred

I shoulda had a hundred-thousand

A hundred-thousand a whole *army* full I shoulda!

I shoulda.

One right after the other! Spitting em out with no years in between!

One after another:

Tail to head: ·

Spitting em out:

Bad mannered Bad mouthed Bad Bad *Bastards*!

A whole *army full* I shoulda!

I shoulda

—nnnnnnn—

I shoulda

She sits there, crumpled, alone.

The prison bars come down.

Scene Nine: The Prison Door

All circle around **Hester** *as they speak.*

All   LOOK AT HER!

WHO DOES SHE THINK

SHE IS

THE ANIMAL

NO SKILLS

CEPT ONE

CANT READ CANT WRITE

SHE MARRIED?

WHAT DO YOU THINK?

SHE OUGHTA BE MARRIED

SHE AINT MARRIED

THATS WHY THINGS ARE BAD LIKE THEY ARE

CAUSE OF

GIRLS LIKE THAT

THAT EVER HAPPEN TO ME YOU WOULDNT SEE ME DOING THAT

YOU WOULDNT SEE THAT HAPPENING TO ME

WHO THE HELL SHE THINK SHE IS

AND NOW SHES GOT TO PAY FOR IT

HAH!

They spit.

All   SHE DONT GOT NO SKILLS

CEPT ONE

CANT READ CANT WRITE

SHE MARRIED?

WHAT DO YOU THINK?

JUST PLAIN STUPID IF YOU ASK ME AINT NO SMART

WOMAN GOT ALL THEM BASTARDS

AND NOT A PENNY TO HER NAME

SOMETHINGS GOTTA BE DONE

CAUSE I'LL BE DAMNED IF SHE GONNA LIVE OFF ME.

All
Hester
All

Welfare   Is she in any pain?

Doctor   She shouldnt be. She wont be having anymore children.

Welfare   No more mistakes.

Chilli   Whats that?

Welfare   An "A."

Amiga Gringa   An "A."

Doctor   First letter of the alphabet.

Welfare   Thats as far as she got.

Hester *holds up her hands—they're covered with blood.*

She looks up with outstretched arms.

Hester   Big hand coming down on me. Big hand coming down on me. Big hand coming down on me

End of Play.

The Looking Song

Words and Music by Suzan-Lori Parks

Im look-ing___ for so-me-one to lose my looks with. Look-ing___ for so-me-one to lose my shape with. Look-ing___ for so-me-one to get my hip re-placed___ with. Look-ing for some-one, could it be___ you?

Im look-ing___ for so-me-one to lose my teeth with. Look-ing___ for so-me-one to go stone deef with. Look-ing___ for so-me-one to lie 6 feet un-der-neath___ with. Look-ing for some-one, could it be___ you?

Well, they say, "Seek___ and ye shall find." So I will look un-til

Introduction to Lynn Nottage

Aimée K. Michel

In 2017 Lynn Nottage was the first female playwright to win the Pulitzer Prize for Drama a second time, receiving the prestigious award for *Sweat*, a play that seemed to speak directly to the political moment in the US. She is quoted in a *Los Angeles Times* article, "Lynn Nottage on her Pulitzer Win for Drama," saying, "No. 1, I'm representing for women, and No. 2, I'm representing for playwrights of color. . . . Winning the second Pulitzer firmly places me in conversation with this culture." Writing plays which speak directly to the political, social, and cultural moment is of importance to Nottage. In "The Listener," an interview with Michael Schulman in the *New Yorker* magazine, she claims to write "morally ambiguous heroes or heroines, people who are fractured within their own bodies, who have to make very difficult choices in order to survive."

Born November 2, 1964, in Brooklyn and raised by her mother, an educator, and her father, a psychologist, in a neighborhood she describes as "working class" and "multicultural," Nottage has spent most of her life in New York City and New England. As a senior at the High School of Music and Art in Manhattan, she was determined to attend Brown University and disregarded the school guidance counselor's discouragement of that choice. The counselor thought she didn't have a chance of getting in. She applied only to Brown and was vindicated when she announced to the counselor that she had been accepted. She then attended Yale School of Drama to study Playwrighting. Upon graduation, her social conscience aroused, she decided to apply to work for Amnesty International and was hired as the National Press Officer, a position she held for four years. In the *New Yorker* interview, she calls this time "one of the most formative and important experiences I could have."

Indeed, it was her time at Amnesty which led her to write her first post-Yale drama *Poof* in 1993. In the course of her work she was confronted with rampant violence against women and Amnesty didn't seem to be addressing it. She claims to have written *Poof* as her own response to the need to address women's issues. In the play a woman who is being abused by her husband wishes him dead. She gets her wish when he spontaneously combusts and turns to a pile of ashes right in front of her. Nottage uses comedy to make the explosive subject matter a little easier to witness and process.

Poof was followed quickly by *Crumbs from the Table of Joy* (1995), a memory play set in 1950s Brooklyn; *Por'Knockers* (1995), a play in which black nationalist militants bomb an FBI building; *Mud, River, Stone* (1997) in which a boy soldier takes Americans hostage in order to reclaim what is owed him; and *Las Meninas* (2002), based on both Velazquez's famous seventeenth-century Spanish painting and a true story of a romance between the Queen of France and a dwarf in the Louis XIV court.

In 2004, Nottage took the New York theater world by storm with her award-winning play *Intimate Apparel* which had premiered regionally at Center Stage in Baltimore and at South Coast Rep in CA. When it moved to New York City, the Roundabout Theater production won the 2004 Steinberg New Play Award, Best Play from the New York Drama Critics' Circle, and the Outer Critics' Circle Award for Outstanding Off-Broadway Play. At the same time that she was writing *Intimate Apparel*, she wrote *Fabulation or the Re-Education of Undine* (2004), which was meant as a companion piece. Whereas *Intimate Apparel* takes place in 1905, *Fabulation* takes place in "The Present" or 2004 when it premiered at Playwrights Horizons. Both plays explore the lives of ambitious black women who build businesses, save their money, and end up robbed and deserted by their husbands. In the *New Yorker* interview, Nottage shares "My family has generations of women abandoned by men," alluding to the fact that these plays are somewhat autobiographical.

After receiving a Guggenheim grant and the PEN/Laura Pels International Foundation for Theater Award, in 2007, Nottage was awarded a MacArthur "Genius" Grant. Shortly after, in 2008, her new play *Ruined* premiered at the Goodman Theater in Chicago. Co-commissioned by the Goodman and the Manhattan Theater Club in New York City, it opened Off-Broadway in 2009. The play was a tremendous success winning the 2009 Pulitzer Prize for Drama, the Drama Desk Award for Outstanding Play, the Outer Critics Circle Outstanding New Off-Broadway Play Award, the Lucille Lortel Outstanding Play Award, and the OBIE Award for Best New American Play. Nottage was inspired to write *Ruined* by Bertolt Brecht's *Mother Courage and her Children*, a play which she greatly admired. She wanted to write a version of *Mother Courage* set in war-torn Congo so she and Kate Whoriskey, a director with whom she had a collaborative relationship, traveled to Africa and interviewed Congolese women in refugee camps. In the play they explore the sexual violence against women that is part of war. The raping of women mutilates their wombs so they can no longer bear children—a form of genocide.

In 2011, Nottage's play *By the Way, Meet Vera Stark* opened at Second Stage Theater in New York City. Returning to satirical comedy, Nottage explores the challenges that black actors have faced finding meaningful roles in the movies where for so long they have played only stereotypical characters.

Nottage's timely play *Sweat* was co-commissioned by the Oregon Shakespeare Festival and Arena Stage as part of their *American Revolutions History Cycle* project and premiered in Ashland in 2015, playing at Arena Stage in 2016 and winning the 2016 Susan Smith Blackburn Prize. It then opened Off-Broadway at the Public Theater in late 2016 where it won Nottage the OBIE Award for Playwrighting. In March 2017, *Sweat* opened on Broadway, marking Nottage's Broadway debut. It won her a second Pulitzer Prize for Drama in 2017 as well as nominations for Tony and Drama Desk Awards. *Sweat* spoke exactly to the political moment in which it premiered. A nation disillusioned by the empty promises of unbridled capitalism is torn apart by people who have worked alongside each other for years suddenly finding each other the enemy. The play ends with Evan, a parole officer, speaking the deepest truth: "Most folks think it's the guilt or rage that destroys us in the end, but I know from experience that it's shame that eats us away until we disappear."

More recent work includes *Mlima's Tale,* which premiered at the Public Theater in New York City in 2018; *The Secret Life of Bees*, a musical adaptation of Sue Monk Kidd's novel by the same name, which premiered at the Atlantic Theater Company in New York City in 2019; and *Floyd's*, which premiered at the Guthrie Theater in Minneapolis, also in 2019.

Awards and accolades continue to honor Nottage's work. In 2017 she was awarded the Award of Merit Medal from the American Academy of Arts and Letters for her entire body of work.

Intimate Apparel, included in this anthology, profoundly articulates Nottage's artistic vision which reveals characters who are trapped in economic and political situations over which they have no control but which cause them great personal pain. The four female characters in the play, Esther, Mrs. Dickson, Mrs. Van Buren and Mayme, are each restricted by the rigid society of 1905 America. The married women are addressed only as Mrs. Dickson and Mrs. Van Buren, giving weight to their married status. But marriage does not bring happiness. Mrs. Van Buren is unable to bear children and because that is the only attribute that gives her value, she is now useless to her wealthy powerful husband. Mrs. Dickson married for security rather than become an old maid, and tolerated a husband addicted to opium. Spinsters Esther and Mayme believe they are nothing without husbands. They are both talented women, Esther as a seamstress and Mayme as a classical pianist, but the color of their skin and their gender limit their potential.

Though the play focuses on Esther, a shy, hard-working, very bright 35-year-old African American woman who has built a thriving business in sewing intimate apparel for women of means, it also lays bare the pain and loneliness of the other women. Nottage has said that Esther was inspired by her great-grandmother, a seamstress who made intimate apparel and married a man with whom she corresponded while he was working on the Panama Canal. As the play opens, Mrs. Dickson, Esther's landlord and friend, encourages her to accept the attentions of an industrious head bellman with prospects while Esther is entranced by a correspondence with a Panamanian, George Armstrong. Esther can neither read nor write so she is dependent on others to facilitate communication with George. However, she is clearly taken with the romantic idea of a man in a foreign place reaching across the distance to her.

Esther has the soul of an artist. She is industrious, talented, and enterprising, and has saved enough money for her dream of running her own beauty salon for black women where they can be pampered as fine ladies. But she is a romantic. Her creations are works of art. They adorn and make beautiful the women who wear them. She wants more in life than a bellman and feels that she deserves it.

Her story is complicated by a touching connection with Mr. Marks, an Orthodox Jewish immigrant who sells her exquisite fabric. In an ideal world, she would end up with Mr. Marks, with whom she shares a passion for the sensuality of clothing. The scenes between Esther and Mr. Marks are poignant and ultimately heartbreaking. They speak the same language and their growing affection for and understanding of each other is palpable. Yet, their religions and backgrounds keep them miles apart. Esther admits: "I touched someone . . . who I knew I wasn't supposed to touch. I touched them because I wanted to."

When George Armstrong arrives to marry her, he is not the man she imagined. She determines to try to make the marriage work but ends deeply betrayed by him. She discovers Mayme wearing a stunning silk smoking jacket which Esther gave to George on their wedding night. Mayme confesses their affair and reveals that George has gambled away all Esther's money. When George arrives at Mayme's door, expecting to be taken in, Esther commands, "Let him go. He ain't real, he a duppy, a spirit. We be chasing him forever," alluding to her acceptance of the proscribed life that is to be hers in a world full of ignorance, prejudice, and defeat.

In the last two scenes of the play Nottage offers redemption to Esther. She boldly crosses the barriers between her and Mr. Marks as she offers him, in friendship, the smoking jacket. *"[Mr. Marks] removes his outer jacket, revealing the fringes of his tallit katan. He carefully puts on the silk jacket."* He asks, 'What do you think?' Esther responds, "It fits wonderfully." And then she returns to her old room in the boarding house where Mrs. Dickson welcomes her with open arms and she picks up again, yet with a new future. **"Esther** *lightly touches her belly. A moment. She walks over to the old sewing machine and begins to sew together pieces of fabric, the beginnings of a new quilt."*

Intimate Apparel

Lynn Nottage

Production History

Intimate Apparel was commissioned and first produced by South Coast Repertory (David Emmes, Producing Artistic Director; Martin Benson, Artistic Director; Paula Tomei, Managing Director) and Center Stage (Irene Lewis, Artistic Director; Michael Ross, Managing Director) in Costa Mesa, California, opening on April 18, 2003. It was directed by Kate Whoriskey; the set design was by Walt Spangler; the costume design was by Catherine Zuber; the lighting design was by Scott Zielinski; the sound design was by Lindsay Jones; the original music was by Reginald Robinson; the arranger and piano coach was William Foster McDaniel; the dramaturg was Jerry Patch; the associate production dramaturg was Rhonda Robbins; the production manager was Tom Aberger; and the production stage manager was Randall K. Lum. The cast was as follows:

Esther	Shané Williams
Mrs. Dickson	Brenda Pressley
Mrs. Van Buren	Sue Cremin
Mr. Marks	Steven Goldstein
Mayme	Erica Gimpel
George	Kevin Jackson

Intimate Apparel was originally produced in New York City by Roundabout Theater Company (Todd Haimes, Artistic Director; Ellen Richard, Managing Director), opening on April 8, 2004. It was directed by Daniel Sullivan; the set design was by Derek McLane; the costume design was by Catherine Zuber; the lighting design was by Allen Lee Hughes; the original music was by Harold Wheeler; the sound design was by Marc Gwinn; the production stage manager was Jay Adler; and the stage manager was Amy Patricia Stern. The cast was as follows:

Esther	Viola Davis
Mrs. Dickson	Lynda Gravatt
Mrs. Van Buren	Arija Bareikis
Mr. Marks	Corey Stoll
Mayme	Lauren Velez
George	Russell Hornsby

Author's Note

For Mayme's song on pages 293–4, any period-appropriate piano accompaniment is acceptable. The projected title card at the end of the play is essential to the storytelling and should be included in all productions.

Characters

Esther, *thirty-five, African American*
Mrs. Dickson, *fifties, African American*
Mrs. Van Buren, *thirties, white American*
Mr. Marks, *thirties, Romanian Jewish immigrant*
Mayme, *thirties, African American*
George, *thirties, Barbadian immigrant*

Place

Lower Manhattan

Time

1905

Production Note

The set should be spare to allow for fluid movement between the various bedrooms.
The action should flow seamlessly from scene to scene. The act endings mark the only
true blackouts in the play.

Act One

Scene One: Wedding Corset—White Satin with Pink Roses

Lower Manhattan, 1905.

A bedroom. It is simple, unadorned with the exception of beautifully embroidered curtains and a colorful crazy quilt.

A clumsy ragtime melody bleeds in from the parlor.

In the distance the sound of laughter and general merriment.

Esther, *a rather plain African American woman (thirty-five), sits at a sewing machine table diligently trimming a camisole with lace. She is all focus and determination.*

Mrs. Dickson (*offstage*)   Don't be fresh, Lionel. I know your mama since before the war. (**Mrs. Dickson**, *fifty, a handsome, impeccably groomed African American woman, enters laughing.*) There you are. Mr. Charles was admiring the bread pudding and I told him that our Esther made it. It seems he has a sweet tooth.

Esther   Mr. Charles is overly generous, come, the pudding ain't nothing special.

Mrs. Dickson   And did I mention that our most available Mr. Charles was promoted to head bellman at just about the finest hotel in New York? Yes.

Esther   But he still fetching luggage.

Mrs. Dickson   Not just any luggage, high-class luggage.

Esther   And is high-class luggage easier to carry?

Mrs. Dickson   I reckon it is easier to haul silk than cotton, if you know what I'm saying. (*She laughs.*) And he sporting a right smart suit this evening.

Esther   Yes, it cashmere.

Mrs. Dickson   You can tell more about a man by where he shops, than his practiced conversation. 'Cause any man who's had enough tonic can talk smooth, but not every man has the good sense to shop at—

Esther and Mrs. Dickson   Saperstein's.

Esther *laughs.* **Mrs. Dickson** *examines the embroidery.*

Mrs. Dickson   Lovely.

Esther   It's for Corinna Mae's wedding night.

Mrs. Dickson   Don't tell me you've been in here all evening? Corinna Mae is getting ready to leave with her fiancé.

Esther   I wish I could find my party face. It really is a lovely affair. You done a fine job.

Mrs. Dickson   Come now, it ain't over yet. Put aside your sewing and straighten yourself up. There. You'll have a dance before this evening's out.

Esther   Please, Mrs. Dickson, I can't, really. I'll just stand there like a wallflower.

Mrs. Dickson   Nonsense, I've danced a half a dozen times, and my feet are just about worn out.

Esther   If I had your good looks I'd raise a bit of dust myself. Ain't nobody down there interested in me.

Mrs. Dickson   Esther, you're being silly. You've been moping around here for days. What's the matter?

Esther   If you must know, I turned thirty-five Thursday past.

A moment.

Mrs. Dickson   Oh Lord, I forgot, child. I sure did. Look at that. With Corinna Mae carrying on and all these people, it slipped my mind. Happy birthday, my sweet Esther.

She gives **Esther** *a big hug.*

Esther   It's fine. You had all this to prepare for. And I been living in this rooming house for so long, I reckon I'm just another piece of furniture.

Mrs. Dickson   Never. You were a godsend when you come to me at seventeen. Yes. I remember thinking how sweet and young you was with a sack full of overripe fruit smelling like a Carolina orchard.

Esther   And now? Twenty-two girls later, if you count Lerleen. That's how many of these parties I have had to go to and play merry. I should be happy for them, I know, but each time I think why ain't it me. Silly Corinna Mae, ain't got no brain at all, and just as plain as flour.

Mrs. Dickson   Your time will come, child.

Esther   What if it don't? Listen to her laughing. God forgive me, but I hate her laughter, I hate her happiness and I feel simply awful for saying so. And I'm afraid if I go back in there, she'll see it all over my face, and it's her day.

Mrs. Dickson   There are a number of young men open to your smile. A sour face don't buy nothing but contempt. Why our Mr. Charles has had three servings of your bread pudding.

Esther   And he shouldn't have had any. (**Esther** *laughs.*) He weighs nearly as much as your horse.

Mrs. Dickson   Nonsense, he weighs more then poor Jessup. Shhh. He is a good man, poised for success. Yes.

Esther   But he's been coming to these parties for near two years and if he ain't met a woman, I'd bet it ain't a woman he after. I've been warned about men in refined suits. But still, Esther would be lucky for his attention, that's what you thinking. Well, I ain't giving up so easy.

Mrs. Dickson   Good for you. But there are many a cautionary tale bred of overconfidence. When I met the late Mr. Dickson he was near sixty and I forgave his infatuation with the opiates, for he come with this rooming house and look how many good years it's given me. Sure I cussed that damn pipe, and I cussed him for making me a widow, but sometimes we get to a point where we can't be so particular.

Esther (*snaps*)   Well, I ain't going down there to be paraded like some featherless bird.

A moment.

I'm sorry, would you kindly take this down to Corinna Mae?

Mrs. Dickson   I'll do no such thing. You can bring it down yourself.

She starts for the door, but abruptly stops.

It tough, Esther, for a colored woman in this city. I ain't got to tell you that. You nimble with your fingers, but all Corinna Mae got be her honey-colored skin. And you good and smart and deserve all the attention in that room, but today's her day and all I ask is that you come toast her as I know she'd toast you. Put aside your feelings and don't say nothing about Sally's piano playing, the girl trying. For God's sake, this a party not a wake.

Esther   Let me fix my hair.

Mrs. Dickson *suddenly remembers the letter tucked in her dress pocket and extends it to* **Esther**.

Mrs. Dickson   And I thought you might want this letter. It come this morning, I didn't want to forget.

Esther   Who'd be writing me?

Mrs. Dickson (*reading*)   Mr. George Armstrong.

Esther   It ain't someone I know. Armstrong? There was an Armstrong that attended my church, but he dead a long time now. Will you read the letter to me? (**Esther** *takes the letter.*)

Mrs. Dickson   I got a house full of people. You best remind me tomorrow. And I will see you downstairs, shortly. Plenty of punch left and it better than New Year's, so best hurry. I made certain everybody be leaving this party happy.

She exits.

Esther *examines the letter, then places it on the sewing table unopened.*

Lights cross-fade, allowing her to linger in half-light during **George**'s *letter. A Panama bunk.*

George, *a muscular, handsome African-Caribbean man, rises from his cot.*

He wipes mud from his face and bare arms, as he speaks with a musical Barbadian accent.

George   Dear Miss Mills,

My name is George Armstrong. I work in Panama alongside Carson Wynn, your deacon's son. We digging a big hole across the land, they say one day ships will pass from one ocean to the next. It is important work, we told. If importance be measured by how many men die, then this be real important work. One man drops for every twenty feet of canal dug, like so many flies. Carson say if we eat a can of sardines, they'll protect us against the mosquitoes and fever. I say, not as long as we be digging. Lord knows our minds deserve a bit of shade. But ain't such a thing to be had, not here at least. Don't think me too forward, but I thought it would be nice to have someone to think about, someone not covered from head to toe in mud, someone to ward off this awful boredom. Carson speaks so highly of his church that I find comfort in his recollections. I ask if I may write you? And if you so please, I'd welcome your words.

Sincerely,

George Armstrong

Scene Two: Gardenia Ball Corset—Pink Silk and Crêpe de Chine

An elegant boudoir.

The silhouette of a naked woman moves gracefully behind a translucent screen. She slides her torso into the fitted lingerie.

Esther sits at the dressing table exploring the carefully arranged silver grooming set. She jumps to attention at the sound of **Mrs. Van Buren**'*s voice, which betrays the slightest hint of a Southern accent.*

Mrs. Van Buren   I feel exposed. I think the straps need to be tightened, Esther.

Esther   No ma'am, that's the way it's meant to be, but I'll add a little more fabric to—

Mrs. Van Buren   No, no, if this is what you made for that singer, it is what I want. All right. I'm coming out.

She emerges from behind the dressing screen wearing a very low corset embossed with lavender flowers. She's an attractive white woman in her early thirties and attempts to carry herself with great poise and confidence.

Oh God, I look ridiculous, and I'm behaving absolutely foolishly, but I'm not sure what else to do. Look at me. I've spent a fortune on feathers and every manner of accouterment.

Esther *begins to tighten the lacing of the corset.*

Mrs. Van Buren   They've written positively splendid things about me in the columns this season.

Esther   I'm sure they did.

Mrs. Van Buren   But does it matter? Has he spent an evening at home? Or even noticed that I've painted the damn boudoir vermilion red?

Esther   You look lovely, Mrs. Van Buren.

Mrs. Van Buren   Ha! I feel like a tart from the Tenderloin. Granted I've never been, but I'm told. Are you sure this is what you made for that . . . singer?

Esther   It is identical to the stitching.

Mrs. Van Buren *examines herself in the mirror, at first with disgust, which gradually gives way to curiosity.*

Mrs. Van Buren   And you say the French women are wearing these?

Esther   So I'm told.

Mrs. Van Buren   I don't believe it. It hardly seems decent. But I suppose the French aren't known for their modesty.

She strikes a provocative, though slightly self-conscious pose.

Esther   Well, it the rage. Some ladies ain't even wearing corsets in private.

Mrs. Van Buren   Is that true?

Esther   Most gals don't like 'em, even fine ladies like yourself. Truth is I ain't known a man to court pain for a woman's glance.

Mrs. Van Buren   You're not one of those suffragettes, are you?

Esther   Oh God no, Mrs. Van Buren

Mrs. Van Buren   Indeed. I'd just as soon not tamper in men's business.

She pours a snifter of brandy.

Esther   Talk and a nickel will buy you five cents worth of trouble.

Mrs. Van Buren *gulps back the brandy.*

Mrs. Van Buren   It's come to this. If Mother dear could see what has become of her peach in the big city.

She clumsily tugs at the bodice.

Esther *runs her fingers gracefully along the seam, down the curve of* **Mrs. Van Buren's** *waist.* **Mrs. Van Buren** *tenses slightly at the sensation of being touched. Distracted, she touches the beading along the corset, in doing so . . .*

Mrs. Van Buren   Do we really need all of these dangling things?

Esther   Oh, I hope you ain't mind, I added a touch of beading along the trim.

Mrs. Van Buren   It is different.

Esther   Do you like it?

Mrs. Van Buren   I confess, I almost do. It's a bit naughty. (*Giggles.*) Yes, I might even wear it beneath my gown tonight. Do you think anyone will notice? It is the annual Gardenia Ball, quite the event of the season.

Esther   So I hear.

Mrs. Van Buren   And do you know what that means?

A moment.

They'll all be there, parading their good fortune. I'll have to smile, be polite, because I'm known for that, but I will dread every last minute, every bit of forced conversation with the Livingstons and the Babcocks. They want to know. All of them do. "When are you going to have a child, Evangeline?" And my answer is always the same, "Why we're working on it, dear, speak to Harold." And dear Harry will be in a sour mood for a week. You probably don't even know what I'm talking about. Have you children?

Esther   No, Mrs. Van Buren. I ain't been married.

Mrs. Van Buren   Never? May I tell you something?

Esther   Yes. If you like.

Mrs. Van Buren   I've given him no children. (*Whispered.*) I'm afraid I can't. It's not for the lack of trying. One takes these things for granted, you assume when it comes time that it will happen, and when it doesn't who is to blame? They think it's vanity that's kept me childless, I've heard the women whispering. If only I were that vain. But it's like he's given up.

Esther   But, you're so beautiful.

Mrs. Van Buren   You think so?

Esther   Yes. I can't imagine he'd ever lose interest.

Mrs. Van Buren   But he has turned to other interests. Trust me. This will stay between us? I'm told you're discreet.

Esther   I just sew, missus. I don't hear anything that I ain't supposed to.

Mrs. Van Buren   You understand why. I'd rather not be a divorcée, at my age it would prove disastrous.

Esther   Do you think there's something wrong with a woman alone?

Mrs. Van Buren   What I think is of little consequence. If I were (*Whispered.*) brave I'd collect my things right now and find a small clean room someplace on the other side of the park. No, further in fact. And I'd . . . But it isn't a possibility, is it?

A moment. Suddenly . . .

Esther   I don't know that I'll marry.

Mrs. Van Buren   Of course you will, it's just a matter of finding the right gentleman.

Esther   Ma'am, I don't want to speak out of turn. But, I been working since I was nine years old with barely a day's rest. In fact, the other evening I was at my sewing machine and I stopped work and all this time had passed, gone. Years really. And I known right there that some things ain't meant to be. And that's all right, ain't it? And I wouldn't have thought no more about it, but then I got this . . .

She stops mid-thought and busies herself with her sewing basket.

Mrs. Van Buren   Yes?

Esther   I'm almost ashamed to say it. At my age it foolish, I know.

Mrs. Van Buren   What is it?

Esther   A gentleman . . . A gentleman has taken interest in me.

Mrs. Van Buren   Really? How wonderful! Is he respectable?

Esther   I don't know, I mean, I don't know him actually. I got me this letter from Panama. A man in Panama. He wrote about two weeks back. I been carrying it around since. But, I ain't so sure I should answer.

Mrs. Van Buren   And why not?

Esther   I ain't much of a writer.

Mrs. Van Buren   Oh—

Esther   No, I ain't a writer at all. The fact is I can't read.

Mrs. Van Buren   Do you have the letter? May I see it?

Esther *hesitates, then pulls the letter from her smock and hands it to* **Mrs. Van Buren***, who quickly peruses it and smiles.*

Mrs. Van Buren   Panama. He has lovely penmanship, that's important. He isn't careless with his stroke, that's the mark of a thoughtful man. It's a good thing, I believe.

Esther   I won't respond, of course, if it ain't appropriate.

Mrs. Van Buren   Nonsense. He's halfway across the world. I'm sure he's perfectly harmless. A bit lonesome perhaps, that's all.

Esther   But, if I have Mrs. Dickson over at the rooming house help me, she'll get all up in my business. And she's got an opinion about everything and I'd rather not be lectured or questioned or bothered. She's just about the busiest . . . in any event, she said to rip it up promptly, a decent woman wouldn't resort to such a dalliance. But as you can see he has taken interest in me.

Mrs. Van Buren   Would you like me to help you write to him, Esther?

Esther   I couldn't ask.

Mrs. Van Buren   You needn't, I insist.

Esther   I never done this before.

Mrs. Van Buren   Nor have I.

Esther   Maybe it ain't such a good idea, Mrs. Van Buren. I ain't really got much to say.

Mrs. Van Buren   Goodness, of course you do—

Esther (*with conviction*) No, I don't! I live in a rooming house with seven unattached women and sew intimate apparel for ladies, but that ain't for a gentleman's eyes. Sure I can tell him anything there is to know about fabric, but that hardly seems a life worthy of words.

Mrs. Van Buren   It is a beginning. Come Esther, don't be shy.

She sits at her dressing table and retrieves a sheet of stationery.

Now, how shall we start?

Esther   I don't know.

Mrs. Van Buren   What sort of things do you like to do?

Esther   I . . . I go to church every Sunday, well practically, but I don't really listen to the sermons, I just like the company and the singing of course . . . And on Tuesdays . . . I take the trolley downtown to Orchard Street, and I climb five flights, in darkness, to this tiny apartment. And, when I open the door my eyes are met . . .

Mr. Marks, *a handsome Orthodox Jewish man, enters with a bolt of gorgeous flowing fabric which he proudly displays.*

Lost in the sweet recollection, **Esther** *resumes speaking.*

Esther   He keeps a wealth of fabric in that apartment. He got everything you need, even things you don't know you need—

Mrs. Van Buren   Esther, you're jumping a bit ahead of yourself.

Lights fade around **Mr. Marks.**

Mrs. Van Buren   Shall we begin with "Dear Mr. Armstrong—"

Esther   Yes. That's good. "Dear Mr. Armstrong—"

Mrs. Van Buren   "I received your letter—"

Lights cross-fade.

George *enters in his work clothing.*

The cross-fade should allow time for **Esther** *and* **George** *to dwell on the stage together, but only for several moments.*

George   Dear Miss Mills,

I received your letter. It two months in the coming, so please forgive me, I've already written you twice since. I am most happy to make your acquaintance, and I'm anxious to hear all about you. As for me, I'd like to report on our good progress, but it isn't the case. This canal seem a near-impossible mission, but here we be, digging until day-end bathed in mud up to our necks. They say a mad Frenchman dreamed up this Panama project, and convinced the devil to give him an army of workers. The price, this great fissure across the land that reach right into the earth's belly. Indeed, chaos is a jackhammer away, that's what be said here anyway. But when the great oceans meet and the gentlemen celebrate, will we colored men be given glasses to raise? Today we severed the roots of a giant flamboyant, and watched it tumble to the ground. I stood thighdeep in crimson blossoms, swathed in the sweet aroma of death and wondered how a place so beautiful could become a morgue. But the days aren't all bad. If you take a moment to listen to the forest around us there is so much life just out of sight. And there be men from every corner of the Caribbean, sharing tales around fires, heads light on rum and laughter. But now, I read your letter. I see you sitting at your sewing machine. I hear the sound of the wheel turning, the tiny stitches drawing together the pieces of satin. They got machines here that take six men to operate, and slice through stone like butter. All this wonder and waste, but your letter be the most splendid thing and shall ride in me pocket, until the next.

Yours considerately,

George Armstrong

Scene Three: Imperial Silk, Embroidered with Blue Thread

Another bedroom in a cramped tenement flat. It is small and cluttered with bolts of fabric.

Mr. Marks *scrambles to put on his suit jacket as a knock sounds on the door. His worn black suit is missing the top button. With haste, he folds up his bedroll and opens the door, breathless.*

Esther *stands in the doorway. She notices the bedroll but chooses to ignore it.*

Esther   Mr. Marks? Am I too early?

Mr. Marks   No, not at all. Come in. Come in. I've a number of new things to show you.

Esther   Good—

Mr. Marks   Ah. Let me get.

He unrolls an extraordinary length of silk.

Feel this one. Japanese silk, your special order for the lady on Fifth Avenue. It took me nearly one month to find this very piece. I had to go everywhere. Lovely. Yes?

Esther   Lovely. Look at how finely embroidered. Beautiful. I never—

Mr. Marks   I have two extra yards left, I give to you for next to nothing. If you'd like.

Esther   Next to nothing is too much for me. You know my answer. What will I do with it?

Mr. Marks   Make something lovely for yourself.

Esther   It will be wasted on me.

Mr. Marks   You'll never see this again. I guarantee. I'll let our Fifth Avenue lady cover the difference. How about that? I see how much you like. I promise it is the very best quality. She don't know what she has, she don't come down here to feel the fabric herself, to feel the difference, the texture, she don't know how remarkable a weave.

Esther   I could make a shawl.

Mr. Marks (*fishing*)   Or a smoking jacket for your gentleman, perhaps.

Esther (*bashfully*)   My gentleman? Oh no.

She self-consciously runs the fabric across her face, then releases it.

You've distracted me, Mr. Marks. You always get me to buy something I don't need.

Mr. Marks   When I see something of quality, I like to share with my favorite customers. Everybody want the same thing. But you want different. I like that.

Esther   Thank you.

He warmly smiles at she. She averts her gaze, allowing her eyes to fall on the spot where he's missing a button.

He self-consciously touches the spot.

Mr. Marks   Ah, look at that. I have lost a button.

He returns his attention to the silk.

I buy at the docks yesterday morning, it come right off a ship from the Orient, I see it and think Esther Mills will like. Of course. Everybody else gabardine, wool, nainsook. (*Flirtatiously.*) But it isn't often that something so fine and delicate enters the store. Look at the way the gold thread is interwoven; a hand took the time to gently wind it through each and every stitch like a magician. It is magnificent, yes. You'll make something exquisite. I can see from your hands that you are blessed with the needle and the thread, which means you'll never be without warmth.

Esther   I'm afraid it was either learn to sew or turn back sheets for fifty cents a day.

Mr. Marks   You make it sound too simple. My father sew, my brother sew, yes, for the finest families. But I don't have the discipline, the fingers. Look at the size of these hands. Like carnati, Romanian sausage. I wish for your hands.

She laughs and returns to examining the fabric, reveling in the tactile pleasure of the texture. There is a sensual way she regards the fabric.

He can't help but notice this.

She brings the fabric to her nose and sniffs.

Mr. Marks *watches her with genuine delight.*

Esther   It's fruit dye. Am I right? It smells like—

Mr. Marks —an imperial palace, it is signed by the artist right there. I wouldn't be surprised if it was created for an empress.

Esther You really want me to buy this, don't you? All right, it means I'll go without sugar for a week, will that make you happy?

Mr. Marks It makes you happy, it makes me happy.

Esther Oh Lord, I do want it.

She affectionately grasps his hand; he abruptly pulls it away.

She is taken aback.

The color won't rub off on you.

Mr. Marks No, no. I'm sorry. It's not that. Please. My religious belief doesn't permit me to touch a woman who isn't my wife or my relative.

Esther Oh, I see.

Mr. Marks It is the rabbinical law, not mine.

Esther Your wife must be a happy woman.

Mr. Marks I am not married. Not yet. My fiancée is in Romania. Um, my family made the arrangement years ago.

Esther Oh? I bet you miss her something awful.

He rubs his hand where she touched him. He laughs, a bit self-consciously.

Mr. Marks I haven't ever met her, actually.

Lights cross-fade.

Scene Four: Heliotrope Handkerchief

Another bedroom. A canopy bed dominates.

Mayme, *a strikingly beautiful African-American woman (thirty), sits at an upright piano. She plays a frenzied upbeat rag. Her silk robe is torn, and her face trembles with outrage.*

Esther *bangs on the door, then finally enters carrying a carpetbag.*

Esther I been knocking for ages. Didn't you hear me? . . . What's going on?

A moment.

Mayme They really do make me sick. Always stinking of booze. And look what he done. It's the only pretty thing I own and look what he done.

She pulls her torn silk robe tight around her body.

Esther That ain't nothing, I can fix it for you.

Mayme   All the pawing and pulling. For a dollar they think they own you.

She quickly washes her face and privates in a basin.

You don't approve of me, Esther, I don't mind. Sit. I'm awfully glad to see ya, 'am. When you knocked on the door, I thought Christ almighty, not another one. I'm so damn tired, I don't know what to do.

She sits down at the upright piano and gracefully plays a slow, well-considered rag.

Esther   Oh, pretty. Did you write that, Mayme?

Mayme   Yeah . . .

Continuing to play.

My daddy gave me twelve lashes with a switch for playing this piece in our parlor. One for each year I studied the piano. He was too proper to like anything colored, and a syncopated beat was about the worst crime you could commit in his household.

She stops playing.

I woke up with the sudden urge to play it.

Esther   You must have gotten a lot of licks in your time.

Mayme   Yeah, baby, I wasn't born this black and blue.

She picks up a bottle of moonshine and takes a belt.

Esther   That there the reason you tired, that ignorant oil is unforgiving. Best let it lie.

Mayme   Oh bother, stop playing mother hen and come show me what you got.

Esther   Anything else, mistress?

Mayme   Hush your mouth, you're far too sweet for sarcasm.

Esther *pulls a corset from her bag; it's pale blue with lines of royal blue glass beads ornamenting the bodice, like* **Mrs. Van Buren**'s.

Mayme (*touched*)   Is that for me?

She leaps up from the piano and holds the corset up to her body.

Esther   I made one just like it for a lady on Fifth Avenue.

Mayme   It's so pretty. This is really for me? No kidding? Can I try it on?

Esther   Of course you can.

Mayme   Feel it. It feels like Fifth Avenue does. You outdone yourself this time, honey.

Esther   Stop talking and put it on.

Mayme *gives* **Esther** *a kiss on the cheek.*

Esther   And look at the flowers, ain't they sweet? It took me a whole day just to sew them on.

Mayme *takes off her robe and puts on the corset.*

Mayme   For shame. This the prettiest thing anybody ever made for me. Truly.

Esther   You know that white lady I talk about sometime, hold on . . .

Mayme *grabs the bed post, as* **Esther** *pulls the corset tight.*

Esther   She keep asking me what they be wearing up in the Tenderloin. All that money and high breeding and she want what you wearing.

Mayme   No kidding?

Esther   What she got, you want, what you got, she want.

Mayme   Onliest, I ain't got the money to pay for it.

She models the corset.

Whatcha think? Do I look like a Fifth Avenue bird?

Esther   Grand. You look grand. Mr. Marks say, that satin foulard was made for the finest ladies in Paris.

Mayme   No kidding.

Esther   I wasn't going to buy it. But, oh Lord, if he didn't talk me into it.

Mayme   Mr. Marks?

A moment.

Who is this Mr. Marks?

Esther   He just a salesman. That's all.

Mayme   It sound to me like you bit sweet on him.

Esther   Me? Oh no, he a Jew.

Mayme *looks into* **Esther**'s *eyes.*

Mayme   And? I been with a Jew, with a Turk even. And let me tell ya, a gentle touch is gold in any country.

Esther   I see the bodice is a bit snug—

Mayme   Is he handsome?

Esther   I ain't noticed.

Mayme   Good patient, Esther. Come, he wouldn't be your first, would he?

Esther   I ain't listenin'.

Mayme (*softening her tone*)   You dear thing.

She laughs long and hard.

Esther *doesn't respond.*

Mayme   No kidding. I can't even remember what it was like. Ain't that something.

Esther   Let's not talk about this.

Mayme   Mercy, what you must think of me.

Suddenly self-conscious, she touches the beading on the corset.

Esther   And if you must know, I'm being courted by a gentleman.

Mayme   Courted by a gentleman. Beg my pardon. Not that Panama man? Oh come on, don't tell me you still writing him.

Esther   He writing me.

Mayme   You'd rather a man all the way across the ocean then down Broadway. Are you expecting him to arrive in the mail like some tonic from a catalogue?

Esther   Please don't make sport, Mayme.

Mayme   I'm just playing with you.

Esther (*wounded*)   I ain't expectin' nothing.

A moment.

Mayme *acknowledges* **Esther's** *hurt.*

She caresses her friend's face.

Mayme   Sure you are. Sure you are, honey. Who ain't?

She sits on the bed, beside **Esther.**

Mayme   I am a concert pianist playing recitals for audiences in Prague and I have my own means, not bad for a colored girl from Memphis . . .

She plays a few bars of classical music, perhaps allowing it to become a rag.

And Madame always takes tea twice a week with her dear friend Miss Esther Mills, who's known in circles for . . . for what? I forget.

Esther *is reluctant to share her dream.*

Mayme   Come on, Miss Esther, don't be proud.

Esther   I own a quaint beauty parlor for colored ladies.

Mayme   Of course.

Esther   The smart set. Someplace east of Amsterdam, fancy, where you get pampered and treated real nice. 'Cause no one does it for us. We just as soon wash our heads in a bucket and be treated like mules. But what I'm talking about is someplace elegant.

Mayme   Go on, missie, you too fancy for me.

Esther   When you come in, Miss Mayme, I'll take your coat and ask, "Would you like a cup of tea?"

Mayme   Why, thank you.

Esther   And I'll open a book of illustrations, and show you the latest styles.

Mayme   I can pick anything in the book?

Esther   Yes.

Mayme   How about if I let you choose?

Esther   Very well. Make yourself comfortable, put your feet up, I know they're tired.

Mayme   Shucks, you don't know the half of it.

Esther   And in no time flat for the cost a ride uptown and back, you got a whole new look.

Mayme   Just like that? I reckon I'd pay someone good money to be treated like a lady. It would be worth two, three days on my back. Yes, it would.

Esther   You think so?

Mayme   I know so.

Esther   And if I told you I got a little something saved? I keep it sewed up in the lining of a crazy quilt.

Mayme   On a cold lonely night wouldn't that quilt be a poor woman's dream.

Esther   I been saving it slowly since I come North. It for that beauty parlor. I ain't told nobody that. Honest, for true.

Mayme   Where'd you get such a damn serious face?

Esther   Why not?

Mayme   Because, we just fooling that's all. I ain't been to Prague, ain't never gonna go to Prague.

Esther   But come, is this what you want to be doing ten years from now, twenty?

Mayme   You think I ain't tried to make a go of it. You think I just laid down and opened my legs 'cause it was easy. It don't look like nothing, but this saloon is better then a lot of them places, ask anybody. Only last night one of Bert Williams' musicians sat up front, and he stayed through the entire show. You think some of those gals in the big revues didn't start right where I am.

Esther   You got this beautiful piano that you play better than anyone I know. There are a dozen church choirs—

Mayme   Let me tell you, so many wonderful ideas been conjured in this room. They just get left right in that bed there, or on this piano bench. They are scattered all over this room. Esther, I ain't waiting for anybody to rescue me. My Panama man come and gone long time now. It sweet that he write you but, my dear, it ain't real.

Esther   Yes, he here in my pocket in a cambric walking suit, he has a heliotrope handkerchief stuffed in his pocket and a sweet way about him. He so far away, I can carry him in my pocket like a feather.

She laughs and produces a letter from her apron.

Mayme   You're funny. You and your silly letter.

Esther   Ain't a week go by without one. It got so I know the postman by name.

She holds out the letter.

Mayme   I ain't interested. Put it away.

Esther   C'mon, Miss Mayme . . . don't be proud, you know you want to read it.

She dangles the letter, threatening to put it away at any moment.

Mayme   Hell, give it here.

She snatches the letter and quickly peruses it, allowing herself a smile.

Ooo.

Esther   What it say?

Mayme   Your man got himself a new pair of socks. Wait . . . uh-oh, he askin' what you look like. Ain't you told him?

Esther   No. I'm afraid, I ain't known what to say.

Mayme   Tell him the truth.

Esther   That I don't look like much.

Mayme   You tell him that you're about as lovely a person as there is.

Esther   You know that ain't so.

Mayme   Of course, it is. And what does it matter? You think half the men that come in here bother looking at my face. No ma'am. He don't care about this.

She grabs **Esther**'s *face and gives her a kiss on the forehead.*

She playfully shows off her physical attributes which are accentuated by the form-fitting lingerie.

Mayme   He interested in this, my dear. This is what he's asking about. (*She laughs.*)

Esther   I wouldn't dare write about something like that. He Christian!

Mayme   And it's in his weakness that he'll find his strength. Hallelujah! C'mon, I'm just playing with you.

Esther   I'm being serious and you got your mind in the gutter.

Mayme   Oh for God's sake, the man just asking what you look like 'cause he want something pretty to think about come sundown.

Esther   You reckon? Then will you help me write something?

Mayme *hands back the letter to* **Esther**.

Mayme   No, what about your white lady? Why not have her do it?

A moment.

Esther *opens her carpetbag.*

Esther   'Cause I'm asking you, my friend.

Mayme   No, my writing ain't perfect.

Esther   Don't bother about the handwriting, we'll tell him I pricked my finger while sewing. He'll understand. Please.

Mayme   Oh.

She fetches a sheet of paper and a pen and sits on the bed.

Esther *sits next to her.*

Mayme I ain't romantic, I find this silly, really I do. Only 'cause it's you. So, how do I begin?

Esther   "Dear George."

Mayme *concentrates, then slowly writes.*

Mayme (*savoring the notion*)   A love letter to a gentleman. Yes, I know. "Dear George, I write you wearing a lavender silk robe with—"

Esther *giggles.*

Lights cross-fade.

George *enters carrying a lantern; he is soaked through by the rain.*

George   Dear Esther,
   Thank you for your sweet words. Your pricked finger delivered the most unexpected lift. It quiet now. The only motion is the rain. The only sound is the rain. It is the white season, and the work all but stop. The rum shop be the onliest business that do prosper. I seen months of hard work lost in an evening and good men befriend the devil overnight. And if I told you it's been months since I've seen a decent a woman it wouldn't be a lie. There are caravans of sweet-faced Indian girls offering up their childhood for a half-day's wage. Yes, many men leave here with less than they

come. I shan't be one. It isn't appropriate, but I will say it. I crave a gentlewoman's touch, even if only be to turn down my collar or brush away the dirt in the evenings. Indeed, I'd like to meet you as a gentleman. I think much about the suit I will wear, and the colors that your eyes find pleasing. I imagine your cobblestone roads and the splendid carriages on the avenues, and a dry place to sit. I think of you running silk thread between your fingers and find a bit of holy relief, for your letters arrive just in time to ward off temptation.

> Yours affectionately,
> George

Lights cross-fade to:

Scene Five: Hand-Dyed Silk

Esther's *boudoir.*

Esther *sits at the sewing machine, working on a silk camisole.*

Mrs. Dickson *enters carrying a letter, which she hands to* **Esther**.

Mrs. Dickson   I don't trust him, not one bit. He writes too often.

Esther   It's open.

Mrs. Dickson   I'm sorry, I opened it by mistake. I didn't mean to, but I'm glad I did.

Esther   'Cause you the landlady don't give you the right to tamper with my things.

Mrs. Dickson   What are your intentions?

Esther   We corresponding. That's all.

Mrs. Dickson   I know these kind of men. Sugared words, but let them stick to the page and go no further. He'll steal your common sense, he will and walk away. It just don't seem like you, Esther, you're too practical a girl for this.

Esther   Don't set your clock by my habits.

Mrs. Dickson   His tone is very familiar. And I don't approve.

Esther   I'm sorry, but I needn't your approval.

Mrs. Dickson   My goodness. I hope you ain't expecting anything to come of this.

Esther   And if I am?

Mrs. Dickson   Our Mr. Charles has asked me twice about you this week. I told him he was most welcome to call.

Esther   Mr. Charles is a fool and a glutton. And I'm sure he don't even know who I am.

Mrs. Dickson   You are a stubborn little country girl. And very particular. And it wouldn't hurt you to be more receptive.

Esther To who? Mr. Charles? Remember it's me you're talking to, not Doreen or Erma, or one of those other silly open-hearted little gals. And yes, I'm writing letters to a man. And it may come to nothing. But I am his sweetheart twice a month, and I can fill that envelope with anything that I want.

Mrs. Dickson Yes. It's an innocent enough flirtation, and I had my share in my youth. And believe me when I say I was romanced by many bright and willing young men.

She takes **Esther**'s *hand.*

It's potent, I know, but I ain't ashamed to admit that my pride ultimately led to compromise. And if you're not careful, Esther—

Esther DON'T! This quilt is filled with my hard work, one hundred dollars for every year I been seated at that sewing machine. It's my beauty parlor. So you see I don't need Mr. Charles for his good job and position.

Mrs. Dickson *pulls the quilt off of the bed.*

Mrs. Dickson You think this is enough? Do you? You think this gonna make you happy when another half dozen girls waltz away in camisoles of your making. When the Bellman's Ball come around another year and you here fluffing ruffles for some girl from Kentucky, who just happy to be wearing shoes.

Esther No, I don't think that. And I'd give this quilt and everything in it to be with someone I care for, I would.

Mrs. Dickson This man in Panama, he's paper and I'll show how easily he goes away.

She rips up the letter.

Esther Mrs. Dickson!

Mrs. Dickson You'll thank me.

She exits.

Esther *picks up the pieces of the letter.*

Lights cross-fade to **George** *in Panama, as he picks up pieces of fabric.*

George Dear Esther, I opened the letter and these tiny bits of fabric tumbled out onto the ground. Imagine my surprise, gray wool, pink silk, and the blue flannel, which I tucked in the back of my shirt this morning—

Lights cross-fade to **Mr. Marks**'s *boudoir.*

Mr. Marks *unrolls a cobalt-blue roll of silk.*

Esther *touches the various fabrics—muslin, taffeta, satin, tulle.*

Mr. Marks *unfurls a vibrant roll of magenta cloth.*

Mr. Marks It is hand-dyed silk, I washed it yesterday and look.

Esther   Yes, beautiful.

Mr. Marks   Have you ever seen anything like that?

Esther   No.

Mr. Marks   It looks fragile, but feel.

She runs her hand across the blue material and smiles.

Esther   Ah, it will feel even better against your back.

Esther   The ladies will like this indeed. You shouldn't have shown me this . . .

She pulls the fabric around her shoulders. He then wraps a strip of magenta cloth around his shoulders.

Mr. Marks   Look at this color.

Esther   It look very good on you, Mr. Marks.

Mr. Marks   Does it?

She laughs.

He laughs.

An awkward moment, fraught with the unspoken attraction that lies between them.

Esther   Your button?

Mr. Marks   I forget.

Esther   If you take off your jacket, I'll sew it on for you.

Mr. Marks   Don't worry. It is fine.

He buttons the remaining buttons on the coat.

Esther   It'll take me no time.

Mr. Marks   No. Thank you. Truly. It is fine.

A moment.

Esther   Why do you always wear black? You sell all of these magnificent colors, and yet every time I see you, you're wearing black.

Mr. Marks   You ask a very complicated question. It's an act of faith, that is the simplest way I know how to explain. It is one of the many ways that I show my devotion to God.

A moment.

Esther   Is marrying someone you don't know another?

Mr. Marks   It is a thousand years of history and struggle behind the answer to that question.

Esther   And yet it seems as simple as taking off a jacket.

A moment.

I'm sorry, I didn't mean to upset you.

Mr. Marks   You haven't upset me.

Esther   If you wrap the magenta, I'll pay you next week.

Mr. Marks   To answer your question, it has always been that way in my family.

Esther   But this a new country.

Mr. Marks   But we come with our pockets stuffed, yes. We don't throw away nothing for fear we might need it later . . . I wear my father's suit. It is old, I know, but this simple black fabric is my most favorite. Why? Because when I wear it, it reminds me that I live every day with a relationship to my ancestors and God.

As he turns to wrap the fabric, she ever so gently touches the back of his collar. He doesn't register the gesture. Or does he?

Lights fade around **Mr. Marks**'s *boudoir as they rise in* **Mrs. Van Buren**'s *boudoir.*

Mrs. Van Buren *wears a lacy kimono and corset made of hand-dyed magenta silk.*

Mrs. Van Buren   Hand-dyed silk? Is it popular?

Esther   It will be by fall.

Mrs. Van Buren   Really? I'll have to weave that tidbit into conversation this evening. My in-laws are coming. The frog and the wart. Oh, and did I tell you? I saw Mr. Max Fiedler of Germany conduct selections from *Don Juan.* I had to endure an encore from the soprano, what was her name? Something Russian, no doubt. I'd rather have gone to the electric show at Madison Square Garden, but you see Harry isn't impressed with electricity. "Miracle upon miracle, but there remain things science will never be able to give us," he says, so he refrains from enthusiasm. By the way, I bled this morning, and when I delivered the news to Harry, he spat at me. This civilized creature of society. We all bleed, Esther. And yet I actually felt guilt, as though a young girl again apologizing for becoming a woman.

She sheds her kimono, revealing a low-cut magenta corset with a pale pink camisole beneath.

Maybe I'll be a bohemian, a bohemian needn't a husband, she's not bound by convention.

Esther   I don't see why you let him do you this way, missus. If you don't mind me saying.

A moment.

Mrs. Van Buren   Have you been to the opera?

Esther, *aware that she overstepped, nervously adjusts the bodice.*

Esther   Never.

Mrs. Van Buren   Oh God, you're lucky. It's one of those things required of me. I'm certain you've found a more engaging means of entertainment.

Esther   I actually only been to the theater once.

Mrs. Van Buren   Really? What did you see?

Esther   Nothing special. A blind gal from Alabama sang spirituals. I need you to lift your arms.

Mrs. Van Buren   Like this?

She seductively lifts her arms.

It's pinching me right here.

Esther *stands behind* **Mrs. Van Buren** *and wraps her arms around her torso. She runs her fingers along the top of the corset, then reaches in to adjust her breast.*

Esther *tightens the bodice as* **Mrs. Van Buren** *continues to speak.*

I've never been to a colored show, I'm told they're quite good.

Esther   I suppose.

Mrs. Van Buren   I should like to see one for myself. You must take me to one of your shows.

Esther   And will you take me to the opera next time you go?

Mrs. Van Buren   I would, if I could. It would be marvelously scandalous, just the sort of thing to perk up this humdrum season.

She touches **Esther**'*s hand with an unexpected tenderness.*

Esther *politely withdraws her fingers.*

Mrs. Van Buren   It is so easy to be with you. (*Whispered.*) Your visits are just about the only thing I look forward to these days. You, and our letters to George, of course. Shall we write something dazzling to him? Something delicious.

A moment.

Esther *seems hesitant.*

Esther   But, if—

Mrs. Van Buren   What? Why not?

Esther   Perhaps something simple this time, I believe there real affection growing.

Mrs. Van Buren   Yes, one would hope. He seems quite taken.

Esther   I don't want him to be disappointed.

Mrs. Van Buren   And he needn't be. We'll send him your warmth and he'll find you irresistible.

Esther   Do you think we could describe this silk?

She runs her fingers down the front of **Mrs. Van Buren**'s *silk corset.*

Esther   Will you tell him what it feel like against your skin? How it soft and supple to the touch. I ain't got the words, but I want him to know this color, magenta red. What it make you feel right now. It—

Mrs. Van Buren   The silk? Are you sure?

Esther   Yes.

Mrs. Van Buren   Mercy, if my friends knew I spend the day writing love letters to a colored laborer, they'd laugh me out of Manhattan.

Esther   People do a lot of things that they don't ever speak of.

Mrs. Van Buren   I smoked opium once, with the most proper of women. She dared me and I did it. And you? What have you done?

A moment.

Esther   I touched someone who I knew I wasn't supposed to touch. I touched them because I wanted to, it was wrong, but I couldn't help myself.

Mrs. Van Buren *takes in* **Esther**'s *words.*

The lights rise on **George** *sitting on his bunk illuminated by a kerosene lantern.*

Esther *remains onstage in half-light, as if listening to* **George** *speaking directly to her.*

George   Dearest Esther,
   It dawn. No work has begun, the morning is still holding the ocean, not yet blue. But I can see past everything green to the horizon. And it is here in half-light that I imagine you. Six months have passed since our first correspondence, and much has changed. A water boy from my parish died, taken by fever two nights past. All their magic machinery and there's nothing could be done for this boy. It got me thinking about his family behind and the wife he'd never meet. He die so easy. Why he? His young life end, and not more than a word from the Yankee chief, 'cept regret that the new boy ain't so quick. This morn I try to remember his small blackened face and cannot even recall his smile, though his hand give me water each and every day since I be here. Why this boy go out my mind, I ask? Tomorrow I too could be sucked into the ground without tears and ride the death train that pass through here five times a day. When I first come, a solid ox was the dream of this man. But I watch the splendid way the American gentlemen touch their fine machines and laugh away the jungle, and I know what great and terrible things their sleep brings. And yet, your America sounds like a wondrous place, a man such as myself would be willing to surrender much for a taste of the modern world. Yes, I see beyond the tilting palms, through the mangroves and across the Caribbean sea to where you sit. I kneel beside you at this moment and I tell you, I am a good strong man. What I've come to feel for you can best be described as love. I love you. There is no other way to say it, will you marry me?
   Most adoringly,
   George

Lights cross-fade to:

Scene Six: White Cotton Bed Linen

Mayme's *boudoir.*

Mayme *hangs a pair of wet stockings on the bedpost.*

Mayme   Why ya smiling so big? Close your mouth 'fore your teeth dry out.

Esther   He's asked me to marry him.

Mayme   What? No kiddin'.

Esther   It in writin'.

Mayme   Show me.

Esther *hands* **Mayme** *the letter.*

Mayme   Our own Miss Esther.

Esther   He say he loves me.

Mayme   And do you love him?

Esther   As much as you can love a man you ain't seen. I'm thirty-five, Mayme, and he wants to marry me. And there ain't gonna be no more opportunities I'm afraid. I've told him yes.

Mayme   Well, goddamn. I'm sure he's a fine man.

Esther   Yes, I suppose. Any man go through this much trouble to court a woman must have his virtues.

Mayme   I reckon.

Esther   He write that he arriving next month.

Mayme   That soon . . . you hardly ready.

Esther   I know. I'm getting married! Oh God, will you come to witness the ceremony?

Mayme   Me? You want to bring me around your new husband?

Esther   It would be nice to have a friend witness.

Mayme   No, I ain't been to church since I was seventeen. It ain't about you, it's just a promise I made to myself years ago. I ain't got nothing to say to God, and it don't seem right to go up into somebody's home and you ain't on speaking terms.

Esther   It just a building.

Mayme   Just the same, I'd rather not be reminded. But thank you, my dear, it's a long time since I been invited anyplace proper.

Esther   Me too.

Mayme *laughs and grabs a bottle of liquor.*

Mayme   Hell, we ought to celebrate. Somebody give me this gin. It look expensive. Whatcha think? Should I open it?

Esther   Sure. Why not.

While speaking, **Mayme** *pours them each a glass of gin.*

Mayme   We gonna toast to one less spinster in New York.

Esther   Oh God, I hope I ain't making a mistake.

Mayme   You'll be fine. You're about the most sensible gal I know. Enjoy this, honey. It's a splendid feeling. Yes, indeed. I was engaged once. You won't tell nobody. A mortician's apprentice who hated music. Need I say more.

Esther   Do you regret not marrying him?

Mayme   Some days. No, some evenings, honey.

She thrusts her glass into the air.

But here's to Esther, you will be a beautiful bride, and may happiness follow.

They toast and drink. **Mayme** *sits at the piano.*

My dear, you're gonna go to socials and other ridiculous functions that married folk attend. Drink lots of lemonade, God forbid, and become an awful gossip. And you know, it won't be appropriate to visit a place like this.

Esther   Who say?

Mayme (*snaps*)   I say.

A moment.

Esther   We friends, ain't no Panama man gonna change that.

Mayme   Well, I hope he is wonderful.

She starts to play piano.

Give me a man that'll come and bake me a cake. Put in some sugar and spice.
Yes, he can put it in my oven any ol' time and watch it rise on up.
Give me a man that'll come and mow my lawn from the front to the back.

Esther *joins in.*

Mayme   Yes, he can tend my garden any ol' time and watch it rise on up.
A woman needs a handyman to take care of her home.
A woman needs a candyman who'll fight the bees for the comb.

Esther *stops singing; she silently contemplates her decision, uncertain.*

Mayme   Give me a man that'll come and bake me a cake.

Load it with some sugar and spice.

Yes, he can put it in my oven any ol' time and watch it rise on up.

Lights cross-fade.

Esther's *boudoir.*

Mrs. Dickson *is packing* **Esther's** *suitcase.*

Esther *crosses into her boudoir.*

Mrs. Dickson   Who is going to sit next to me at the table? There is Bertha, but she has no conversation. Oh, I could move Erma down closer, but she and Bertha don't speak. It'll be an absolute mess at the dinner table without you. That's for certain. Oh, it's gonna be a shame to let this room to anybody else. It has so many of your sweet touches. Yes.

Esther   You wasn't always pleased with my conversation if I recall.

Mrs. Dickson   Who told you that? Well, they lie.

She holds up a dress.

Oh no. Not this little frumpy thing, really Esther. My grandmother wouldn't even wear a collar like so and she was a right proud Christian soldier. Yes.

Esther   Well, I like it. It's the most refined thing I own. I paid five whole dollars for it.

Mrs. Dickson   You'll scare off your gentleman, and it ain't worth five dollars of misery. You needn't be a prude. Trust me, your man'll have needs, and it's your duty to keep his member firmly at home. Yes.

Esther   Excuse me?

Mrs. Dickson   I shan't repeat it. But there ain't no greater disappointment than a husband without much . . . vigor. Believe me, I know. And sometime he gotta be pleasured to ensure your own satisfaction. You understand. I ain't an expert, but I do have some experience. And I'll tell you, give and take make for the best of partnerships. Never mind what the minister tells you about decency, what go on between a man and wife be their own business. He will test you and he will try you, but don't let him beat on you, don't take no shit from him, understand.

Esther   Mrs. Dickson.

Mrs. Dickson   Excuse me for saying, but if he raises his hand once, he'll do it again. I thought we should have this conversation before you go off. I don't mean to scare you, but I know you come as an innocent and we're friends so I feel I can speak plainly.

Esther   Thank you, but I do believe I'm old enough to handle things for myself.

Mrs. Dickson   Just the same, I thought I'd say it. Now whatcha want me to do with this dress?

Esther   It that bad?

Mrs. Dickson   Let's just say we'll give it to Deacon Wynn and let the church ladies fight over it. Yes.

She sits on the bed.

You really going to do this, ain't you?

Esther   You didn't expect me to be here for the rest of my life?

Mrs. Dickson   I guess I sort of did. I'm so used to hearing your sewing machine and foot tapping up here. Yes, I reckon I'm going to miss it.

Esther   Another gal will move into this room, and by supper you'll be fussing about something new.

Mrs. Dickson   You say that with such certainty. You hurt my feelings, Miss Esther Mills.

She dabs her eyes with a handkerchief.

Eighteen years is a long time. Yes. I don't reckon I've known anyone else that long. It'll be lonely.

Esther   You have plenty of suitors to keep you busy.

Mrs. Dickson   But ain't a working man amongst them.

A moment.

You know you don't have to do this.

Esther   Yes, I do. I stay on here, I'll turn to dust one day, get swept up and released into the garden without notice. I've finally found someone. Just as you found Mr. Dickson.

Mrs. Dickson   I married him, because I was thirty-seven years old, I had no profession and there wasn't a decent colored fella in New York City that would have me.

Esther   But you come to love each other.

Mrs. Dickson   I suppose. He give me some laughs. But you see, my mother wanted me to marry up. She was a washerwoman, and my father was the very married minister of our mission. He couldn't even look out at her there in the church pews, but she'd sit there proudly every Sunday, determined to gain God's favor. Marry good. She didn't ever want me to be embarrassed of my fingers the way she was of hers. I'd watch her put witch hazel and hot oil on her delicate hands, but they remained raw and chapped and she kept them hidden inside gray wool gloves. In the winter they'd bleed so bad sometimes, but she'd plunge her hands into the hot water without flinching, knead and scrub the clothing clean. Fold and press for hours and hours, the linen, the bedding, the stockings, and the britches, sometimes wearing the frayed gloves so as not to leave bloodstains on her precious laundry. She wouldn't even let me help her, she didn't want my hands to show the markings of labor. I was going to marry up. Love was an entirely impractical thing for a woman in her position. "Look what love done to me," Mama used to say. "Look what love done to me."

A moment.

So I did what was necessary to gain favor. I allowed myself to be flattered by gentlemen. You understand? Yes, this "pretty" gal done things, un-pretty things, for this marble mantle, gaslights in every room, a player piano, and an indoor toilet.

Esther   But Mr. Dickson was a good man.

Mrs. Dickson   Bless his broken-down soul. He had fine suits and perfect diction, and was too high on opium to notice that he was married. But I would not be a washerwoman if it killed me. And I have absolutely marvelous hands to prove it.

She laughs, displaying her hands.

But you have godly fingers and a means, and you deserve a gentleman. Why gamble it all away for a common laborer?

Esther   . . . Love.

Mrs. Dickson   Don't you let a man have no part of your heart without getting a piece of his.

Lights cross-fade to **George**.

George   Dear Esther, I held in the port of Havana, Cuba, awaiting passage to New York City. A passenger come down with cholera. So here I wait, fighting patience. We sail tomorrow—

Cross-fade to **Mr. Marks**'s *boudoir, where* **Mr. Marks** *has just finished preparing a cup of tea.*

Esther *hesitantly enters.*

Mr. Marks   Miss Mills, where have you been? I thought I'd lost you to a competitor.

A moment.

I keep looking out the window at Mr. Friedlander's shop, he's giving away thread with each purchase. Yesterday, stress tonic. Tomorrow, who knows? I saw this morning Mrs. Simons, Mrs. Simons my cousin's wife, go into Mr. Friedlander's. His fabric is inferior, I tell her this. But she wants the stress tonic . . . then go to the pharmacy I say. Where have you been? I've been going crazy. I couldn't bear to lose you to Friedlander.

Esther   I'm sorry, I—

Mr. Marks   No, I'm sorry. You've been busy, of course. I thought something might have happened to you.

Esther   Don't tell me you were worried about me.

Mr. Marks   Well, yes. I didn't have your address, otherwise I would have inquired about your health.

Esther   I'm very well, thank you.

A moment.

She smiles.

He shyly looks away.

Mr. Marks   I found something I think you'll love. (*Excited.*) Do you have a moment?

Esther   Yes.

Mr. Marks   I'll get it.

He fingers through the bolts of fabric, but suddenly stops himself. He struggles for a moment with whether to broach a question.

I just made tea, would you have a cup of tea with me?

Esther   Thank you, that would be nice.

He clears a chair for her. She sits, a bit disarmed by the invitation.

He pours her a cup of tea, then one for himself. He sits down on a chair across from her.

A moment.

He touches the spot where the button is missing.

Mr. Marks   Is the tea hot enough? Milk? Would you like sugar, of course?

Esther   No, thank you, it's fine.

She smiles.

Mr. Marks   You have a lovely smile.

She stops smiling.

He stands up, embarrassed by his candor.

Let me show you the fabric.

Esther   Actually, I have a special request. I'll need fabric for a wedding gown, something simple, Mr. Marks. The bride don't got a lot of money to throw away.

Mr. Marks   Satin? Chiffon? Cotton? Silk? Yes. Tulle?

Esther   Satin, I think.

Mr. Marks   She hasn't told you?

Esther   Silk.

He pulls down several bolts of fabric.

She examines each one, her excitement muted.

Mr. Marks   That one you're touching is very popular. And the price will please you. Thirty cents a yard.

Esther   Twenty?

Mr. Marks   Twenty-five cents. The bride will like.

Esther   It's too much. Something less expensive. I'll dress it up with lace and ribbons.

She points to a faded old roll.

How about this one?

Mr. Marks   It's a wedding. This is for an older woman—

Esther   I ain't so young.

Mr. Marks   —the bride's mother perhaps.

A moment.

You are getting married?

Esther (*a moment*)   Yes. You seem surprised.

Mr. Marks (*he is*)   No, no. Not at all. My congratulations.

He pulls out his finest wedding fabric.

Please. I'm sure the rich lady who ordered this didn't appreciate the delicacy of the fabric. She gave no thought to who crafted this perfection, the labor that went into making it. How many hands touched it. Look. Beautiful. You deserve to wear it on your wedding day.

Esther   It's so beautiful, it looks like little fairy hands made it. It's too fine for me.

Mr. Marks   Come, touch it and then refuse. Please. Touch.

He watches her run her fingers across the fabric. He also touches it, sensually. She closes her eyes. He continues to watch her, savoring the moment.

It is exquisite. Miss Mills, many fine ladies have worn it against their skin, but it was made for you. I know this . . .

She holds the fabric to her face and begins to weep.

. . . May it be your first gift.

He wants to offer comfort, but he cannot touch her.

Esther   I won't let you.

Mr. Marks   It would be my pleasure.

She accepts the length of fabric.

They gaze at each other, neither able to articulate the depth of their feelings.

A moment.

They exit the stage, as the lights rise on **Mayme** *seated at the piano.*

She plays a rag.

Mrs. Van Buren *enters, smoking a cigarette and nursing a glass of brandy. She studies her image in the vanity mirror.*

Mr. Marks *reenters, fiddling with the buttons on his jacket. He takes out a needle and thread and contemplates whether to sew on a new button.*

Mrs. Dickson *enters, carrying a wedding veil; she toys with the delicate fabric.*

George *enters in an ill-fitted suit, his best. He moves downstage with the uncertainty of a new arrival.*

Esther*, dressed in a wedding gown, nervously enters.*

Mrs. Dickson *places the veil on* **Esther***'s head.*

Everyone but **George** *and* **Esther** *exit.*

Esther *joins* **George** *downstage, each of them in a separate pool of light.*

They look at each other, for the first time, then look out into the world.

There is a flash—as from an old-fashioned flash camera.

The sepia-tone image is captured.

A projected title card appears above their heads: "Unidentified Negro Couple ca. 1905."

Blackout.

End of Act One.

Act Two

Scene One: The Wedding Corset—White Satin Embroidered with Orange Blossoms

Esther stands in a pool of light; she wears a spectacular white wedding gown.

Another pool of light engulfs **George**; *he wears a worn gray dress suit frayed around the sleeves, certainly his best.*

Lights rise.

A spare studio flat; an iron bed dominates the room.

George *and* **Esther** *stand on either side of the bed, which is covered with the crazy quilt.*

A silence divides them.

Finally **Esther** *speaks.*

Esther   Don't really feel much different. I guess I expected somethin' to be different. It was a nice ceremony. Didn't you think? I wish my family coulda witnessed it all. My mother in particular. When the minister said man and wife I nearly fainted, I did. I been waiting to hear those words, since . . . they nearly took my breath away. Man and wife, and the truth is we barely know each other. I've written you near everything there is to know about me, and here we is and I fear I ain't got no more to say.

Note: **George***'s accent is a touch heavier and more distinctly Barbadian than in the first act.*

George   We ain't need to say nothin' now. We got plenty of time for that. It late.

He takes off his jacket and tosses it across the bed. He loosens his top button.

She picks up the jacket, quickly surveys the label, then neatly folds it, placing it at the bottom of the bed.

Esther   Do you wish to bathe? I'll fetch the basin.

He kneels on the bed and extends his hand to her.

George   Why don't yuh come sit by me. Let me see yuh.

She sinks on the bed with her back to him. He gently strokes her cheek.

She trembles.

Are yuh afraid of me? Yuh shaking.

Esther   Am I? None of this be familiar.

George   Give yuh hand 'ere.

She gingerly passes her hand to him.

He sits next to her, kissing each of her fingers, then places her hand on his crotch.

See. It ain't scary at all.

She leaves her hand resting on his crotch, uncomfortable.

A moment.

I expected yuh to be—

Esther   Prettier.

George   No, I was gonna say—

Esther   It's okay, I lived with this face all my life, ain't no surprises. We should say what we think now and get it out of the way.

George   I suppose from yuh letters—

Esther   I described my character. And I think you'll find me truthful.

He begins to unbutton her dress.

She stiffens at his touch.

You're very handsome. More than I thought and I must say it do make me a little uncomfortable.

She withdraws her hand from his crotch.

And the other thing I think you must know, I ain't been with a man before. I been kissed and done some kissing, but you know what I'm saying. And it might be awkward on this first night, even if we man and wife—

George   Then we'll make it less awkward.

He slips her dress off of her shoulders and plants a kiss on her bare back.

She's wearing a stunning wedding corset of white satin embroidered with orange blossoms.

Real nice. Pretty. I like it.

He runs his fingers across the delicate lace covering her breasts.

Esther   Wait. I made something for you.

She stands up and quickly fetches the smoking jacket.

Here.

George   What it?

Esther   It's Japanese silk. Put it on.

He clumsily pulls the smoking jacket around his muscular body.

He clearly isn't comfortable with the delicacy of the garment.

Careful.

He explores the jacket with his weather-worn fingers.

It ain't too small?

George   Nah. But I afraid, I soil it.

He removes the jacket and tosses it on the bed.

He pulls her into his arms.

Esther   Not yet.

George   Yuh got somethin' in mind?

Esther   Couldn't we wait a bit?

George   Minister say man and wife.

Esther   Please, I'd like to know about your mother or about your birthplace, Bar-ba-dos. Something I don't know. That wasn't in the letters. Something for us, right now.

A moment.

George   Like what?

She pulls away and picks up the smoking jacket.

Esther   I come here from North Carolina at seventeen after my mother died of influenza, God bless her loving spirit. My father died two years later, he was a slave you see and didn't take to life as a freeman. He'd lost his tongue during a nasty fight over a chicken when I was a baby, so I never heard him speak, no complaints, no praise, no gentle words, no goodbye. He was . . . silent. Broken really. I come to this city by myself, worked my way North little by little, picking berries in every state until I get here. An old woman in the rooming house teach me to sew intimate apparel, saying folks'll pay you good money for your discretion. It was just about the best gift anybody give me. It was as though God kissed my hands when I first pulled the fabric through the sewing machine and held up a finished garment. I discovered all I need in these fingers.

A moment.

I wanted you to know that about me.

George   My parents were chattel . . . born to children of chattel.

He takes off his shirt.

We cut sugar cane and die and that our tale for as long as anybody could say. Nothin' worthy of a retelling, really. I come here so the story'll be different, that I hopin'. Now ifyuh don' mind, I spent many nights on a hard wood floor, a bed be long overdue.

She gives him her hand.

We married. I ain' gonna commit no crime 'ere, a man and wife don't 'ave no quarrel in the bedroom.

He gently pulls her onto the bed.

The lights slowly fade as she succumbs to his embrace.

Ragtime piano.

Mayme *and* **Mrs. Van Buren** *enter, dressed in their twin corsets.*

They stand over the wedding bed.

Mayme   What is he like?

George *climbs out of bed; he stands in a pool of light and slowly goes through the ritual of dressing.*

Esther *kneels on her bed wrapped in the crazy quilt.*

Esther   He handsome enough.

Mrs. Van Buren   Come, what did he say when he saw you?

Esther *climbs out of bed.*

As they speak, if necessary, **Mayme** *and* **Mrs. Van Buren** *may help* **Esther** *dress.*

Esther   He ain't say much of nothing. He just stood there for a moment regarding me with his eyes. Yellow, cotton and cane eyes. I didn't have no tongue.

Mrs. Van Buren   He must be something of a romantic. He traveled halfway across the world because of some promise on a paper.

Esther   And he still smell of salt and ground nuts. It make me sick and it make me excited.

Mrs. Van Buren   I was tipsy on my wedding night. I recall being in love with the notion of love, and everything took on a rosy glow. Harry was foolish and confident and I was frightened to death.

Mayme   Is he as we imagined?

Esther   Yes, he is sturdy enough and quite a pleasure to behold. His hands thick, stained dark from work. North Carolina field hands. But he got a melodious voice, each word a song unto itself.

Mayme *and* **Mrs. Van Buren** *reluctantly retreat into the darkness.*

Esther *and* **George** *button their shirts.*

Esther   And when he finally fell asleep I placed my head on his chest, and listened for the song of cicadas at dusk, and imagined the sweet aroma of the mango trees and the giant flamboyant with its crimson tears.

Esther *and* **George** *stand on either side of the bed, dressed.*

Scene Two: Valenciennes Lace

George/Esther's *boudoir.*

A rag plays.

George *smoothes down his overgrown hair, pleased with himself.*

His clothing is worn but that doesn't seem to trouble him.

Esther *takes in* **George** *from the corner of her eye, quickly averting her gaze when he glances over.*

He smiles to himself.

Esther   Do you want me to fix you something?

George   I ain't really hungry, you know.

Esther   Where are you going? It Sunday. I promised Mrs. Dickson we'd dine with her this afternoon after the church social.

George   That woman ask too many questions for me liking.

Esther   That's what ladies do. She's just being attentive.

He grabs his hat and toys with it for a moment.

He ventures to speak, but stops himself.

Finally:

George   Say Mrs. Armstrong, you got two dollars?

Esther   What for?

George   I need a proper hat if yuh want me to look for real work. It near three months now, and this a farmer's hat I tol'. The rag man wouldn' even give me a penny for it.

Esther   Two dollars. That's a lot of money. I tol' you I'd make you a worsted suit. Right smart.

He gently touches her hand.

George   C'mon, Mrs. Armstrong. Just two dollars.

Esther   But this is the last time. Hear?

Reluctant, she goes over to the quilt and opens the seam with her scissors. She digs in and pulls out two dollars.

There.

George   That all you got?

Esther   Yes. Why do you need to go out?

George   I tell some fellas I stop off for a quick ale, be back 'fore yuh know.

Esther   But it Sunday. I'll put on some tea, and sit, let me mend your shirt. You can't go out with a hole in your shirt.

She touches the hole in his shirt.

What will they say about your wife? I won't hear the end of it from Mrs. Dickson.

George   She a real madam. "Yuh working, George?" "Oh, nuh?" (*Chupses.*) I ain' been this idle since a boy in St. Lucy. But that busylickum ain' 'ear nothing.

(*Chupses again.*) I got me pats on the back from white engineers, and a letter of recommendation from the Yankee crew chief heself. But 'ere, I got to watch buildings going up left and right, steel girders as thick as tamarind trees, ten, twelve stories high. Thursday last I stood all day, it cold too, waitin' for the chief, waiting to interview. Do yuh have tools, boy? Yes! Do yuh know how to operate a machine, boy? Yes. But 'e point just so to the Irishman, the German, and the tall Norwegian who's at least fifty years plus five. And I got more experience than the lot. I tell 'e so. Next time, 'e say. Next time, George. Can you believe? And when everyone gone, 'e pass me this damn note like it money.

He takes a letter from his pocket and unfolds it.

Look.

He hands the note to her.

She examines it, pretending to read.

What do you t'ink?

He watches her ever so carefully . . .

Esther   I don't know what to say. I suppose he mean what he say.

She anxiously places the letter on the bed.

George   But what do you t'ink? You t'ink what he say true?

Esther   Why wouldn't he be truthful?

Frustrated, he takes off his shirt and tosses it to her.

He then throws himself across the bed and lights a cigarette.

She goes about mending his shirt by hand.

Did you try over at that butcher's? Like I asked. I know they could use an extra man 'cause it's always crowded in there. Especially on Friday.

George   I don' know. We'll see.

Esther   There are worse things you could do. And I thought maybe we could go to the church social before Mrs. Dickson's.

George   I ain' a church man, really.

She stops sewing.

Esther   You do believe, don't you? Why in letters you said—

George   I say a lot of t'ings.

A moment.

She returns to sewing.

He feels the quilt.

Esther   Please, I ain't been to a social. I sat up in Saint Martin's for years, and didn't none of them church ladies bother with me until I walked in on your arm, and suddenly they want Mrs. Armstrong over for tea.

George   Yuh and yuh monkey chaser yuh mean?

Esther   Oh that ain't so. Most of them folks ain't been nowhere to speak of. But they are fine people, and who knows where help will come from?

George   I want to build t'ings, not polish silver or port luggage. Them fine jobs for yuh Yankee gentlemen, but not me. I ain' come 'ere for that! They'll have me a bootblack 'fore long, let the damn Italians blacken their hands, I say. Mine been black long enough. A man at the saloon, smart looking fella, say the onliest way for a colored man in this country is for 'e to be 'e own man. Have 'e own business, otherwise 'e always be shining the white man nickel. You understand, no? And really, how it look to people. Me, sitting 'ere, waitin' on fortune, you out there courtin' it.

Esther   I am your wife, and whatever I got, yours. And George mind your smoking on the bed. The Chinaman two floors down burn up that way.

He puts out the cigarette.

George   Listen, this fella at the saloon talk about a man sellin' a stable with a dozen strong draft horses. 'E in a bit of debt, and need money quick quick. A dozen horses for nothin'. Did you 'ear what I say?

Esther   That saloon talk. That man'll take your money to Shanghai. It just a dream, it ain't gonna feed you today.

George   You t'ink I stupid?

Esther   No. But supposin' he honest, where would you get the money for twelve horses?

George   Where, Mrs. Armstrong?

He gently strokes the quilt.

Am I wrong?

Esther   My quilt? Never mind with that money. It just there and it gonna stay there.

George   Yuh a squirrel, for true. That's what yuh call them city rats, no?

Esther   A squirrel ain't a rat. That money for my beauty parlor, I told you that.

George (*laughs*)   That funny.

Esther   Why's that funny to you?

George   You ownin' a beauty parlor.

Esther   Yes.

He studies her.

She self-consciously returns to sewing.

George   Look at yuh. How yuh know pretty from the lookin' glass?

A moment.

Esther (*wounded*)   I make pretty things.

He pops up off the bed and takes her in his arms.

George   I sorry, Mrs. Armstrong, I ain' know what I say. Yuh be real sweet, if you done up yuh hair, nice. Put a little paint on yuh lips.

He runs his hand across her mouth. He grabs her and tries to do a quick dance.

Esther   I ain't that kind of woman.

George   No, yuh ain'.

He lets go of her arm. Gently.

Please, Esther.

Esther   No. That eighteen years there.

George (*chupses*)   Yuh vex me so. Where's me shirt?

Esther   It ain't finished.

He grabs the shirt from her and puts it on.

Esther   Be careful, you'll tear—

George   I going o'er to the Empty Cup for an ale. I see yuh later.

Esther   That a notorious place.

George   How yuh know?

Esther   I know. (*He chupses dismissively.*) Why are you so cross with me? You got your ale money and enough for God knows what else. Ain't that so?

George   Yes, it yuh nickel. How do t'ink that make me feel?

Esther   I come here with nothing.

George   Don't look at me so.

Esther   I slept in a cold church for nine days, and picked up breadcrumbs thrown to pigeons.

George   Yes. Yuh done good, but five hundred days digging don' amount to nothing 'ere. It always gray, why it so gray? Work on the Isthmus, it hard, but at least the sun shine.

Esther   I know you here 'cause of me, and I want you to be happy. We stood in that church, and promised before God to take care of each other. That means something, even if it gray. You listenin'?

George   I listenin'.

Esther   You got a good arm George Armstrong, and I'd be proud to walk in on it whether it shining shoes or picking cotton.

George   I just tired of comin' home to put me hand in yuh pocket.

He grabs his hat and coat.

She attempts to turn down his collar.

He brushes her hand away.

I off.

Esther   What about Mrs. Dickson and the social?

George   I be back for supper.

He grabs his coat and exits.

She picks up his work letter and crumples it up.

Cross-fade to **Mr. Marks**'s *boudoir.*

Mr. Marks *hums a rag as he searches through the piles of fabric.*

Esther *enters.*

Mr. Marks   Here it is. Scottish wool, it isn't as expensive as one would think. It is very good.

Esther   Are you humming a rag, Mr. Marks?

Mr. Marks   No, it's a Romanian song. I can't remember the words. It is driving me mad.

Esther (*smiles*)   I'm very happy to see that you replaced the button on your suit.

Mr. Marks (*proudly*)   You noticed. It was time, don't you think?

He displays the fabric.

You wanted Scottish wool, yes?

Esther   Scottish wool. Yes.

She feels the fabric.

It's so heavy. Would you wear a suit made of this?

Mr. Marks   Well, yes. You see how soft it is. I bought it from a gentleman who said it came from his village. He had a wonderful story about his mother caring for the sheep like small children. He said every night she'd tell them a fairy tale, and each morning give the creatures a kiss and a sprinkle of salt. The neighbors would watch and laugh. Watch and laugh. But come time to shear the animals, what wonderful wool they produced for his mother. Like no other.

She feels the fabric, lovingly.

He revels in her delight.

He could have been a thief for all I know, but the color is a lovely coffee, very subtle. Don't you think? So I pay too much, but not enough for the quality. Ah! Yes. I have something else to show you. It's here. Where is it? Where are you? Here we are.

He unfurls a roll of lace.

I almost let it go last week, but I was waiting for you. I wanted you to see it.

Esther Oh, yes.

Mr. Marks I knew you'd like it. (*Elated.*) The wait was worth seeing your smile again.

He playfully drapes the lace around her neck.

They find themselves standing dangerously close to each other.

They are so close that they can inhale each other's words.

A moment.

Miss Mills, if I may say—

Esther Armstrong.

She removes the lace.

Mr. Marks I apologize. I forget. I forget.

A moment.

He takes the lace and places it on the cutting board.

Esther It is pretty, thank you, but today I've come for fabric for a gentleman's suit. Next time.

Mr. Marks Yes. Just a minute, I have some other wools, gabardine, if you'd like to see? I have no story for them, but they are sturdy and reliable, will give you no problems.

As he turns to search for another bolt of fabric, she gently runs her fingers across the lace.

He turns with the dark drab suit fabrics.

He slowly rolls the lace, his disappointment palpable.

Next time.

Esther Mr. Marks?

Mr. Marks Yes?

She wants to say something, but she can't quite find the words.

Is there—?

Esther No. No . . . I'm sorry . . . I can't do this. (*Distraught.*) I thought I'd be able to, but I can't. I can't come here anymore. I—

Mr. Marks Why do you say this? Did I do something to offend, tell me, did I—

Esther   No.

Mr. Marks   Then—

Esther   Please, I think you know why.

A moment.

Mr. Marks   How many yards will you need for the gentleman's suit?

Esther   Four yards. The Scottish wool . . . and if you would, please wrap the Valenciennes lace.

Cross-fade to **Mrs. Van Buren's** *boudoir.*

Light pours into her room.

Scene Three: Rose Chemise

Mrs. Van Buren's *boudoir.*

Mrs. Van Buren *sits on the bed cradling a snifter of brandy.*

She's upbeat, almost cheerful.

However, **Esther** *is distracted, consumed by her own thoughts.*

Mrs. Van Buren   He's gone to Europe.

Esther   I'm sorry to hear that.

Mrs. Van Buren   You needn't be. It's a relief actually. Some business obligation, I don't expect to see him for months. He'll find ways of prolonging his stay, no doubt. Anyway, I'm considering a visit with friends in Lenox this summer. It'll be good to escape the city. Don't you think? You could come, of course, I'll recommend your services to several women.

Esther   I thank you, but I can't.

She drapes the Valenciennes lace over the bed post.

Here. I found a strand of lace for your rose chemise. I know it ain't exactly what you wanted, but—

Mrs. Van Buren   I had all but forgotten. I ordered it over four weeks ago. Four whole weeks. It's not like you to—

Esther   I been busy.

Mrs. Van Buren   Oh? Indeed. How is our Mr. Armstrong?

Esther   Good. Well, he . . . good. Work scarce, and he so particular. He wanting, but his pride make him idle. And I try, I do, but he ain't really take to this city.

Mrs. Van Buren   But he will. I am certain. Oh Esther, it must be wonderful to be in love.

Esther   I suppose.

A moment.

Mrs. Van Buren *quickly examines the lace; indifferent, she tosses it onto the bed.*

Esther *bristles at her employer's lack of interest.*

Mrs. Van Buren   Is everything all right?

Esther   Yes.

Mrs. Van Buren   Such a long face so early in the day. I won't allow it.

Esther *doesn't smile.*

Mrs. Van Buren   Come.

Esther   I'd like to settle matters. Please. You ain't paid me in two months and I need the money.

Mrs. Van Buren   Of course, I hadn't realized.

She sits at her dressing table. Smiling to herself.

You know what? I miss writing our letters. I do! I've been absolutely without purpose for months.

Esther (*snaps*)   Let's not talk about the letters!

Mrs. Van Buren (*surprised*)   Fine, we won't.

Esther   I'm sorry, Mrs. Van Buren

Mrs. Van Buren   Something is wrong.

Esther   No. Nothing.

She sits on the edge of **Mrs. Van Buren**'s *bed.*

She carefully refolds the lace, attempting to hold back tears, but they come anyway.

Mrs. Van Buren   Esther, what is it?

Esther   The other day George asked me to read a letter. I took it in my hand and I lied. I lie every day. And I'm a Christian woman.

Mrs. Van Buren *takes* **Esther**'s *hand and sits down on the bed next to her.*

Mrs. Van Buren   We do what we must, no? We are ridiculous creatures sometimes.

A moment.

Esther   Do you love Mr. Van Buren?

Mrs. Van Buren   I am a married women, such a question is romantic.

Esther   But I fear my love belongs someplace else.

Mrs. Van Buren   And why is that?

Esther   I shouldn't say. No, I can't. Perhaps I'm wrong.

Mrs. Van Buren   Perhaps not.

She pulls **Esther** *close and plants a kiss on her lips.*

Esther *for a moment gives in to the sensation of being touched, then abruptly pulls away.*

Shocked.

Mrs. Van Buren   I'm sorry. I didn't mean to do that. I'm sorry. Please don't go. I just wanted to show you what it's like to be treated lovingly.

Esther   Don't say that. You don't love me.

Mrs. Van Buren   How do you know? Please. We will forget this and continue to be friends.

Esther   Friends? How we friends? When I ain't never been through your front door. You love me? What of me do you love?

Mrs. Van Buren   Esther, you are the only one who's been in my boudoir in all these months. And honestly, it's only in here with you, that I feel . . . happy. Please, I want us to be friends?

Esther   I'm sorry. I can't.

Mrs. Van Buren (*screams*)   Coward!

A moment.

I'm sorry.

She digs into her dressing-table drawer and produces a wad of money.

She tosses the money on the bed.

There.

Esther   I'm not the coward.

She picks up the money.

Cross-fade to **Mayme**'s *boudoir.*

Mayme *plays a slow, seductive rag.*

George *enters; he watches her gracefully regard the instrument.*

He places money on top of the piano, then straddles the piano bench behind her.

He kisses her neck and cups her breasts in his hands.

Cross-fade to **Esther**'s *boudoir.*

Esther *sits alone, waiting.*

Cross-fade to **Mayme**'s *boudoir.*

Scene Four: Gentleman's Suit

Mayme's *boudoir.*

Esther *enters.*

Mayme *is dressed in a red flowing dressing gown and bubbles over with excitement.*

Mayme   I've saved up every penny I have. It's been two months and I want something new, Esther. Simple, this time, without all the pronouncement. Something a young gal might wear on her wedding night.

Esther   Wedding night? What ain't I heard? I don't believe those words got any place in your mouth.

Mayme   Seriously.

Esther   What's going on? C'mon, are you gonna tell me?

Mayme   It ain't nothing really. A fella, perhaps.

Esther   I thought you didn't feel nothing for these fools.

Mayme   Nothing ain't never felt so good.

Esther   Who is he?

Mayme   He ain't nobody really, but he real sweet. Like a schoolboy almost. We call him Songbird, 'cause he sing to speak. He come in like all them others. Hands crude and calloused, a week's wage in his pocket. But when we done I didn't want him to leave and I asked him to have a drink. Fool drunk up all my liquor, but it ain't bother me. In fact I was fixin' to run out and git some more, but he placed his hands around my waist, real gentle and pulled me close. I actually wanted him to kiss me, I didn't even mind his sour tongue in my mouth, I wanted him there, inside me. He ain't like a lot of the colored men who pass through here with anger about their touch. He a gentleman. Comes three times a week on schedule like the iceman. He was here last night until midnight, but he don't ever stay later. He just leaves his scent, which lingers until two A.M. or three, and I lie awake until it disappears.

Esther   He sounds wonderful.

Mayme   Yeah, I reckon.

Esther   What?

Mayme   Whatcha think? He got a wife. Yeah. A rich wife. But she troubles him, he say. Troubles him to no end. You should hear him go on about this poor gal. Made me feel bad for her.

Esther   She terrible, I'm sure. But just the same, you on uneasy ground.

Mayme   You find it shocking?

Esther   Yes, I find it shocking.

Mayme   Hush your mouth, you wouldn't understand. You want to see what my songbird give me?

She pulls **George***'s Japanese smoking jacket from beneath her pillow.*

She displays it proudly.

Mayme   And you know me, I don't usually take gifts from men, but when he give me this, it took my breath away. It's so pretty. Look, Esther. Feel it.

Esther   He give you this?

Mayme   Yup.

Esther   He must like you a bunch to give you something so fine.

Mayme   What can I tell you, the man got taste, honey.

Esther   I've only seen fabric like this just once before. It's Japanese silk.

Mayme   How'd you know?

Esther   It's expensive fabric. Very hard to find. You see the pictures were embroidered by an imperial artist, he signed it there. He give you this?

Mayme   He say I his gal. But this time a little part of me is hoping he telling the truth.

Esther   And what about his wife?

Mayme   What about her? I'm sure she just a sorry gal.

Esther   How you know she ain't a good person? And he just saying what you want to hear. That his words are a smooth tonic to make you give out what ain't free. How you know his wife ain't good?

Mayme   I don't know. But do it matter?

Esther   Yeah it do. You ever think about where they go after they leave here? Who washes their britches after they been soiled in your bed?

Mayme   No, I don't actually. Why would I?

Esther   'Cause there's some poor woman out there waiting, getting up every five minutes, each time a carriage pass the window or a dog bark. Who thinks a great deal of her husband, thinks so much of him that she don't bother to ask questions, she just know that there are places that he go that gentlewomen don't belong.

Mayme   I don't want to hear it.

Esther   She thinks he's playing cards or simply restless. But still when the door opens and he lies down next to her, that poor stupid woman don't feel angry, because his body is warm and she ain't alone.

Mayme   What?! You troubled because he married? They all married. You ain't completely clean of this business. Truth. No, I don't care to think about those women. I don't care to think about the kind of lives that keep them sitting in their windows, worrying while their husbands—

Esther   I pity your heart. You are the worst sort of scavenger.

Lights rise on **George** *and* **Esther**'s *boudoir.*

George *stands in a brand-new suit.*

Mayme   What's the matter with you?

Esther   I don't feel so good. That's all.

Mayme   I thought you'd be happy for me.

Esther   I think I'm gonna go home, if you don't mind.

Lights cross-fade.

Esther *and* **George**'s *boudoir.*

George *stands in a new wool suit.*

George   Yuh t'ink I'd be taken for a Yankee gentleman? I do t'ink so, no? I'd like one them tall hats, whatcha call 'em? Like that fella across the way, yuh know, the one always be talkin' about 'e rich brother in Chicago. (*Affecting an American accent.*) Yes, sir, my name George Armstrong and I from New York, yes sir, born here. (*He laughs.*) It fit real nice. But, it seem to me that the fellas be wearin' shorter jackets with a touch of color.

Esther *pins his pants.*

Esther   Sporting fellas, they ain't gentlemen. This Scottish wool. It white-folk quality and it'll keep you warm through the winter. There is a lovely story—

George   Yeah? I'm sure it excitin'.

She runs her hands down his legs, then adjusts the hem.

He does not respond to her touch.

Esther   Be that way, I won't tell it then. There. You look good, George. Really. Now take off the pants so I can hem them proper.

George   Nah, don't bother. I need them for this evenin'.

Esther   This evening? Why? Don't go out. I bought fresh pork chops from Mrs. Franklin's son. I was gonna smother them in onions, the way you like. But it ain't worth the trouble if you ain't gonna eat. And . . . and I have something for you, I was going to save it for later . . . but . . .

A moment.

Do you want to see?

George (*excited*)   Sure.

Esther   Close your eyes. C'mon. And don't smile.

He closes his eyes.

She puts a rose in her hair and a touch of color on her lips.

She nervously slips off her dress, revealing an elaborate corset similar to **Mayme***'s.*

You can open your eyes.

She awkwardly poses, awaiting his reaction.

His disappointment is palpable.

He clearly was expecting something else.

He chuckles to himself with a mixture of amusement and disgust.

George   What yuh doing?

Esther   Don't you like it?

George   Come, put yuh clothin' on.

Esther   What's the matter? Ain't this to your liking? Ain't this what you want?

She places his hands around her waist.

Feel it. It satin. See.

George   No, don't do this Esther. C'mon, this ain' yuh. 'Ear.

Esther (*timidly*)   If I ain't mistaken, a man has certain obligations.

A moment.

Why won't you touch me?

A moment.

George   You want me to touch yuh?

Esther   Yes.

He grabs her around the waist.

He plants a heavy hard kiss on her mouth.

She nevertheless succumbs to his touch.

George   Like so? You want me to touch you. That all you want of George? You want me to bend and please, so you can feel mighty. No.

He pushes her away.

'Least in Panama a man know where 'e stand. 'E know 'e chattel. That as long as 'e have a goat 'e happy. 'E know when 'e drunk, 'e drunk and there ain' no judgment if so. But then 'e drink in words of this woman. She tell 'e about the pretty avenues, she tell 'e plentiful. She fill up 'e head so it 'ave no taste for goat milk. She offer 'e the city stroke by stroke. She tantalize 'e with Yankee words. But 'e not find she. Only this woman 'ere, that say touch me, George. And ask 'e to lie down on what she promise, lie down on 'e stable with a dozen strong horses for the work sites, ask 'e to lie down as they haul lumber and steel. Strong sturdy beasts. They are. 'E lie down, but what 'e get? No, he ain't gonna lie down no more.

Esther   Stop it. Why you talking this way?

George   I t'ink yuh know.

A moment.

He eyes the quilt.

Esther   No. Please don't ask me again.

George   But it there dreamin' a fine fine house wit it own yard. It taunt 'e so, 'e can't even show what kind of man 'e be. What 'e hands can do.

Esther   No. That half my life. Thousands of tiny stitches and yards of fabric passed through that old machine.

George   And for what, huh? For it sit?

Esther   No.

George   Stop sayin' no! Ain't you see. If 'e own wife ain't willin' to believe in 'e, who will? 'E stand in work lines that wind around city blocks. But 'e don't have to no more, 'cause 'e know a fella got twelve draft horses and want to sell them quick quick. And 'e buy them and in two years, they'll have enough money for a beauty parlor even. They'll have the finest stable in New York City. People'll tip their hats and pay tribute. They'll call them Mr. and Mrs. Armstrong. The Armstrongs. Them church ladies will clear the front row just for them. And 'e will—

Esther (*wants to believe him*)   He will what?

George   'E will sit with she and nod graciously to the ladies. 'E will come home for supper every evenin'. (*Seductively.*) 'E will lie with she.

Esther   Only she?

He strokes her back tenderly, she savors his touch. He kisses her neck, her back, her shoulders, her breasts. He embraces her, almost too much so.

She nevertheless surrenders to the unexpected affection.

Are you telling me the truth? Is this the truth?

George   Yes.

Esther   Please, you're not just saying that. You're not laughing at me are you?

George   No, I ain' laughin'.

Finally, she breaks the embrace.

She hesitates, then tears into the quilt, wrenching it apart with her bare hands. She pulls the money out and examines it, before placing it in his outstretched hands.

Esther   There. There. There.

She's almost relieved to be shedding the money.

Surprised, he smiles and gathers the money into a pile.

George   So much 'ere. Sweet mercy, look at it all. Good lord, that fella ain' gonna believe it. I gonna place the money square in 'e hand, wipe that silly Yankee grin off 'e lips. I show 'e.

Esther   George, it's late, you ain't gotta do this now . . . put it back. It'll still be there in the morning.

George   Woman, how yuh get so much?

Esther   Leave it. Come. George, I said put it back, it'll be there in the morning! . . .

He beckons him to the bed.

He looks at her pleading outstretched hand, but instead chooses to fetch a worn bag for the wrinkled money.

Humiliated, she studies her husband with growing horror.

Aghast, she slowly lowers her hand and pulls on her dress. George?

He continues to take unbridled delight in the money.

Esther   George?

George (*snaps*)   What?

Esther (*whispered*)   Do you love me?

George   What the matter wit' you? You look as though you seen a duppy.

Esther   Do I?

George   Why yuh look at me strange?

Esther   I asked you something.

George   Yuh my wife, ain't yuh?

Esther   Am I? (*Whispered.*) I didn't write them letters.

George   I didn' hear what yuh said.

Esther (*louder, almost too much so*)   I said I didn't write them letters.

He studies her with disbelief.

All this time I was afraid that you'd find me out. This good noble man from Panama.

She retrieves a pile of letters tied with a satin ribbon.

I have all of your letters here. I look at them every day. I have one that looks as though it's weeping, because the words fade away into nothing, and another that looks as if it's been through a hard day, because there's a smudge of dirt at each corner, and it smells of kerosene and burnt sugar. But I can't tell you what it say, because I don't read. I can't tell whether there are any truths, but I keep them, 'cause George give me his heart, though it covered in mud and filthy, but he give it to me in one of these letters. And I believed him. I believed him!

A moment.

But you ain't the man in these letters, because that gentleman would have thanked me. Who wrote them letters, George? Tell me!

He considers.

YOU TELL ME!

George   An old mulatto man. I paid him ten cents for each letter, ten cents extra for the fancy writing.

Esther   I ain't really Mrs. Armstrong, am I? I been holding on to that, and that woman ain't real. We more strangers now than on the eve of our wedding. At least I knew who I was back then. But I ain't gonna let you hurt that woman. No! She's a good decent woman and worthy. Worthy!

George   Esther!

He reaches out to her.

Esther   No, don't touch me!

She backs away from him.

George   Please. I ain' a thief. No. They warn't my words, but that don't mean I ain't feel them t'ings. I go now, and I gonna bring yuh back them horses.

Esther   I hope they real strong horses.

George   You'll see. And, we'll begin here.

Lights cross-fade.

Mayme's *boudoir.*

Ragtime music plays, fast and furious.

Scene Five: Smoking Jacket

Mayme's *boudoir.*

Mayme *is lying on the bed wrapped in the Japanese smoking jacket.*

She sits up, pours herself a shot of moonshine, and slams it back.

A knock sounds on the door.

Mayme   Hold on, hold on.

She opens the door.

Esther, *calm, enters.*

Mayme's *unable to disguise her surprise.*

Mayme   Esther. What . . . I got someone coming shortly. You can't stay.

She nervously wraps the robe around her body.

I can't put him off. You understand. Come back later and we'll catch up.

Esther *grabs* **Mayme**'s *arm.*

Mayme   What's wrong?

Esther *gathers her strength.*

Esther   He gone.

Mayme   Who gone?

Esther   George.

Mayme   You ain't serious.

Esther   He has another woman.

Mayme   How do you know?

Esther   She told me so.

Mayme   She did? Well, she must be a cruel heartless heifer.

Esther   You think so?

Mayme   Yes.

Esther   But, she ain't. When I left home this morning I intended to do harm to his whore. I was going to march into her room and scratch her face with my scissors. I was going to scar her. Make her ugly. Make her feel what I'm feeling. But, she gonna know soon enough.

Mayme   You gotta go now.

Esther   No.

Mayme   Please, we'll talk about it later. I got someone coming.

Esther   Do you know what I done? I tore a hole in my quilt and give him my beauty parlor. Half my life bent at the machine, and I give it to him, just like that.

Mayme   Oh, Esther. Why?

Esther   I wanted to be held. (*Distracted.*) I thought if . . . He ain't come home last night. I sat at the sewing machine all night, trying to make something, I just kept sewing together anything I could find until I had a strip a mile long, so long it fill up the apartment.

A moment.

Mayme *runs her fingers along the fabric of the jacket.*

Esther   Do you know where he is, Mayme?

Mayme   Why would I know?

Esther   Because you're wearing the jacket I give him on our wedding night.

Mayme   How come you ain't say nothing before?

Horrified, she rips off the jacket.

Esther   What am I gonna say?

Mayme   Yeah, yeah. Last night Songbird come around the saloon in a new suit with bottomless pockets, throwing dice all night, and boasting of easy money. I ask him where he got the money and he say his luck turn and he was gonna ride it out. If you can imagine that. He was gonna buy himself draft horses. The world changing and he wants big strong horses. He made me laugh. He promised to take me out someplace special, but I didn't have nothing nice to wear. And honestly it made me think about how long it been since I done something for myself. Gone someplace like you said, where a colored woman could go to put up her feet and get treated good for a change. And I see the dice rolling, and I think Lord, God, wouldn't a place like that be wonderful. But every time the dice roll, that place is a little further away. Until it all gone. And then I put my arms around this man, and I know who he is. He George. And maybe I known all along.

Esther   Why didn't you stop him?

Mayme   Because, he belong to me as well.

*She places the jacket in **Esther**'s hands.*

Mayme   But this yours.

Esther   Foolish country gal.

Mayme   No, you are grand, Esther. And I ain't worthy of your forgiveness, nor will forget what you done for me. You ain't never treat me like a whore. Ever.

George *knocks on door.*

Esther   Please don't answer that door.

George *rattles door and knocks.*

Esther   Please don't, please don't answer.

Mayme   He's going to leave.

George *(knocks and rattles door more urgently, shouts)*   Mayme!

He rattles door again.

Esther   LET HIM GO!

Mayme *moves toward the door.* **Esther** *grabs her arm.*

Esther   Let him go. He ain't real, he a duppy, a spirit. We be chasing him forever.

George *knocks and rattles door even more persistently.*

Eventually he stops.

Silence.

Mayme *sits on her bed.*

Esther *exits with the smoking jacket.*

Cross-fade to **Mr. Marks**'s *boudoir, as* **Esther** *moves into* **Mr. Marks**'s *boudoir.*

Scene Six: Japanese Silk

Mr. Marks's *boudoir.*

Mr. Marks *unfurls a roll of ocean-blue fabric.*

As he turns, he finds himself facing **Esther**.

Esther   Hello, Mr. Marks.

Mr. Marks (*surprised*)   Miss Mills, I'm sorry, Mrs. Armstrong. How have you been?

Esther   I seen worse days. And you?

Mr. Marks   I've seen better days. (*He laughs.*)

Esther   I've been meaning to stop in. I walked past here a half dozen times trying to get up the courage to come in. You remember you sold me a rather special length of fabric some time ago.

Mr. Marks   Please, remind me.

Esther   Japanese silk, with—

Mr. Marks   Of course, I remember it.

Esther   Well, I made it into a man's smoking jacket, at your suggestion. (*She holds it up.*)

Mr. Marks   It is very nice, it will please your husband, I'm sure.

Esther   I want you to have it.

Mr. Marks   Me? I can't—

Esther   Yes, you will.

He accepts the jacket, genuinely touched by the gesture.

Mr. Marks   Thank you.

Esther   I can't stay.

She begins to leave.

Mr. Marks   Wait, one moment.

He removes his outer jacket, revealing the fringes of his tallit katan.

He carefully puts on the silk jacket.

What do you think?

Esther   It fits wonderfully.

She takes a step toward him, hesitates, then takes another step forward. She raises her hands.

May I?

He nervously holds his breath and nods yes.

She reaches toward him, expecting him to move away.

She smoothes the shoulders of the garment, then expertly runs her hands down the jacket's lapels, straightening the wrinkled material.

He does not move.

Silence.

Their eyes are fixed upon one another, then she reluctantly walks away, exiting the boudoir without a word.

He is left alone onstage to contemplate the moment.

A gentle rag plays.

Lights cross-fade; we're in **Esther***'s original boudoir.*

Scene Seven: Patchwork Quilt

Esther*'s boudoir.*

Mrs. Dickson*'s rooming house.*

Mrs. Dickson *folds laundry, humming a ragtime tune.*

Esther *enters.*

Esther   The girl downstairs told me I could find you up here.

Mrs. Dickson   My Lord, Mrs. Armstrong. I been telling everyone how you forgot us.

Esther   It ain't been that long.

Mrs. Dickson   Feel so.

The women hug.

Look at you. I was about to take some tea, come on into the kitchen, I'm glad for the company. These new girls are always out and about. They trouble me so these days, but whatcha gonna do? And I want to hear about everything.

Esther   Have you rented this room?

Mrs. Dickson   Why do you ask?

Esther   I don't much feel like saying why. If you please, just a yes or no would suit me fine.

Mrs. Dickson   No.

Esther   Well, then, you won't mind another person at supper this evening. It's Friday and you don't know how I been missing your carrot salad.

Mrs. Dickson   Of course. Esther—

Esther   I'm fine.

She takes **Mrs. Dickson's** *hand.*

Esther   And I'd love that cup of tea.

Mrs. Dickson   Come on downstairs and we'll catch up. I'll tell you about Corinna Mae, girl's as big as a house, I swear to God.

Esther, *barely listening, takes in the room.*

Mrs. Dickson   She didn't waste any time getting pregnant and already talking nonsense about her man. When they first was married he was good enough for her, but to hear it now you'd think the man didn't have no kind of sense.

Esther   I don't care to hear about Corinna Mae.

Mrs. Dickson   Oh, I just thought—

Esther   I'd like to sit here for a moment.

Mrs. Dickson   Oh, yes. I gotta bring a few more things in off the line before the sunset, I'll see you downstairs shortly.

Esther   Of course. Mrs. Dickson, thank you for not asking.

Mrs. Dickson *lovingly takes* **Esther**'s *hand, giving it a supportive squeeze.*

Mrs. Dickson *picks up the laundry basket and exits.*

Esther *lightly touches her belly.*

A moment.

She walks over to the old sewing machine and begins to sew together pieces of fabric, the beginnings of a new quilt.

Lights shift: sepia tone, the quality of an old photograph.

A slow, gentle rag plays in the distance.

As the lights fade, projected title card: "Unidentified Negro Seamstress, ca. 1905."

Blackout.

End of Play.

Selected Bibliography

Barlow, Judith E. *Plays by American Women: The Early Years*. Avon Books, 1981.

Barlow, Judith E. *Plays by American Women, 1930–1960*. Applause, 2001.

Betsko, Kathleen and Rachel Koening. *Interviews with Contemporary Women Playwrights*. Beech Tree Books, 1987.

Bjerre, Thomas. "Thomas Ærvold Bjerre." *Oxford Research Encyclopedias*.

Chinoy, Helen Krich and Linda Walsh Jenkins. *Women in American Theatre*. Theatre Communications Group, 2007.

Crothers, Rachel. "He and She." https://www.emporia.edu/Theatre/Documents/HeAndShe_FinalScript.PDF Emporia State University, March 10, 2018.

Dramatists Guild Foundation. "A Conversation with DGF Traveling Master Paula Vogel." *Traveling Masters Program*, July 21, 2016.

France, Rachel. *A Century of Plays by American Women*. Richards Rosen Press, 1979.

Gelt, Jessica. "Lynn Nottage on Her Pulitzer Win for Drama: I'm Representing for Women." *Los Angeles Times*, April 10, 2017.

Hartmann, Susan M. *Home Front and Beyond: American Women in the 1940s*. Twayne Publishing, 1998.

Hatch, James V. *Black Theater, USA: Forty-Five Plays by Black Americans, 1847–1974*. Free Press, 1974.

Henley, Beth. *Beth Henley Collected Plays: 1980–1989*. Smith & Kraus, 2000.

Henley, Beth. *Beth Henley Collected Plays: 1990–1999*. Smith & Kraus, 2000.

Hodges, Benjamin A., ed. *The Plays that Changed My Life: America's Foremost Playwrights on the Plays that Influenced Them*. Applause Theatre and Cinema Books, 2009.

Kilgore, Emilie S. *Landmarks of Contemporary Women's Drama*. Methuen, 1992.

Kolin, Philip C. *Understanding Adrienne Kennedy*. University of South Carolina Press, 2005.

Nottage, Lynn. *Intimate Apparel and Fabulation or the Re-Education of Undine*. Theatre Communications Group, 2006.

Parks, Suzan-Lori. *The America Play and Other Works*. Theatre Communications Group, 1995.

Parks, Suzan-Lori. *The Red Letter Plays*. Theatre Communications Group, 2001

Paulson, Michael. "Two Female Playwrights Arrive on Broadway. What Took So Long?" *New York Times*, March 22, 2017.

Savran, David. *The Playwright's Voice*. Theatre Communications Group, 2005.

Shange, Ntozake. *See No Evil*. Momo's Press, 1984.

Shange, Ntozake. *Three Pieces*. St. Martin's Press, 1992.

Schulman, Michael. "The Listener." *The New Yorker*, March 27, 2017, pp. 30–33.

Sullivan, Victoria and James Hatch, eds. *Plays By and About Women*. Random House, 1973.

Vogel, Paula. *The Mammary Plays: How I Learned to Drive; The Mineola Twins*. Theatre Communications Group, 1998.

Vogel, Paula. *The Baltimore Waltz and Other Plays*. Theatre Communications Group, 2005.

Weinert-Kendt, Rob. "Southern Without the Comfort" *New York Times*, January 11, 2012.

Winer, Linda. "Paula Vogel." *Women in Theatre: Dialogues with Notable Women in American Theatre*, CUNY TV, October 11, 2002.